About the Editor

HANS J. HILLERBRAND received his doctorate in Germany, though he has spent his career in the United States, most recently as the chair of the Department of Religion at Duke University in Durham, North Carolina. He has published many articles and books on the Reformation, and was the editor in chief of *The Oxford Encyclopedia of the Reformation.* Dr. Hillerbrand is a former president of the American Society for Reformation Research, the American Society of Church History, and the American Academy of Religion.

The Protestant Reformation

The Protestant Reformation

Revised Edition

edited
BY HANS J. HILLERBRAND

HARPER ● PERENNIAL

NEW YORK • LONDON • TORONTO • SYDNEY • NEW DELHI • AUCKLAND

HARPER ⬤ PERENNIAL

The materials printed here are either in the public domain or are used by permission.

A hardcover edition of this book was published in 1968 by Walker and Company.

THE PROTESTANT REFORMATION. Copyright © 1968, 2009 by Hans J. Hillerbrand. All rights reserved. Printed in the United States of America. No part of this book may be used or reproduced in any manner whatsoever without written permission except in the case of brief quotations embodied in critical articles and reviews. For information address HarperCollins Publishers, 195 Broadway, New York, NY 10007.

HarperCollins books may be purchased for educational, business, or sales promotional use. For information please e-mail the Special Markets Department at SPsales@harpercollins.com.

First HarperTorchbooks edition published 1968.

First Harper Perennial edition published 2009.

Library of Congress Cataloging-in-Publication Data is available upon request.

ISBN 978-0-06-114847-7

HB 01.13.2023

Contents

Introduction to the Revised Edition

This collection of important primary sources pertaining to the Protestant Reformation of the sixteenth century has had an amazingly persistent history. Originally published some thirty years ago, it still enjoys the confidence of students (and teachers!) of the Reformation. The reason may well be that, in contrast to most other source collections, *The Protestant Reformation* offers lengthy excerpts from important primary sources, rather than short snippets, so as to provide the reader with an understanding of the broader cogency and dynamic of an author's arguments.

However, since the time of the original publication, the study of the Reformation of the sixteenth century has taken several important turns that have altered the traditional understanding. Accordingly, these new perspectives need to be noted.

For a long time, historians—not surprisingly, mostly Protestant in their orientation—declared the "Reformation" of the sixteenth century to have been one of the most significant epochs of European history. Leopold von Ranke, the founder of modern historical scholarship, saw the Reformation as the beginnings of modernity. He spoke of the "Age of the Reformation," roughly marked by the years 1517 to 1555, to denote that this movement defined an entire epoch. Ranke's conceptualization became the standard interpretative scheme of historians from the middle of the nineteenth century onward. Thomas Carlyle, in England, opined that Martin Luther's 95 Theses had exerted more influence on the course of European history than did the Battle of Waterloo.

Nonetheless, historians of the Reformation told the story very much along partisan lines: Catholic historians tended to view the events as a sad and tragic aberration; Protestant historians in turn had a way of insisting that the Protestant reformers revived an authentic Christianity which had lain suppressed and perverted for over a thousand years. Only in the twentieth century did these partisan perspectives give way to a more irenic point of view. Nowadays, Catholic scholars are prone to extol the positives of the reformers, while Protestant scholars have been inclined to argue that the insights customarily associated with the Protestant Reformation were nothing but restatements of positions known in the fifteenth century.

This latter point has been significant. It was nurtured by the increasing realization that the break between the late Middle Ages and what happened after 1517 was by no mans as radical as Ranke and the Protestant historians had argued. Numerous lines of continuity between the late Middle Ages and the sixteenth century have been recognized, in theology as well as in intellectualism; the newness of Luther's notions has been questioned; and above all the state of affairs in church and society before 1517 is now seen in a far more mellow light than had traditionally been the case. The notion of a corrupt, worldly, perverted church was replaced by the picture of a church full of vitality and spirituality, despite obvious (and understandable) deviations from the professed ideal.

In short, recent historiography has questioned the significance of the changes brought about by the Reformation. Were those changes simply the continuation of developments that had their beginning in the late Middle Ages or were they something new, a real break with the past? The former notion points to the long-term qualitative changes in all areas of society and church in the decades and centuries prior to 1517. It suggests, supported by a myriad of detailed studies and monographs, that what Protestant historians of earlier generations self-confidently stated to be the "theological discoveries" of the Reformation—the emphasis on divine grace rather than human merit; the repudiation of papal power, pilgrimages, and canon law; the centrality of Scripture; the use of the vernacular; etc.—can be confidently stated to have had manifestations well before 1500. If seen this way, the traditional understanding of the Reformation will evaporate: There will be nothing exciting to record because the truly exciting, indeed revolutionary changes occurred well before Martin Luther started his university career. The latter notion argues on behalf of a revolutionary change. Take, for example, the concept of sainthood. The medieval view of sainthood was that it was an extraordinary gift from God, bestowed upon some humans for their meritorious efforts. The saints were seen as bearers of extraordinary spiritual power, which not only placed them close to God but also compelled all others to approach them, solicit their aid, venerate their relics. The Reformation repudiated the notions of merit, satisfaction, purgatory and indulgences, virginity, celibacy, the monastic profession.

The lack of a sharp break with the past, triggered by Luther and others early in the sixteenth century, has led some historians to place the sixteenth-century Reformation into a much wider time frame, and to consider the traditional notion of an age of the Middle Ages followed by an age of the Reformation a serious distortion of historical reality. Nowadays, the common practice is to speak of "Early Modern Europe" extending from the middle of the fifteenth to the eighteenth century (with considerable disagreement among scholars as to the exact chronological parameters). Needless to say, the use of such periodization entails a minimizing of the import of the Reformation.

These new perspectives must also be related to the shift that has occurred in historical scholarship during the last generation. Increasingly, historians have abandoned their traditional emphasis on political and intellectual history in favor of history "from the bottom up" and social history. This has had ramifications for the study of the Reformation. Particularly in North America, Reformation studies have focused on social aspects of religion and religious change. Broadly speaking, this has entailed a focus on the interaction of religion and society. It has brought about, for example, a concern for issues of gender and social status as these related to religion in the sixteenth century. Women authors of reform pamphlets received recognition. The connection between the German peasants' war and the emerging Anabaptist conventicles was emphasized.

This current uncertainty about the significance of the Reformation may be related to the fact that historians of different interests—cultural historians, social historians, theological historians, etc.—have used the areas of their particular expertise to reflect on the larger issues in the period from 1400 to 1600, and they have understandably come up with divergent results: It should come as no surprise that social historians will view the sweep of events between 1400 and 1600 differently than will a religious historian. Accordingly, the divergent perspectives of the Reformation, when seen in this broader context, become rather obvious.

Another strand of recent scholarship has focused attention on the latter part of the sixteenth century and has argued that the truly revolutionary developments and events occurred at that time. This perspective, known as the "Confessionalization Thesis," argues that the "confessions" (i.e., the several religious traditions old and new) increasingly permeated all aspects—law, music, literature, government—of the societies in which they were prominent. While insisting on the primacy of religion in this development, the emphasis on Confessionalization nonetheless shifts attention from what was customarily understood as the Reformation to a time roughly three generations later.

This new edition seeks to accommodate these trends while retaining the basic orientation of the original edition. It includes texts written by women as well as texts dealing with popular religion. Its basic assumption, however, continues to be that religion—no matter how variously dependent on societal forces—must be seen as the pivotal element in the story of the sixteenth century.

Needless to say, I hope that this sentiment is appreciated by the reader and that my effort to have this new edition affirm both ideas and their practice has been successful.

HANS J. HILLERBRAND
DUKE UNIVERSITY
JUNE 2007

Chronology

1546   Death of Luther

War of Schmalkald

1547   Death of Henry VIII; accession of Edward VI

1548   Augsburg Interim

1549   Book of Common Prayer

1553   Death of Edward VI; accession of Mary Tudor

1555   Peace of Augsburg

Abdication of Charles V; accession of Philip II

1559   Acts of Uniformity and Supremacy in England

Treaty of Cateau Cambresis

1560   Accession of Charles IX in France

1562   First religious war in France

1564   Death of Calvin

1567   Revolt in the Netherlands

PART I

MARTIN LUTHER AND THE GERMAN REFORMATION

I

The Grievances [Gravamina] of the German People. [1521]

Grievances, or complaints, were part of the late medieval political scene, which vested representative bodies with the power and authority to lodge formal complaints in order to redress abuses. A first such set of grievances was formulated at the Council of Constance (1414–1418) under eighteen headings. This was done with the endorsement of the German higher clergy, an indication, it would seem, that these grievances were directed not so much against the church as against the papacy and Rome. Subsequently, such "gravamina" were periodically voiced by German diets, or legislatures. In 1510, Emperor Maximilian I instructed the humanist Jakob Wimpfeling to draft a list of grievances. In a list published in 1519, Wimpfeling warned of the German church's widespread unhappiness with the burdens placed on it by Rome. Two years later, when the new emperor, Charles V, sought the concurrence of the German diet to condemn Martin Luther, the diet responded by presenting a new version of Wimpfeling's document. A portion of this document is reprinted here.[1]

---

1. The document, of March 1521, is found in *Deutsche Reichstagsakten, Jüngere Reihe*. Vol. II, Gotha, Germany, 1896, pp. 670–704.

LITERATURE

Gerald Strauss, *Manifestations of Discontent in Germany on the Eve of the Reformation*. Bloomington, IN, 1971.

13. *Concerning Regulations of the Papal Chancery.* These regulations are made for the benefit and advantage of Roman courtiers, and often changed or reinterpreted so as to allow the transfer of ecclesiastical benefices, especially in Germany, into Roman hands and to compel us to buy back or lease these benefices from Rome. This is against both statutory law and equity.

18. *Concerning the Pope's Prevention of the Elections of Prelates.* The pope also seeks to prevent, according to his pleasure, in these cathedral churches the election of bishops, priors, deans, etc. When a bishop is duly elected according to canon law, he replaces him (through confirmation by the consistory) and burdens the elected bishop from Germany with excessive financial charges and taxes.

19. *Concerning Papal Dispensation and Absolution.* Also, popes and bishops reserve to themselves the absolution from certain sins and cases from which, they say, only they can grant absolution. When such a "case" occurs, the people are not granted absolution unless much money changes hands. No dispensation is issued unless a great amount of money is paid. And if a poor man cannot pay, he will not receive the dispensation. Certain rich individuals, however, will receive letters of indulgence from his holiness the pope dealing with murder, perjury or some like misdeed to be committed at some future date. Any outrageous priest will then grant absolution. Thus money and the love of money becomes the cause of great vice and sin.

20. *Concerning the Ravages of Papal Courtiers.* Germans also suffer much from the greed of papal courtiers. When ecclesiastical

benefices in a principality fall vacant, honorable senior clergy, who have properly occupied their benefices for several years, are cited by these courtiers to appear in Rome. There they are subjected to humiliating chicaneries and are coerced to make annual payments to these courtiers in line with certain statutes, cited by these courtiers, called Chancery Rules, newly revised. In this way, honorable older clerics, ignorant of the bureaucrats' cunning, are deprived of their benefices. They also thereby defraud the donors, for if one dies, his will would not be honored.

21. *Many Benefices Are Acquired Under the Pretext of Papal Family Relations.* Also, splendid and good benefices frequently come through the doings of officials, relatives, or courtiers of the pope to incompetent, bad, and ignorant individuals. They gain the right to hold offices "provisionally," or through "regression," "reservation," "pension," or "incompatibility." This causes these benefices to become less attractive and decline in importance, more and more remain attached to the papal court, will not soon fall vacant. Worship is made impossible and the will of the donor is inappropriately dishonored.

22. *Concerning Indulgences.* It is also most objectionable that His Holiness allows so many indulgences to be sold in the German nation. The poor, simple people are thereby misled and cheated out of their savings. When His Holiness sends nuncios and ambassadors to a country, he empowers them to offer indulgences, from which they retain a portion of the income for their expenses and wages. At one time, indulgences were sold for Rome in the hope to make a greater profit, as merchants are wont to do. Bishops and secular authorities, who are astute, also receive a share for their assistance. All this is obtained from poor and simple people with cunning.

28. *How Much Reform Is Needed.* Thus, the poor Christian believers experience much eternal damnation, and the German

nation is financially drained, as is easily seen daily in the spiritual leader. It is highly necessary that, therefore, amelioration and reform of our nation are undertaken in order to prevent further decline and damnation of our land. Therefore, we beseech our imperial majesty most urgently to render support for further reform.

31. *How Priests Arrested for Their Misdeeds Escape Punishment.* If one of them is arrested by a secular court and brought to trial, he will say "I have been ordained." The bishops, counselors, and ecclesiastical judges will promptly demand of secular authorities that he be transferred to their custody, even though he never wore ecclesiastical attire or tonsure nor ever exhibited a behavior appropriate for that estate. If the secular court does not release him within twenty-four hours, the judges are placed under the ban. This has encouraged many a clergy to do malice, trusting in documents, called *litterae formati*. Generally, they are let go free, without having made good the damage they cause. This is the cause of frequent rebellion, hostility, and disobedience.

32. *How Secular Property Is Transferred into Ecclesiastical Hands.* Also, since the spiritual estate is supplied with constitutions, bylaws, and rules by the papacy never to sell or transfer real or other assets of the church to the laity, it is prudent for his Imperial Majesty to make a law and rule for the secular estate, that no secular individual may deed any part of his real property to an ecclesiastical estate. This prohibition should apply to inheritance as well. If such a law is not passed, it is altogether possible that the secular estate will possibly, over time, be bought out by the spiritual estate, and that the clergy through such purchases and especially through leases (which they obtain daily) acquire the assets of common folk so that the secular estate of the Holy Roman Empire eventually are partially, perhaps even completely, at the mercy of the church.

37. How *Ecclesiastical Courts Confirm Jewish Usury*. Everyone knows that the Jews support themselves in German lands through usury, and thereby burden and corrupt the poor Christian people. If at several places, where Jews are living, secular authority sets out to curb the collections of debts due to usury or even curb usury itself, the Jews will call upon an ecclesiastical court for help with the result that the Christians are placed under the ban. For even though the poor people state and swear that the moneys were not received on usurious terms, the courts know full well from general knowledge that Jews do not lend except usuriously and that the poor, in their great need, perjure themselves to their detriment. Canon and civil law most emphatically prohibits judicial or other aid in matters of usury, but nonetheless bishops and prelates permit it.

39. *Sinners Are Given Fines to Pay Rather Than Spiritual Penance to Do*. Although spiritual penance ought to be imposed upon sinners for one reason only, namely to gain salvation of their souls, ecclesiastical judges tend to penalize so formidably that sinners are obliged to buy their way out. This practice causes enormous amounts of money to flow into the church's treasury.

43. *Excommunication Is Issued Indiscriminately, Even in Trivial Matters*. Notwithstanding the original and authentic purpose of spiritual censure and excommunication, namely, to aid and inspire the Christian life and faith, this weapon is flung at us for even the most inconsequential debts—some of not more than a few pennies—or for the failure to pay court or administrative costs when the principal has already been paid. With these procedures the lifeblood is drained out of the poor, unlearned laity, who are driven to distraction by the fear of the ban of the church.

47. *Improper Interdicts and Suspensions of Worship*. Also, if a layperson wounds or kills a priest, an interdict is placed over the town or village where the deed occurred, even when it was done in self-

defense or under legally extenuating circumstances. No service of worship is held in the churches until the perpetrator, council, or community of that place declare their penance. Also, interdicts are imposed for debts and other financial matters, although the church law does not allow this. This is not observed, with the explanation that the interdict is imposed because of "disobedience," deemed to be all the more serious since it stems from trivia. This explanation, so blatantly against common sense and law, is what the prelates offer.

50. *How They Demand a Share of Pilgrims' Offerings.* In some bishoprics, which have pilgrimage shrines, bishops and prelates demand one-third or one-fourth of all offerings collected. There is no basis in canon law for such a demand.

51. *About the Expenses Connected with the Dedication of Churches.* Also, when churches and other chapels are dedicated, the poor people are burdened with additional expenses, even wishing for major donations, notably the bishops and their suffrages.

54. *How There Are Too Many Vagrant Mendicant Priests.* Also, the poor are greatly oppressed by the mendicant monks and their excessive begging, especially certain begging monks who are in towns and villages in violation of their own rules. Frequently, there are two, three, or four of these begging monks in a village or town. Poor people, who have sustained themselves honorably, honestly, and with integrity, have a wife and poor children who cannot maintain themselves because of their frailties, are deprived of their alms and help, but those go somewhere else. Such is annually authorized by the bishops for the payment of a fee.

56. *Too Many Priests Are Ordained, Many of Them Unlearned and Unfit.* Also, archbishops and bishops frequently ordain poor and uneducated men who have neither a sufficient livelihood nor a proper background. Frequently, because of their poverty or natural wickedness, they engage in reckless and disreputable machina-

tions and bring the ecclesiastical estate into disrepute, setting a bad example for the common people. Before an ordination, a bishop is obliged to hear six references on the candidate's fitness for ordination, to record how the candidate is worthy and properly prepared. As things stand at present, these witnesses are not likely ever to have seen the candidate or heard of him. Thus our Christian laws are nothing but pretense and sham.

58. *Concerning Synods, How They Ought to Be Held Frequently.* Also, if the bishops personally attended their synods of their prelates and ecclesiastical subjects, the shortcomings noted above would be alleviated.

62. *The Common People Are Burdened to Contribute Money for Processions and Prayers for the Soul.* Also, priests and pastors have become accustomed to burden their flock with special payments for processions and displays of the Holy Sacrament, determining the amount of such payments. They also pester the poor, who cannot afford to have special prayers offered on the anniversary days of their friends' deaths. They shame them into paying an amount for a sung Mass, less for one that is read. The priests know that their benefices oblige them to say anniversary Masses whenever required. Thus, by saying a single Mass, a priest may receive two or three salaries simultaneously.

63. *Priests Demand Payment from Parishioners Who Leave the Parish.* Also, if a man or woman marries and moves to another parish, their priest demands a gulden as a departure letter. The parishioners have no choice but to pay it, for if they refuse, the priest withholds the sacraments from him.

64. *Gravesites Must Be Purchased for the Dead.* If an individual, especially a layperson, dies in an accident, drowns, is murdered, or is otherwise found dead without having received the sacrament, church law precludes a church burial only in cases of clear and known mortal sin. But the priests refuse burial in the church cem-

etery for those who died this way, unless their wives, children, or relatives make a payment to the priest.

66. *Some Priests Behave Like Laymen and Begin Brawls in Taverns.* Also, most parish priests and other clerics sit with the common people in inns and taverns. They frequent public dances and walk about in secular attire, brandishing long knives. They cause much inappropriate quarreling and argumentation, which lead to fights. The poor people are wounded or maimed; they are excommunicated and given heavy fines, and damages are placed on them. The priests force them to agree to make a settlement payment.

67. *Concerning the Bad Examples of Priests Living with Their Servant Women.* Also, most parish priests and other clerics keep house with easy-going women and their children. They live dishonorable and detestable lives, as a shameful example for their parishioners.

69. *How Some Priests Have Inappropriately Become Tavern Keepers and Gamblers.* Priests have at times set themselves up as tavern keepers. At church fairs, when they have proprietary rights, they and their helpers, often also priests, put up tables for playing dice, or cards, and they take the winnings. They shamelessly claim that they belong to them, since they are the superior authority, even though both secular and church law, and all governmental authority, prohibit this.

70. *Regular Clergy, Monks, and Mendicants.* It is well known that the prosperous monastic orders, such as the Benedictines, Cistercians, and others, have succeeded in daily taking property from the laypeople. The monasteries have grown wealthier. In return, they do not offer the customary services, obligations, and taxes to His Imperial Majesty or other secular authorities, as in earlier times, when they were much poorer. Even worship, such as celebrating the Mass, is done less responsibly than in earlier times.

It is highly appropriate that monasteries and other ecclesiastics not be allowed to acquire, though purchase or any other means, secular assets.

71. *How Priests Persuade the Old and the Sick Not to Bequeath Their Estates to Their Rightful Heirs.* Priests and monks are with the sick, if they know them to be rich in money or land. With learned words they persuade these people to will much of their property to them, so that their poor heirs, children, or other friends receive less than is their due.

74. *How Secular Subjects Are Brought Before Ecclesiastical Courts Because of Debts.* Clergy frequently cite secular subjects to come before ecclesiastical courts because of debts, when the secular authorities failed to honor their claims. The poor people are put in a miserable way under the ban and are forced to pay the trial costs and damages.

77. *How Servants of Priests May Cite Poor People Before an Ecclesiastical Law Court.* Priests drag not only laypeople into ecclesiastical courts, but so also their administrative officials, bailiffs, sheriffs, subjects, and their female servants. They see this as part of their authority.

85. *How Priests Take Issues That Should be Adjudicated by Secular Courts to Ecclesiastic Courts.* There are many legal matters that, according to law, could be settled in either an ecclesiastical or a secular court. It happens often that when a secular judge assumes jurisdiction over a case, an ecclesiastical judge steps forward threatening the secular judge with excommunication unless he surrenders the case. Thus the ecclesiastical judges hear whatever cases they wish. If our Imperial Majesty and his secular subjects are willing to accept this would need to be determined. According to our laws, both ecclesiastical and lay courts, depending on who first brought forward the case, may handle offenses such as per-

jury, adultery, black magic, or the like. But the ecclesiastical judges, against all laws, boldly usurp such cases, which causes great troubles for secular authority.

91. *How Money Buys Approval of Concubinage and Usury.* Also, if a man and a woman cohabit without being married, the priests impose an annual fee and the couple are left alone, though they live in sin and shame. The same also happens with usurers, which means that they do not merely suffer from their temporal goods but also have been misled against God and the salvation of their souls. Moreover, many other Christians are scandalized and offended. Priests also tolerate without much ado that a married person whose spouse has disappeared but might still be living is, without any further search for the missing partner, allowed to cohabit with another person. They call this *"tolerates,"* and it serves to bring contempt upon the holy sacrament of marriage and the offense of pious Christians.

95. *How Innocent People Who Happen to Live Near an Excommunicated Person Are Themselves Excommunicated.* In some places, as many as ten or twelve neighbors of an excommunicated individual are also placed under the ban together with that individual, although they have nothing to do with the matter. This is done for no other reason than the clergy's authority is accepted more expeditiously and the poor people must reach an agreement with them or with their poor children move away. No distinction is made in the ability of the poor and innocent people to pay to have the ban removed, or if they willfully and obstinately had contact with the excommunicated individual. After all, they have no obligation to expel that individual from their area. And even though their own church law prohibits the Interdict for financial reasons, they do not observe it. The priests impose the ban, alleging the crime of disobedience as the cause so that their illegal and unjust action is covered up.

97. *How Priests Demand Weekly Payments from Artisans.* Also, in many places the priests demand a weekly tax or tribute from millers, innkeepers, bakers, shoemakers, blacksmiths, tailors, shepherds, cowhands, and other artisans. If they refuse to pay, they are threatened with the ban.

101. *How Priests Withhold the Sacraments for Trivial Offenses.* Also, if someone owes a debt to the priest or to the parish, and because of poverty is unable to repay it and asks for a short extension of the loan, the priest withholds the sacraments from that person, thereby spiritually tortured, although according to the subject matter this should be handled by a secular judge.

2

Summary Instruction for Indulgence Preachers.

The sale of the jubilee indulgence for the construction of St. Peter's in Rome was regulated by a "Summary Instruction," issued by the Archbishop of Mainz, Albert of Hohenzollern. Here the details for the administration of the indulgence were set forth.[2] It was this document, together with reports of John Tetzel's indulgence preaching, that triggered Martin Luther's 95 Theses and the ensuing controversy.

LITERATURE

Martin Brecht, *Martin Luther: His Road to Reformation, 1483–1521*. Philadelphia, 1985.

Albert, by the grace of God and the Apostolic Chair, Archbishop of Magdeburg and Mainz, Primate and Chancellor of the Holy Roman Empire in Germany, Elector, Administrator of the Churches in Halberstadt, Margrave in Brandenburg, Duke of Stettin, etc.

To all who read this letter: Salvation in the Lord. We do here-

---

2. *Instructio Summaria* in W. Köhler, ed., *Dokumente zum Ablassstreit.* Tübingen, Germany, 1934, pp. 104–16.

with proclaim that our most holy Lord Leo X, by divine providence present Pontiff, has given and bestowed to all Christian believers of either sex who lend their helpful hand for the reconstruction of the cathedral church of St. Peter; the Prince of the Apostles, in Rome, complete indulgence (as well as other graces and freedoms) which the Christian believer may obtain according to the apostolic letter dealing with this matter...

Here follow the four principal graces granted in the apostolic bull. These can be obtained separately. Utmost industriousness should be exercised in order to commend each grace most emphatically to the faithful. The first grace is the complete remission of all sins. Nothing can be called greater than this grace, since man, living in sin and deprived of divine grace, obtains complete forgiveness by these means and enjoys anew the grace of God. Moreover, through such forgiveness of sin the punishment which one is obliged to undergo in purgatory on account of the offense of the divine Majesty is all remitted and the pain of purgatory is altogether done away with. And even though nothing satisfactory and worthy could be given in exchange for such a grace—since it is a gift of God and a grace beyond price—yet we decree the following rules in order that Christian believers may obtain it all the more easily:

In the first place: Everyone who is contrite in heart and has confessed with his mouth—or at least has the intention of confessing at a suitable time—shall visit the designated seven churches in which the papal coat of arms is displayed and pray in each church five devout Lord's Prayers, and five Hail Mary's in honor of the five wounds of our Lord Jesus Christ whereby our redemption took place, or one Miserere [Ps. 51], which psalm seems particularly appropriate to obtain forgiveness of sins...

Where, however, persons are so weak that they could not easily come to such a church, their confessor or penitentiary should cause to be brought an altar to a suitable place according to his discretion. When such persons visit this place and offer their prayers near the altar or before, they shall receive the indulgence as though they had visited the seven churches.

Those on a sickbed are to be given a holy picture, before or near which they shall offer several prayers according to the decision of the confessor. Thus they shall receive the indulgence in this manner as though they had visited the seven churches. Wherever any person for a certain reason desires to be relieved of the necessity to visit said altars and churches, it may be granted him by the penitentiary. However, a larger amount will become necessary under such circumstances. Concerning the contribution to the chest, for the building of said church of the chief of the apostles, the penitentiaries and confessors are to ask those making confession, after having explained the full forgiveness and privilege of this indulgence: How much money or other temporal goods they would conscientiously give for such full forgiveness? This is to be done in order that afterwards they may be brought all the more easily to make a contribution. Because the conditions of men are many and diverse, it is not possible to establish a general fee. We have therefore fixed the following rates:

Kings, queens, and their sons, archbishops and bishops, and other great rulers should pay, upon presenting themselves to places where the cross is raised, twenty-five Rheinish guilders.

Abbots, prelates of cathedral churches, counts, barons, and others of the higher nobility and their wives shall pay for each letter of indulgence ten such gold guilders. Other lesser prelates and nobles, as also the rectors of famous places, and all others who take in, either from steady income or goods or other means, 500 gold guilders should pay six guilders.

Other citizens and merchants, who ordinarily take in 200 gold florins, should pay three florins.

Other citizens, merchants, and artisans, with families and income of their own, shall pay one such guilder; those of lesser means, pay only one-half... Those who do not have any money should offer their contribution with prayer. For the kingdom of heaven should be open to the poor no less than to the rich.

Even though a wife cannot obtain from the property of her husband without his will, she can still dispose of her dowry or other property elsewhere, which will enable her to contribute even against the will of her husband. If she does not have any property or is hindered by her husband, she is to provide her contribution with prayer. This applies also to sons who are under paternal authority. Where, however, poor wives and sons yet under paternal authority are able to beg or to receive gifts from rich and devout persons, they are to put those contributions into the chest. If they have no opportunity to obtain the necessary amount, they may obtain said treasure of grace through prayer and intercession both for themselves and also for the dead... The second principal grace is a letter of indulgence, entailing the greatest, exceedingly quickening and hitherto unheard of powers, which will continue beyond the eight years designated in the present bull... The content of this letter shall be explained by the preachers and confessors to the best of their ability... The third principal grace is the participation in all the possessions of the church universal... Contributors toward said building, together with their deceased relatives, who have departed this world in a state of grace, shall from now on, and for eternity, be partakers in all petitions, intercessions, alms, fasting, prayers, in each and every pilgrimage, even those to the Holy Land; furthermore, in the stations at Rome, in masses, canonical hours, flagellations, and all other spiritual goods which have been, or shall be, brought forth by the universal, most holy Church militant or by any of its members. Believers who purchase confessional letters may also become participants in all these things. Preachers and confessors must insist with great perseverance upon these advantages, and persuade believers not to neglect to acquire these benefits along with their confessional letter. We also declare that in order to obtain these two most important graces, it is not necessary to make confession, or to visit the churches and altars, but merely to procure the confessional letter...

The fourth distinctive grace is for those souls which are in purgatory, and is the complete remission of all sins, which remission the Pope brings to pass through his intercession, to the advantage of said souls, in this wise: that the same contribution shall be placed in the chest by a living person as one would make for himself. It is our wish, however, that our subcommissioners should modify the regulations regarding contributions of this kind which are given for the dead, and that they should use their judgment in all other cases, where, in their opinion, modifications are desirable.

It is, furthermore, not necessary that the persons who place their contributions in the chest for the dead should be contrite in heart and have orally confessed, since this grace is based simply on the state of grace in which the dead departed, and on the contribution of the living, as is evident from the text of the bull. Moreover, preachers shall exert themselves to give this grace the widest publicity, since through the same, help will surely come to departed souls, and the construction of the church of St. Peter will be abundantly promoted at the same time...

3

John Tetzel: *A Sermon.* [1517]

The Dominican monk John Tetzel was charged with the sale of the indulgence in Saxony and Brandenburg. It is not altogether clear if Tetzel's rhetoric got away from him or if his instructions—the "Summary Instructions"—were not accurately understood by him. At any rate, if the contemporary accounts can be trusted, his preaching was rather flamboyant. Here are excerpts from one of his sermons.[3]

LITERATURE

Martin Brecht, *Martin Luther: His Road to Reformation, 1483–1521.* Philadelphia, 1985.

What are you thinking about? Why do you hesitate to convert yourself? Why don't you have fears about your sins? Why don't you confess now to the vicars of our most holy pope? Don't you have the example of St. Lawrence, who, compelled by the love of God, gave away his inheritance and suffered his body to be burned? Why do you not take the examples of Bartholomew, Stephen, and of other saints who gladly suffered the most gruesome deaths for the sake and salvation of their souls? You, however, do not give up

---

3. As cited in Hans J. Hillerbrand, *The Reformation. A Narrative History.* New York, 1965, p. 41.

great treasures; indeed you give not even moderate alms. They gave their bodies to be martyred, but you delight in living well joyfully. You, priest, nobleman, merchant, wife, virgin, you married people, young, old, enter into your church which is for you, as I have said, St. Peter's, and visit the most holy cross. It has been placed there for you, and it always cries and calls for you. Are you perhaps ashamed to visit the cross with a candle and yet not ashamed to visit a tavern? Are you ashamed to go to the apostolic confessors but not ashamed to go to a dance? Behold, you are on the raging sea of this world in storm and danger, not knowing if you will safely reach the harbor of salvation. Do you not know that everything which man has hangs on a thin thread and that all of life is but a struggle on earth? Let us then fight, as did Lawrence and the other saints, for the salvation of the soul, not the body that is today but not tomorrow. Today it is well, but not tomorrow. Today alive and tomorrow dead.

You should know that all who confess and in penance put alms into the coffer according to the counsel of the confessor, will obtain complete remission of all their sins. If they visit, after confession and after the Jubilee, the cross, and the altar every day, they will receive that indulgence which would be theirs upon visiting in St. Peter's the seven altars, where complete indulgence is offered. Why are you then standing there? Run for the salvation of your souls! Be as careful and concerned for the salvation of your souls as you are for your temporal goods, which you seek both day and night. Seek the Lord while he may be found and while he is near. Work, as St. John says, while it is yet day, for the night comes when no man can work.

Don't you hear the voices of your wailing dead parents and others who say, "Have mercy upon me, have mercy upon me, because we are in severe punishment and pain. From this you could redeem us with small alms and yet you do not want to do so." Open your ears as the father says to the son and the mother to the daughter..., "We have created you, fed you, cared for you, and left you our temporal goods. Why then are you so cruel and harsh that you do not want to save us, though it only takes a little? You let us lie in flames so that we only slowly come to the promised glory." You may have letters which let you have, once in life and in the hour of death...full remission of the punishment which belongs to sin. Oh, those of you who made a vow, you usurers, robbers, murderers, and criminals—now is the time to hear the voice of God. He does not want the death of the sinners, but that they be converted and live. Convert yourself then, Jerusalem, Jerusalem, to the Lord, thy God. Oh, you blasphemers, gossipers, who hinder this work openly or secretly, what about your affairs? You are outside the fellowship of the Church. No Masses, sermons, prayers, sacraments, or intercession help you. No field, vineyard, trees, or cattle bring fruit or wine for you. Even spiritual things vanish, as many an illustration could point out. Convert yourself with all your heart and use the medicine of which the Book of Wisdom says, "The Most High has made medicine out of the earth and a wise man will not reject it."

4

Frederick the Wise, Elector of Saxony:
The Wittenberg Book of Holies. [1509]

L ate medieval spirituality was character-
ized by a great interest in relics of the
saints. Elector Frederick of Saxony was a
devoted and committed collector of relics. Here is a section from
the printed catalogue of his collection in Wittenberg, on All Saints'
Day on public display.[4]

LITERATURE

Martin Brecht, *Martin Luther: His Road to Reformation, 1483–1521.*
Philadelphia, 1985.

One piece of the stone on which Jesus stood while weeping
over Jerusalem. One piece of the stone from which Christ got on
the donkey. Two pieces of the ground where the Lord Christ was
arrested. Five pieces of the table on which the Lord Christ held
the Last Supper with his disciples. One piece of the bread of which
Christ ate with his disciples during the Last Supper. One piece of
the land which was bought for the thirty pieces of silver for which
Christ was betrayed. One piece of the Holy Land. Three pieces of

---

4. Lucas Cranach, *Wittenberger Heiligthumsbuch.* Wittenberg, Germany,
1509, E 2i, E 2j b, F 2, F 2ij, H 2ij b, I 2ff.

the stone where the Lord sweated blood. One piece of the ground where the Lord sweated blood. One piece of the stone sprinkled with the blood of Christ. Three pieces of the Mount of Olives and of the rod of Aaron. Two pieces of the rod of Moses. One piece of the burning bush which Moses saw. One piece of an object sprinkled with the blood of Christ. Eleven pieces of Mount Calvary. Two pieces of the Mount of Olives. One piece of the cloth with which the Lord wiped his disciples' feet. One piece of the robe of Christ. One piece of the seamless robe of Christ. One piece of the robe of Christ. One piece of his purple robe. Two pieces of the cloth which St. Veronica received from the Lord. Three pieces of the white robe in which the Lord was ridiculed by Herod. Three pieces of the cloth with which our Lord's holy eyes were blindfolded. One piece of the beard of the Lord Jesus. One piece of the wax of the candles which touched the sudarium of Christ. One piece of the wedge with which the cross of Christ was held in place. Three pieces of the stone on which the cross stood. Three pieces of the place where the cross of Christ was found. Twelve pieces of the pillar where the Lord Christ was scourged and flogged.

One piece of the rope with which Jesus was tied. Three pieces of the rod with which the Lord Jesus was scourged. Three pieces of the whip with which the Lord Jesus was flogged. One piece of the stone upon which the Lord Jesus sat when he was crowned. One piece of the stone which was crushed while the Lord carried the cross. One piece of the sponge with which the Lord was given vinegar and gall.

Two pieces of the crown of the Lord Jesus. Eight complete thorns of the crown of the Lord Jesus.

One large piece of one nail which was driven through the hands or feet of the Lord Jesus.

A thorn which wounded the holy head of the Lord Jesus.

One piece of the holy cross.

Three pieces of the holy cross.

Three pieces of the three kinds of wood of the cross of Christ.

A particularly large piece from the holy cross. Twenty-five pieces of the holy cross.

One piece of the stone which lay on the grave of Christ. Twenty-two pieces of the grave of Christ. One piece of the stone from which Christ descended into heaven. Seventy-six pieces of holy remains. Bones from holy places which because of the faded writing can no longer be read and identified.

All in all: five thousand and five pieces. An indulgence of one hundred days for each piece. There are eight rooms and each room has an indulgence of one hundred and one days in addition. Blessed are those who participate therein.

5

Martin Luther: *Letter to Archbishop Albert of Mainz.* [1517]

Luther sent a copy of his 95 Theses in which he denounced the practices of John Tetzel to the person he thought a key figure, Archbishop Albert of Brandenburg, and included the following letter.[5]

LITERATURE

Martin Brecht, *Martin Luther: His Road to Reformation, 1483–1521.* Philadelphia, 1985.

In the name of Jesus I bid you the grace and mercy of God, Reverend Father in Christ, Most Illustrious Elector. You must graciously forgive that I, that scum of the earth, am so bold as to dare to address a letter to you. The Lord Jesus is my witness that I am not unaware of my unworthiness and insignificance, which has caused me to delay for some time what I am now boldly doing. I am strongly moved by the faithful devotion, which I confess to owe to you, Reverend Father in Christ. May you therefore cast

---

5. As printed in Hans J. Hillerbrand, *The Reformation. A Narrative History.* New York, 1965, pp. 49–51. The edition used is the facsimile edition, Munich, 1884.

a gracious eye upon me, as I am earth and ashes, and with clemency becoming a bishop graciously hear and understand my concern.

There is sold in the country under the protection of your illustrious name the papal indulgence for the building of St. Peter's in Rome. I do not complain so much about the great claim of the indulgence preachers whom I have not personally heard. But I am greatly concerned about the false notion existing among the common people, which has become a cause of public boast. These unfortunate souls seemingly believe they are assured of their salvation as soon as they purchase letters of indulgence. They also believe that the souls leave purgatory as soon as they put the money into the chest. Furthermore, this grace of indulgence is said to be so powerful that no sin is too large not to be forgiven, even in the impossible case when someone had—to use their words—assaulted the Mother of God. Finally, it is claimed that a person can free himself by this indulgence from all punishment and guilt…

How is it possible that the indulgence preachers convey security and fearlessness to the people through false fables and further promises about indulgences? Indulgences do not contribute to the salvation and sanctification of souls but only remit temporal punishment which is imposed according to canon law. Therefore works of piety and charity are infinitely more valuable than indulgences and yet they are preached neither with such splendor nor diligence. Indeed, they must surely give way to the more important preaching of indulgences. Yet it should be the foremost and only care of all bishops to teach the gospel and the love of Christ to the people. Christ nowhere commanded to preach indulgences, but emphatically insisted on the preaching of the gospel. What great danger and shame wait for a bishop who allows the Gospel to be silenced, but suffers the pompous proclamation of indulgences and is more concerned about indulgences than the gospel.

Will not Christ say to him, "Ye strain at a gnat, and swallow a camel"?

But this, Most Reverend Father in the Lord, is not all. The *Instructions* to the indulgence commissioners issued under your name state—surely without your knowledge and consent—that all of the most precious graces offered consist in the invaluable divine gift of man's reconciliation with God and the remission of all punishment in purgatory. It is also said that those who purchase such letters of indulgences need not be contrite. What can I do, Most Magnificent Bishop and Illustrious Elector, but beseech you, through our Lord Jesus Christ, to cast your eyes of paternal concern on this matter.

6

Martin Luther: *Preface to the First Volume of His Latin Writings.* [1545][6]

Martin Luther's formulation of a new theology, which occurred as he pursued his teaching responsibilities at the University of Wittenberg and eventually led to the Reformation, was related to an intensely personal religious experience. Luther had become a monk in order to have a "gracious God" whom he would serve by doing good. Despite his utterly conscientious exercise of his religious vocation as a monk, brutal self-analysis confronted him with the realization that he was nothing but a sinner, deserving to be eternally damned by God's righteousness.

As the following excerpt indicates, Luther despaired over this reality, but then found deliverance in a new understanding of the term "righteousness of God."

The setting of Luther's recollection of that breakthrough is a description of the *res indulgentiara*, the indulgences affair, to share with the reader how the Reformation began. Luther described his own spiritual state at the time, the nature of his problem, and his solution—a new understanding of the notion of "the righteousness

6. Lewis W. Spitz, ed., *Luther's Works.* Vol. 34, *Career of the Reformer IV.* Philadelphia, 1960, pp. 336–37.

of God." Faced with an exegetical problem, he found an exegetical answer.

LITERATURE

Martin Brecht, *Martin Luther: His Road to Reformation*. Philadelphia, 1985.

Meanwhile, I had already during that year returned to interpret the Psalter anew. I had confidence in the fact that I was more skilful, after I had lectured in the university on St. Paul's epistles to the Romans, to the Galatians, and the one to the Hebrews. I had indeed been captivated with an extraordinary ardor for understanding Paul in the Epistle to the Romans. But up till then it was not the cold blood about the heart, but a single word in chapter 1 [:17], "In it the righteousness of God is revealed," that had stood in my way. For I hated that word "righteousness of God," which, according to the use and custom of all the teachers, I had been taught to understand philosophically regarding the formal or active righteousness, as they called it, with which God is righteous and punishes the unrighteous sinner.

Though I lived as a monk without reproach, I felt that I was a sinner before God with an extremely disturbed conscience. I could not believe that He was placated by my satisfaction. I did not love, yes, I hated the righteous God who punishes sinners, and secretly, if not blasphemously, certainly murmuring greatly, I was angry with God, and said, if, indeed, it is not enough that miserable sinners, eternally lost through original sin, are crushed by every kind of calamity by the law of the Decalogue, without having God add pain to pain by the gospel and also by the gospel threatening us with righteousness and wrath. Thus I raged with a fierce and troubled conscience. Nevertheless, I beat importunately upon

Paul at that place, most ardently desiring to know what St. Paul wanted.

At last, by the mercy of God, meditating day and night, I gave heed to the context of the words, namely, "In it the righteousness of God is revealed as it is written, He who through faith is righteous shall live." There I began to understand that the righteousness of God is that by which the righteous lives by a gift of God, namely by faith. And this is the meaning: The righteousness of God is revealed by the gospel, namely, the passive righteousness with which merciful God justifies us by faith, as it is written, "He who through faith is righteous shall live." Here I felt that I was altogether born again and had entered paradise itself through open gates. There a totally other face of the entire Scripture showed itself to me. Thereupon, I ran through the Scriptures from memory. I also found in other terms an analogy, as, the work of God, that is, what God does in us, the power of God, with which He makes us strong, the wisdom of God, with which He makes us wise, the strength of God, the salvation of God, the glory of God.

And I extolled my sweetest word with a love as great as the hatred with which I had before hated the word "righteousness of God." Thus that place in Paul was for me truly the gate to paradise. Later I read Augustine's *The Spirit and the Letter,* where contrary to hope I found that he, too, interpreted God's righteousness in a similar way, as the righteousness with which God clothes us when He justifies us. Although this was heretofore said imperfectly and he did not explain all things concerning imputation clearly, it nevertheless was pleasing that God's righteousness with which we are justified was taught.

7

Martin Luther:
The Freedom of a Christian. [1520]

This pamphlet was one of the three major treatises Luther wrote in 1520, the other two being the *Babylonian Captivity of the Church* and the *Open Letter to the Christian Nobility*. Taken together, they constitute an incisive exposition of his thought. Luther wrote the tract on Christian freedom in October, at a time of increasing uncertainty about papal action against him. Published in both German and Latin, it quickly became popular and its title offered a slogan that was widely echoed. Its theme was that of Christian freedom, but in a broader sense it delineated the principles of Luther's program of ecclesiastical reform.

Luther's other two tracts of 1520 sought to do the same—the *Open Letter* by demanding a reform in the structure of the Church, the *Babylonian Captivity* by questioning Catholic sacramental teaching. The pamphlet on Christian freedom discussed the principles of the new life in Christ as it grew out of a new understanding of the nature of the Christian gospel. What must a Christian do? On the basis of the righteousness of faith, the cornerstone of his new gospel, Luther repudiated the rigidity of Catholic morality and offered his own reconstruction. The treatise opened with the assertion that "a Christian is a perfectly free lord of all, subject to none," bound to his neighbor only in love. Luther repudiated the Aristotelian notion that good works make a good man and insisted a good man does good works, and does so freely and without legal regimentation. Luther's tract aimed to show how a vibrant and dynamic faith makes this possible. A slightly condensed version of the entire tract is reprinted below.[7]

LITERATURE

Eberhard Jüngel, *The Freedom of a Christian: Luther's Significance for Contemporary Theology.* Minneapolis, 1988.

Many have considered Christian faith an easy thing, and not a few have given it a place among the virtues. They do this because they have not had experience in it and have never tasted the great virtue there is in faith. It is impossible to write well about it or to understand what has been written about it unless one has at one time or another experienced the courage which faith gives a man when trials oppress him. But he who has had even a faint taste of it can never write, speak, meditate, or hear enough concerning it. It is a living "spring of water welling up to eternal life," as Christ calls it in John 4 [: 14].

As for me, although I have no wealth of faith to boast of and know how scant my supply is, I nevertheless hope that I have attained to a little faith, even though I have been assailed by great and various temptations; and I hope that I can discuss it, if not more elegantly, certainly more to the point, than those literalists and subtle disputants have previously done, who have not even understood what they have written.

To make the way smoother for the unlearned—for only them

---

7. Harold J. Grimm, ed., *Luther's Works.* Vol. 31, *Career of the Reformer I.* Philadelphia, 1957, pp. 327–79.

do I serve—I shall set down the following two propositions concerning the freedom and the bondage of the spirit:

A Christian is a perfectly free lord of all, subject to none.

A Christian is a perfectly dutiful servant of all, subject to all.

These two theses seem to contradict each other. If, however, they should be found to fit together, they would serve our purpose beautifully. Both are Paul's own statements, who says in 1 Cor. 9 [: 19], "For though I am free from all men, I have made myself a slave to all," and in Rom. 13 [: 8], "Owe no one anything, except to love one another." Love by its very nature is ready to serve and be subject to him who is loved. So Christ, although He was Lord of all, was "born of woman, born under the law" [Gal. 4: 4], and therefore was at the same time a free man and a servant, "in the form of God" and "of a servant" [Phil. 2: 6–7].

Let us start, however, with something more remote from our subject, but more obvious. Man has a twofold nature, a spiritual and a bodily one. According to the spiritual nature, which men refer to as the soul, he is called a spiritual, inner, or new man. According to the bodily nature, which men refer to as flesh, he is called a carnal, outward, or old man, of whom the Apostle writes in 2 Cor. 4 [: 16], "Though our outer nature is wasting away, our inner nature is being renewed every day." Because of this diversity of nature, the Scriptures assert contradictory things concerning the same man, since these two men in the same man contradict each other, "for the desires of the flesh are against the Spirit, and the desires of the Spirit are against the flesh," according to Gal. 5 [: 17].

First, let us consider the inner man to see how a righteous, free, and pious Christian, that is, a spiritual, new, and inner man, becomes what he is. It is evident that no external thing has any influence in producing Christian righteousness or freedom, or in producing unrighteousness or servitude. A simple argument will furnish the proof of this statement. What can it profit the soul if the body is well, free, and active, and eats, drinks, and does as it pleases? For in these respects even the most godless slaves of vice may prosper. On the other hand, how will poor health or imprisonment or hunger or thirst or any other external misfortune harm the soul? Even the godliest people, and those who are free because of clear consciences, are afflicted with these things. None of these things touch either the freedom or the servitude of the soul. It does not help the soul if the body is adorned with the sacred robes of priests or dwells in sacred places or is occupied with sacred duties or prays, fasts, abstains from certain kinds of food, or does any work than can be done by the body and in the body. The righteousness and the freedom of the soul require something far different since any wicked person could do the things which have been mentioned. Such works produce nothing but hypocrites. On the other hand, it will not harm the soul if the body is clothed in secular dress, dwells in unconsecrated places, eats and drinks as others do, does not pray aloud, and neglects to do all the above-mentioned things which hypocrites can do.

Furthermore, to put aside all kinds of works, even contemplation, meditation, and all that the soul can do, does not help. One thing, and only one thing, is necessary for Christian life, righteousness and freedom. That one thing is the most holy word of God, the gospel of Christ, as Christ says, John 11 [:25], "I am the resurrection, and the life: he who believes in me, though he die, yet shall he live"; and John 8 [:36], "If the Son makes you free, you will be free indeed"; and Matt. 4 [:4], "Man shall not live by bread alone, but by every word that proceeds from the mouth of God." Let us then consider it certain and firmly established that the soul can do without anything except the word of God and that where the word of God is missing there is no help at all for the soul. If it has the word of God it is rich and lacks nothing since it is the word of life, truth, light, peace, righteousness, salvation, joy, liberty, wisdom, power, grace, glory, and of every incalculable blessing. This is why the prophet in the entire Psalm [119] and in many other places yearns and sighs for the word of God and uses so many names to describe it.

On the other hand, there is no more terrible disaster with which the wrath of God can afflict men than a famine of the hearing of His word, as He says in Amos [8: 11]. Likewise there is no greater mercy than when He sends forth His word, as we read in Psalm 107 [: 20]: "He sent forth His word, and healed them, and delivered them from destruction." Nor was Christ sent into the world for any other ministry except that of the word. Moreover, the entire spiritual estate—all the apostles, bishops, and priests—has been called and instituted only for the ministry of the word.

You will ask, "What then is the word of God, and how shall it be used, since there are so many words of God?" I answer: The Apostle explains this in Romans 1. The word is the gospel of God concerning His Son, who was made flesh, suffered, rose from the dead, and was glorified through the Spirit who sanctifies. To preach Christ means to feed the soul, make it righteous, set it free, and save it, provided it believes the preaching. Faith alone is the saving and efficacious use of the word of God, according to Rom. 10 [: 9]: "If you confess with your lips that Jesus is Lord and believe in your heart that God raised Him from the dead, you will be saved." Furthermore, "Christ is the end of the law, that every one who has faith may be justified" [Rom. 10: 4]. Again, in Rom. 1 [: 17], "He who through faith is righteous shall live." The word of God cannot be received and cherished by any works whatever but only by faith. Therefore it is clear that, as the soul needs only the word of God for its life and righteousness, so it is justified by faith alone and not any works; for if it could be justified by anything else, it would not need the word, and consequently it would not need faith.

This faith cannot exist in connection with works—that is to say, if you at the same time claim to be justified by works, whatever their character—for that would be the same as "limping with two different opinions" [1 Kings 18: 21], as worshipping Baal and kissing one's own hand [Job 31: 27–28], which, as Job says, is a very great iniquity. Therefore the moment you begin to have faith you learn that all things in you are altogether blameworthy, sinful, and damnable, as the Apostle says in Rom. 3 [: 23], "Since all have sinned and fall short of the glory of God," and "None is righteous, no, not one; all have turned aside, together they have gone wrong," Rom. 3 [: 10–12]. When you have learned this you will know that you need Christ, who suffered and rose again for you so that, if you believe in Him, you may through this faith become a new man insofar as your sins are forgiven and you are justified by the merits of another, namely, of Christ alone.

Since, therefore, this faith can rule only in the inner man, as Rom. 10 [: 10] says, "For man believes with his heart and so is justified," and since faith alone justifies, it is clear that the inner person cannot be justified, freed, or saved by any outer work or action at all, and that these works, whatever their character, have nothing to do with this inner person. On the other hand, only ungodliness and unbelief of heart, and no outer work, make him guilty and a damnable servant of sin. Wherefore it ought to be the first concern of every Christian to lay aside all confidence in works and increasingly to strengthen faith alone and through faith to grow in the knowledge, not of works, but of Christ Jesus, who suffered and rose for him, as Peter teaches in the last chapter of his first epistle, 1 Pet. [5: 10]. No other work makes a Christian. Thus when the Jews asked Christ, as related in John 6 [: 28], what they must do "to be doing the work of God," He brushed aside the multitude of works which He saw they did in great profusion and suggested one work, saying, "This is the work of God, that you believe in Him whom He has sent" [John 6: 29]; "for on Him has God the Father set His seal" [John 6: 27].

Therefore true faith in Christ is a treasure beyond comparison which brings with it complete salvation and saves man from every evil, as Christ says in the last chapter of Mark [16: 16]: "He who believes and is baptized will be saved; but he who does not believe will be condemned." Isaiah contemplated this treasure and foretold it in chapter 10: "The Lord will make a small and consuming word upon the land, and it will overpower with righteousness" [cf. Is. 10: 22]. This is as though he said, "Faith, which is a small and perfect fulfillment of the law, will fill believers with so great a righteousness that they will need nothing more to become righteous." So Paul says, Rom. 10[: 10], "For man believes with his heart and so is justified."

Should you ask how it happens that faith alone justifies and offers us such a treasure of great benefits without works in view of the fact that so many works, ceremonies, and laws are prescribed in the Scriptures, I answer: First of all, remember what has been said, namely, that faith alone, without works, justifies, frees, and saves; we shall make this clearer later on. Here we must point out that all of divine Scripture is divided into two parts: commandments and promises. Although the commandments teach things that are good, the things taught are not done as soon as they are taught, for the commandments show us what we ought to do but do not give us the power to do it. They are intended to teach humans to know themselves, that through them they may recognize their inability to do good and may despair of their own ability. That is why they are called the Old Testament and constitute the

Old Testament. For example, the commandment "You shall not covet" [Ex. 20: 1] is a command which proves us all to be sinners, for no one can avoid coveting no matter how much he may struggle against it. Therefore, in order not to covet and to fulfill the commandment, a man is compelled to despair of himself, to seek the help which he does not find in himself elsewhere and from someone else, as stated in Hos. [13: 9]: "Destruction is your own, O Israel: your help is only in me." As we fare with respect to one commandment, so we fare with all, for it is equally impossible for us to keep any one of them.

Now when a person has learned through the commandments to recognize his helplessness and is distressed about how he might satisfy the law—since the law must be fulfilled so that not a jot or tittle shall be lost, otherwise man will be condemned without hope—then, being truly humbled and reduced to nothing in his own eyes, he finds in himself nothing whereby he may be justified and saved. Then the second part of Scripture comes to our aid, namely, the promises of God which declare the glory of God, saying, "If you wish to fulfill the law and not covet, as the law demands, come, believe in Christ in whom grace, righteousness, peace, liberty, and all things are promised you. If you believe, you shall have all things; if you do not believe, you shall lack all things." That which is impossible for you to accomplish by trying to fulfill all the works of the law—many and useless as they all are—you will accomplish quickly and easily through faith. God our Father has made all things depend on faith so that whoever has faith will have everything, and whoever does not have faith will have nothing. "For God has consigned all individuals to disobedience, that He may have mercy upon all," as it is stated in Rom. 11 [: 32]. Thus the promises of God give what the commandments of God demand and fulfill what the law prescribes so that all things may be God's alone, both the commandments and the fulfilling of the commandments. He alone commands, He alone fulfills. Therefore the promises of God belong to the New Testament. Indeed, they are the New Testament...

From what has been said it is easy to see from what source faith derives such great power and why a good work and all good works together cannot equal it. No good work can rely upon the word of God or live in the soul, for faith alone and the word of God rule in the soul. Just as the heated iron glows like fire, because of the union of fire with it, so the word imparts its qualities to the soul. It is clear, then, that a Christian has all that he needs in faith and needs no works to justify him; and if he has no need of works, he has no need of the law; and if he has no need of the law, surely he is free from the law. It is true that "the law is not laid down for the just" [1 Tim. 1: 9]. This is that Christian liberty, our faith, which does not induce us to live in idleness or wickedness but makes the law and works unnecessary for any person's righteousness and salvation.

This is the first power of faith. Let us now examine the second. It is a further function of faith that it honors him whom it trusts with the most reverent and highest regard since it considers him truthful and trustworthy. There is no other honor equal to the estimate of truthfulness and righteousness with which we honor him whom we trust. Could we ascribe to a man anything greater than truthfulness and righteousness and perfect goodness? On the other hand, there is no way in which we can show greater contempt for an individual than to regard him as false and wicked and to be suspicious of him, as we are when we do not trust him. So when the soul firmly trusts God's promises, it regards Him as truthful and righteous. Nothing more excellent than this can be ascribed to God. The very highest worship of God is this, that we ascribe to Him truthfulness, righteousness, and whatever else should be ascribed to one who is trusted. When this is done, the soul consents to His will. Then it hallows His name and allows itself to be treated according to God's good pleasure, for clinging to God's promises, it does not doubt that He who is true, just, and wise will do, dispose, and provide all things well.

Is not such a soul most obedient to God in all things by this faith? What commandment is there that such obedience has not completely fulfilled? What more complete fulfillment is there than obedience in all things? This obedience, however, is not rendered by works but by faith alone. On the other hand, what greater rebellion against God, what greater wickedness, what greater contempt of God is there than not believing His promise? For what is this but to make God a liar or to doubt that He is truthful—that is, to ascribe truthfulness to one's self but lying and vanity to God. Does not a man who does this deny God and set himself up as an idol in his heart? Then what good are works done in such wickedness, even if they were the works of angels and apostles? Therefore God has rightly included all things, not under anger or lust, but under unbelief, so that they who imagine that they are fulfilling the law by doing the works of chastity and mercy required by the law (the civil and human virtues) might not be saved. They are included under the sin of unbelief and must either seek mercy or be justly condemned...

The third incomparable benefit of faith is that it unites the soul with Christ as a bride is united with her bridegroom. By this mystery, as the Apostle teaches, Christ and the soul become one flesh [Eph. 5: 31–32]. And if they are one flesh and there is between them a true marriage—indeed the most perfect of all marriages, since human marriages are but poor examples of this one true marriage—it follows that everything they have they hold in common, the good as well as the evil. Accordingly the believing soul can boast of and glory in whatever Christ has as though it were its own, and whatever the soul has Christ claims as His own. Let us compare these and we shall see inestimable benefits. Christ is full of grace, life, and salvation. The soul is full of sins, death, and damnation. Now let faith come between them and sins, death, and damnation will be Christ's, while grace, life, and salvation will be the soul's; for if Christ is a bridegroom, He must take upon Himself the things which are His bride's and bestow upon her the things that are His. If He gives her His body and very self, how shall He not give her all that is His? And if He takes the body of the bride, how shall He not take all that is hers?

Here we have a most pleasing vision not only of communion but also of a blessed struggle and victory and salvation and redemption. Christ is God and man in one person. He has neither sinned nor died, and is not condemned, and He cannot sin, die, or be condemned; His righteousness, life, and salvation are unconquerable, eternal, omnipotent. By the wedding ring of faith He shares in the sins, death, and pains of hell which are His bride's. As a matter of fact, He makes them His own and acts as if they were His own and as if He Himself had sinned; He suffered, died, and descended into hell that He might overcome them all. Now since it was such a one who did all this, and death and hell could not swallow Him up, these were necessarily swallowed up by Him in a mighty duel; for His righteousness is greater than the sins of all men, His life stronger than death, His salvation more invincible than hell. Thus the believing soul by means of the pledge of its faith is free in Christ, its bridegroom, free from all sins, secure against death and hell; and is endowed with the eternal righteousness, life, and salvation of Christ its bridegroom. So He takes to Himself a glorious bride, "without spot or wrinkle, cleansing her by the washing of water with the word" [cf. Eph. 5:26–27] of life, that is, by faith in the word of life, righteousness, and salvation. In this way He marries her in faith, steadfast love, and in mercies, righteousness, and justice, as Hos. 2 [: 19–20] says…

From this you once more see that much is ascribed to faith, namely, that it alone can fulfill the law and justify without works. You see that the first commandment, which says, "You shall worship one God," is fulfilled by faith alone. Though you were nothing but good works from the soles of your feet to the crown of your head, you would still not be righteous or worship God or fulfill the first commandment, since God cannot be worshipped unless you ascribe to Him the glory of truthfulness and all goodness which is due Him. This cannot be done by works but only by the faith of the heart. Not by the doing of works but by believing do we glorify God and acknowledge that He is truthful. Therefore faith alone is the righteousness of a Christian and the fulfilling of all the commandments, for he who fulfills the first commandment has no difficulty in fulfilling all the rest.

Hence all of us who believe in Christ are priests and monarchs in Christ, as 1 Pet. 2 [: 9] says: "You are a chosen race, God's own people, a royal priesthood, a priestly kingdom, that you may declare the wonderful deeds of Him who called you out of darkness into His marvelous light."

The nature of this priesthood and kingship is something like this: First, with respect to the kingship, every Christian is by faith so exalted above all things that, by virtue of a spiritual power, he is lord of all things without exception, so that nothing can do him any harm. As a matter of fact, all things are made subject to him and are compelled to serve him in obtaining salvation. Accordingly Paul says in Rom. 8 [: 28], "All things work together for good for the elect," and in 1 Cor. 3 [: 21–23], "All things are yours whether life or death or the present or the future, all are yours; and you are Christ's." This is not to say that every Christian is placed over all things to have and control them by physical power—a madness with which some churchmen are afflicted—for such power belongs to kings, princes, and other men on earth. Our ordinary experience in life shows us that we are subjected to all, suffer many things, and even die. As a matter of fact, the more Christian a person is, the more evils, sufferings, and deaths must be endured, as we see in Christ the first-born prince Himself, and in all His brethren, the saints. The power of which we speak is spiritual. It rules in the midst of enemies and is powerful in the midst of oppression. This means nothing else than that "power is made perfect in weakness" [2 Cor. 12: 9] and that in all things I can find profit toward salvation [Rom. 8: 28], so that the cross and death itself are compelled to serve me and to work together with me for my salvation. This is a splendid privilege and hard to attain, a truly omnipotent power, a spiritual dominion in which there is nothing so good and nothing so evil but that it shall work together for good to me, if only I believe. Yes, since faith alone suffices for salvation, I need nothing except faith exercising the power and dominion of its own liberty. Lo, this is the inestimable power and liberty of Christians.

Not only are we the freest of rulers, we are also priests forever, which is far more excellent than being kings, for as priests we are worthy to appear before God to pray for others and to teach one another divine things. These are the functions of priests, and they cannot be granted to any unbeliever. Thus Christ has made it possible for us, provided we believe in Him, to be not only His brethren, co-heirs, and fellow-kings, but also His fellow priests...

From this anyone can clearly see how a Christian is free from all things and over all things so that he needs no works to make him righteous and save him, since faith alone abundantly confers all these things. Should he grow so foolish, however, as to presume to become righteous, free, saved, and a Christian by means of some good work, he would instantly lose faith and all its benefits, a foolishness aptly illustrated in the fable of the dog who runs along a stream with a piece of meat in his mouth and, deceived by the reflection of the meat in the water, opens his mouth to snap at it and so loses both the meat and the reflection.

You will ask, "If all who are in the church are priests, how do these whom we now call priests differ from laymen?" I answer: Injustice is done those words "priest," "cleric," "spiritual," "ecclesiastic," when they are transferred from all Christians to those few who are now by a mischievous usage called "ecclesiastics." Holy Scripture makes no distinction between them, although it gives the name "ministers," "servants," "stewards" to those who are now proudly called popes, bishops, and lords and who should according to the ministry of the word serve others and teach them the faith of Christ and the freedom of believers. Although we are all equally priests we cannot all publicly minister and teach. We ought not to do so even if we could. Paul writes accordingly in 1 Cor. 4 [: 1], "This is how one should regard us, as servants of Christ and stewards of the mysteries of God."...

To return to our purpose, I believe that it has now become clear that it is not enough or in any sense Christian to preach the works, life, and words of Christ as historical facts, as if the knowledge of these would suffice for the conduct of life; yet this is the fashion among those who must today be regarded as our best preachers. Far less is it sufficient or Christian to say nothing at all about Christ and to teach instead human laws and the decrees of the Fathers. Now there are not a few who preach Christ and read about Him that they may move men's affections to sympathy with Christ, to anger against the Jews, and such childish and effeminate nonsense. Rather ought Christ to be preached to the end that faith in Him may be established that He may not only be Christ but be Christ for you and me, and that what is said of Him and is denoted in His name may be effectual in us. Such faith is produced and preserved in us by preaching why Christ came, what He brought and bestowed, what benefit it is to us to accept Him. This is done when that Christian liberty which He bestows is rightly taught and we are told in what way we Christians are all kings and priests and therefore lords of all and may firmly believe that whatever we have done is pleasing and acceptable in the sight of God, as I have already said.

What person is there whose heart, upon hearing these things, will not rejoice to its depth, and when receiving such comfort will not grow tender so that he will love Christ as he never could by means of any laws or works? Who would have the power to harm or frighten such a heart? If the knowledge of sin or the fear of death should break in upon it, it is ready to hope in the Lord. It does not grow afraid when it hears tidings of evil. It is not disturbed when it sees its enemies. This is so because it believes that the righteousness of Christ is its own and that its sin is not its own but Christ's, and that all sin is swallowed up by the righteousness of Christ. This, as has been said above, is a necessary consequence on account of faith in Christ. So the heart learns to scoff at death and sin and to say with the Apostle, "O death, where is thy victory? O death, where is thy sting? The sting of death is sin, and the power of sin is the law. But thanks be to God, who gives us the victory through our Lord Jesus Christ" [1 Cor. 15: 55–57]...

Now let us turn to the second part, the outer person. Here we shall answer all those who, offended by the word "faith" and by all that has been said, now ask, "If faith does all things and is alone sufficient unto righteousness, why then are good works commanded? We will take our ease and do no works and be content with faith." I answer: Not so, you wicked, not so. This would indeed be proper if we were wholly inner and perfectly spiritual beings. But such we shall be only at the last day, the day of the resurrection of the dead. As long as we live in the flesh we only begin to make some progress in that which shall be perfected in the future life. For this reason the Apostle in Rom. 8 [: 23] calls all that we attain in this life "the first fruits of the Spirit" because we shall indeed receive the greater portion, even the fullness of the Spirit, in the future. This is the place to assert that which was said above, namely, that a Christian is the servant of all and made subject to all. Insofar as he is free he does no works, but insofar as he is a servant he does all kinds of works. How this is possible we shall see.

Although, as I have said, a person is abundantly and sufficiently justified by faith inwardly, in his spirit, and so has all that he needs, except insofar as this faith and these riches must grow from day to day even to the future life; yet he remains in this mortal life on earth. In this life he must control his own body and have dealings with others. Here the works begin; here individuals cannot enjoy leisure; here they must indeed take care to discipline their bodies by fasting, watchings, labors, and other reasonable discipline and to subject it to the Spirit so that it will obey and conform to the inner person and faith and not revolt against faith and hinder the inner person, as it is the nature of the body to do if it is not held in check. The inner person, who by faith is created in the image of God, is both joyful and happy because of Christ in whom so many benefits are conferred upon him; and therefore it is his one occupation to serve God joyfully and without thought of gain, in love that is not constrained.

While they are doing this, behold, they meet a contrary will in their own flesh, which strives to serve the world and seeks its own advantage. This the spirit of faith cannot tolerate, but with joyful zeal it attempts to put the body under control and hold it in check, as Paul says in Rom. 7 [: 22–23], "For I delight in the law of God, in my inmost self, but I see in my members another law at war with the law of my mind, and making me captive to the law of sin," and in another place, "But I pommel my body and subdue it, lest after preaching to others I myself should be disqualified" [1 Cor. 9: 27], and in Galatians [5: 24], "And those who belong to Christ Jesus have crucified the flesh with its passions and desires."

In doing these works, however, we must not think that a person is justified before God by them, for faith, which alone is righteousness before God, cannot endure that erroneous opinion. We must, however, realize that these works reduce the body to subjection and purify it of its evil lusts, and our whole purpose is to be directed only toward the driving out of lusts. Since by faith the soul is cleansed and made to love God, it desires that all things, and especially its own body, shall be purified so that all things may join with it in loving and praising God. Hence a person cannot be idle, for the need of his body drives him and he is compelled to do many good works to reduce it to subjection. Nevertheless, the works themselves do not justify him before God, but he does the works out of spontaneous love in obedience to God and considers nothing except the approval of God, whom he would most scrupulously obey in all things.

The following statements are therefore true: "Good works do not make a good person, but a good person does good works; evil works do not make a wicked person, but a wicked person does evil works." Consequently, it is always necessary that the substance or person himself be good before there can be any good works, and that good works follow and proceed from the good person; as Christ also says, "A good tree cannot bear evil fruit, nor can a bad tree bear good fruit" [Matt. 7: 18]. It is clear that the fruits do not bear the tree and that the tree does not grow on the fruits, also that, on the contrary, the trees bear the fruits and the fruits grow on the trees. It is necessary, therefore, that the trees exist before their fruits and the fruits do not make trees either good or bad, but rather as the trees are, so are the fruits they bear; so a man must first be good or wicked before he does a good or wicked work, and his works do not make him good or wicked, but he himself makes his works either good or wicked.

Illustrations of the same truth can be seen in all trades. A good or a bad house does not make a good or a bad builder, but a good or a bad builder makes a good or a bad house. And in general, the work never makes the worker like itself, but the worker makes the work like himself. So it is with the works of people. As individuals are, whether believers or unbelievers, so also are their works—good if it was done in faith, wicked if it was done in unbelief. But the converse is not true, that the work makes the person either a believer or an unbeliever. As works do not make a person a believer, so also they do not make him righteous. But as faith makes a person a believer and righteous, so faith does good works. Since, then, works justify no one, and a person must be righteous before he does a good work, it is very evident that it is faith alone which, because of the pure mercy of God through Christ and in His word, worthily and sufficiently justifies and saves the person. Christians have no need of any work or law in order to be saved since through faith they are free from every law and do everything out of pure liberty and freely. They seek neither benefit nor salvation since they already abound in all things and are saved through the grace of God because in their faith they now seek only to please God.

It is indeed true that in the sight of others a person is made good or evil by his works, but this being made good or evil only means that the man who is good or evil is pointed out and known as such, as Christ says in Matt. 7 [: 20], "Thus you will know them by their fruits." All this remains on the surface, however, and very many have been deceived by this outward appearance and have presumed to write and teach concerning good works by which we may be justified without even mentioning faith. They go their way, always being deceived and deceiving [2 Tim. 3: 13], progressing, indeed, but into a worse state, blind leaders of the blind, wearing themselves with many works and still never attaining to true righteousness [Matt. 15: 14] ...

From this it is easy to know how far good works are to be rejected or not, and by what standard all the teachings of men concerning works are to be interpreted. If works are sought after as a means to righteousness, are burdened with this perverse leviathan, and are done under the false impression that through them one is justified, they are made necessary and freedom and faith are destroyed; and this addition to them makes them no longer good but truly damnable works. They are not free, and they blaspheme the grace of God since to justify and to save by faith belongs to the grace of God alone. What the works have no power to do they nevertheless by a godless presumption through this folly of ours pretend to do and thus violently force themselves into the office and glory of grace. We do not, therefore, reject good works; on the contrary, we cherish and teach them as much as possible. We do not condemn them for their own sake but on account of this godless addition to them and the perverse idea that righteousness is to be sought through them; for that makes them appear good outwardly, when in truth they are not good. They deceive men and lead them to deceive one another like ravening wolves in sheep's clothing [Matt. 7: 15] ...

Lastly, we shall also speak of the things which people do toward their neighbors. Individuals do not live for themselves alone in this mortal body to work for it alone, but they live also for all people on earth; rather, they live only for others and not for themselves. To this end they bring their bodies into subjection that they may the more sincerely and freely serve others, as Paul says in

Rom. 14 [: 7–8], "None of us lives to himself, and none of us dies to himself. If we live, we live to the Lord, and if we die, we die to the Lord." They cannot ever in this life be idle and without works toward their neighbors, for they will necessarily speak, deal with, and exchange views with people, as Christ also, being made in human likeness [Phil. 2: 7], was found in form as a man and conversed with people, as Baruch 3 [: 38] says.

Humans, however, need none of these things for their righteousness and salvation; therefore they should be guided in all their works by this thought and contemplate this one thing alone, that they may serve and benefit others in all that they do, considering nothing except the need and the advantage of their neighbors. Accordingly, the Apostle commands us to work with our hands so that we may give to the needy, although he might have said that we should work to support ourselves. He says, however, "that he may be able to give to those in need" [Eph. 4: 28]. This is what makes caring for the body a Christian work, that through its health and comfort we may be able to work, to acquire, and lay by funds with which to aid those who are in need, that in this way the strong member may serve the weaker, and we may be sons of God, each caring for and working for the other, bearing one another's burdens and so fulfilling the law of Christ [Gal. 6: 2]. This is a truly Christian life. Here faith is truly active through love [Gal. 5: 6], that is, it finds expression in works of the freest service, cheerfully and lovingly done, with which a man willingly serves another without hope of reward; and for himself he is satisfied with the fullness and wealth of his faith…

Although Christians are thus free from all works, they ought in this liberty to empty themselves, take upon themselves the form of a servant, be made in human likeness, be found in human form, and to serve, help, and in every way deal with their neighbors as they see that God through Christ has dealt and still deals with them. This they should do freely, having regard for nothing but divine approval.

They ought to think: "Although I am unworthy and condemned, my God has given me in Christ all the riches of righteousness and salvation without any merit on my part, out of pure, free mercy, so that from now on I need nothing except faith which believes that this is true. Why should I not therefore freely, joyfully, with all my heart, and with an eager will do all things which I know are pleasing and acceptable to such a Father who has overwhelmed me with his inestimable riches? I will therefore give myself as a Christ to my neighbor, just as Christ offered Himself to me; I will do nothing in this life except what I see is necessary, profitable, and salutary to my neighbor, since through faith I have an abundance of all good things in Christ."

Behold, from faith thus flow forth love and joy in the Lord, and from love a joyful, willing, and free mind that serves one's neighbor willingly and takes no account of gratitude or ingratitude, of praise or blame, of gain or loss. For people do not serve that they may put others under obligations. They do not distinguish between friends and enemies or anticipate their thankfulness or unthankfulness, but they most freely and most willingly spend themselves and all that they have whether they waste all on the thankless or whether they receive a reward. As their Father does, distributing all things to all people richly and freely, making "his sun rise on the evil and on the good" [Matt. 5: 45], so also the son does all things and suffers all things with that freely bestowing joy which is his delight when through Christ he sees it in God, the dispenser of such great benefits.

Therefore, if we recognize the great and precious things which are given us, as Paul says [Rom. 5: 5], our hearts will be filled by the Holy Spirit with the love which makes us free, joyful, almighty workers and conquerors over all tribulations, servants of our neighbors, and yet lords of all. For those who do not recognize the gifts bestowed upon them through Christ, however, Christ has been born in vain; they go their way with their works and shall never come to taste or feel those things. Just as our neighbor is in need and lacks that in which we abound, so we were in need before God and lacked His mercy. Hence, as our heavenly Father has in Christ freely come to our aid, we also ought freely to help our neighbor through our body and its works, and each one should become as it were a Christ to the other that we may be Christs to one another and Christ may be the same in all; that is, that we may be truly Christians.

Who then can comprehend the riches and the glory of the Christian life? It can do all things and has all things and lacks nothing. It is lord over sin, death, and hell, and yet at the same time it serves, ministers to, and benefits all people. But alas in our day this life is unknown throughout the world; it is neither preached about nor sought after; we are altogether ignorant of our own name and do not know why we are Christians or bear the name of Christians. Surely we are named after Christ, not because He is absent from us, but because He dwells in us, that is, because we believe in Him and are Christs one to another and do to our neighbors as Christ does to us. But in our day we are taught by the doctrine of men to seek nothing but merits, rewards, and the things that are ours; of Christ we have made only a taskmaster far harsher than Moses.

We have a preeminent example of such a faith in the blessed Virgin. As is written in Luke 2 [: 22], she was purified according to the Law of Moses according to the custom of all women, although she was not bound by that law and did not need to be purified. Out of free and willing love, however, she submitted to the law like other women that she might not offend or despise them. She was not justified by this work, but being righteous she did it freely and willingly. So also our works should be done, not that we may be justified by them, since, being justified beforehand by faith, we ought to do all things freely and joyfully for the sake of others...

Anyone knowing this could easily and without danger find his way through those numberless mandates and precepts of pope, bishops, monasteries, churches, princes, and magistrates upon which some ignorant pastors insist as if they were necessary to righteousness and salvation, calling them "precepts of the Church," although they are nothing of the kind. For a Christian, as a free person, will say, "I will fast, pray, do this and that as men command, not because it is necessary to my righteousness or salvation; but that I may show due respect to the pope, the bishop, the community, a magistrate, or my neighbor, and give them an example. I will do and suffer all things, just as Christ did and suffered far more for me, although He needed nothing of it all for Himself, and was made under the law for my sake, although He was not under the law." Although tyrants do violence or injustice in making their demands, yet it will do no harm as long as they demand nothing contrary to God...

This ignorance and suppression of liberty very many blind pastors take pains to encourage. They stir up and urge on their people in these practices by praising such works, puffing them up with their indulgences, and never teaching faith. If, however, you wish to pray, fast, or establish a foundation in the Church, I advise you to be careful not to do it in order to obtain some benefit, whether temporal or eternal, for you would do injury to your faith which alone offers you all things. Your one care should be that faith may grow, whether it is trained by works or sufferings. Make your gifts freely, and for no consideration, so that others may profit by them and fare well because of you and your goodness. In this way you shall be truly good and Christian. Of what benefit to you are the good works which you do not need for keeping your body under control? Your faith is sufficient for you, through which God has given you all things.

See, according to this rule the good things we have from God should flow from one to the other and be common to all, so that everyone should "put on" his neighbor and so conduct himself toward him as if he himself were in the other's place. From Christ the good things have flowed and are flowing into us. He has so "put on" us and acted for us as if He had been what we are. From us they flow on to those who have need of them so that I should lay before God my faith and my righteousness that they may cover and intercede for the sins of my neighbor which I take upon myself and so labor and serve in them as if they were my very own. That is what Christ did for us. This is true love and the genuine rule of a Christian life. Love is true and genuine where there is true and genuine faith. Hence the Apostle says of love in 1 Cor. 13 [: 5] that "it does not seek its own."

We conclude, therefore, that Christians live not in themselves but in Christ and in their neighbors. Otherwise they are not Christians. They live in Christ through faith, in their neighbors through love. By faith they are caught up beyond themselves into God. By love they descend beneath themselves into their neighbors. Yet they always remain in God and in His love, as Christ says in John 1 [: 51], "Truly, truly, I say to you, you will see heaven opened, and the angels of God ascending and descending upon the Son of man."...

Our faith in Christ does not free us from works but from false opinions concerning works, that is, from the foolish presumption that justification is acquired by works. Faith redeems, corrects, and preserves our consciences so that we know that righteousness does not consist in works, although works neither can nor ought to be wanting; just as we cannot be without food and drink and all the works of this mortal body, yet our righteousness is not in them but in faith; and yet those works of the body are not to be despised or neglected on that account. In this world we are bound by the needs of our bodily life, but we are not righteous because of them. "My kingship is not of this world" [John 18: 36], says Christ. He does not, however, say, "My kingship is not here, that is, in this world." And Paul says, "Though we live in the world we are not carrying on a worldly war" [2 Cor. 10: 3], and in Gal. 2 [: 20], "The life I now live in the flesh I live by faith in the Son of God." Thus what we do, live, and are in works and ceremonies, we do because of the necessities of this life and of the effort to rule our body. Nevertheless we are righteous, not in these but in the faith of the Son of God.

Hence the Christians must take a middle course and face those two classes of people. They will meet first the unyielding, stubborn ceremonialists who like deaf adders are not willing to hear the truth of liberty [Ps. 58: 4] but, having no faith, boast of, prescribe, and insist upon their ceremonies as means of justification. Such were the Jews of old, who were unwilling to learn how to do good. These they must resist, do the very opposite, and offend them boldly lest by their impious views they drag many with them into error. In the presence of such people it is good to eat meat, break the fasts, and for the sake of the liberty of faith do other things which they regard as the greatest of sins. Of them we must say, "Let them alone; they are blind guides." According to this principle Paul would not circumcise Titus when the Jews insisted that he should [Gal. 2: 3], and Christ excused the apostles when they plucked ears of grain on the Sabbath [Matt. 12: 1–8]. There are many similar instances. The other class of people whom a Christian will meet are the simple-minded, the ignorant, the weak in faith, as the Apostle calls them, who cannot yet grasp the liberty of faith, even if they were willing to do so [Rom. 14: 1]. These they must take care not to offend. They must yield to their weakness until they are more fully instructed. Since they do and think as they do, not because they are stubbornly wicked, but only because their troth is weak, the fasts and other things which they consider necessary must be observed to avoid giving them offense. This is the command of love, which would harm no one but would serve all men. It is not by their fault that they are weak, but by that of their pastors who have taken them captive with the snares of their traditions and have wickedly used these traditions as rods with which to beat them. They should have been delivered from these pastors by the teachings of faith and freedom. So the Apostle teaches us in Rom. 14: "If food is a cause of my brother's falling, I will never eat meat" [cf. Rom. 14: 21 and 1 Cor. 8: 13]; and again, "I know and am persuaded in the Lord Jesus that nothing is unclean in itself; but it is unclean for anyone who thinks it unclean" [Rom. 14: 14].

For this reason, although we should boldly resist those teachers of traditions and sharply censure the laws of the popes by means of which they plunder the people of God, yet we must spare the timid multitude whom those impious tyrants hold captive by means of these laws until they are set free. Therefore fight strenuously against the wolves, but for the sheep and not also against the sheep. This you will do if you inveigh against the laws and the lawgivers and at the same time observe the laws with the weak so that they will not be offended, until they also recognize tyranny and understand their freedom. If you wish to use your freedom, do so in secret, as Paul says, Rom. 14 [: 22], "The faith that you have, keep between yourself and God"; but take care not to use your freedom in the sight of the weak. On the other hand, use your freedom constantly and consistently in the sight of and despite the tyrants and the stubborn so that they also may learn that they are all impious, that their laws are of no avail for righteousness, and that they had no right to set them up.

Since we cannot live our lives without ceremonies and works, and the perverse and untrained youth need to be restrained and saved from harm by such bonds; and since all should keep their bodies under control by means of such works, there is need that the minister of Christ be far-seeing and faithful. He ought so to govern and teach Christians in all these matters that their conscience and faith will not be offended and that there will not spring up in them a suspicion and a root of bitterness and many will thereby be defiled, as Paul admonishes the Hebrews [Heb 12: 15]...

In brief, as wealth is the test of poverty, business the test of faithfulness, honors the test of humility, feasts the test of temperance, pleasures the test of chastity, so ceremonies are the test of the righteousness of faith. "Can a man," asks Solomon, "carry fire in his bosom and his clothes and not be burned?" [Prov. 6: 27]. Yet as people must live in the midst of wealth, business, honors, pleasures, and feasts, so also must they live in the midst of ceremonies, that is, in the midst of dangers. Indeed, as infant boys need beyond all else to be cherished in the bosoms and by the hands of women to keep them from perishing, yet when they are grown up their salvation is endangered if they associate with women, so the inexperienced and perverse youth need to be restrained and trained by the iron bars of ceremonies lest they in unchecked ardor rush headlong into vice after vice. On the other hand, it would be death for them always to be held in bondage to ceremonies, thinking that these justify them. They are rather to be taught that they have been so imprisoned in ceremonies, not that they should be made righteous or gain great merit by them, but that they might thus be kept from doing evil and might more easily be instructed to the righteousness of faith. Such instruction they would not endure if the impulsiveness of their youth were not restrained...

We do not despise ceremonies and works, but we set great store by them; but we despise the false estimate placed upon works in order that no one may think that they are true righteousness, as those hypocrites believe who spend and lose their whole lives in zeal for works and never reach that goal for the sake of which the works are to be done, who, as the Apostle says, "will listen to anybody and can never arrive at a knowledge of the truth" [2 Tim. 3: 7]. They seem to wish to build, they make their preparations, and yet they never build. Thus they remain caught in the form of religion and do not attain unto its power [2 Tim. 3: 5].

8

Martin Luther: *Invocavit Sermons.* [1522]

ollowing Luther's refusal at the Diet at Worms to recant, the question arose if the sundry pronouncements of reform should to be translated into practice; he was nowhere in sight. He had called a wide variety of Catholic practices into question as unscriptural—the mass, monastic vows, and clerical celibacy. Nonetheless, religious life continued unchanged in Wittenberg. Late in 1521 some advocates of reform became determined to turn theory into practice. In December one of them celebrated an "evangelical" communion, and did so in ordinary clothing, and early the following year heated disagreements arose over the necessity of further changes in ecclesiastical practices. Luther, informed of this development, returned to Wittenberg early in March and shortly thereafter preached a series of sermons in which he elaborated his own understanding of ecclesiastical reform. Portions of two of these sermons are reprinted here. They illustrate Luther's characteristic concentration on the essential, and show that he found fault with the impatient reformers for having done the right thing at the wrong time. Inner change, he pointed out, had to precede outer change, and he charged that the reverse had been advocated in Wittenberg. Moreover, he said, the gospel should never be turned into rigid regimentation; a "may" cannot be translated into a "must." Here spoke a moderate, if not conservative reformer who abhorred external regimentation and felt it wise to make haste slowly. A selection from the very first sermon follows.[8]

LITERATURE

Neil R. Leroux, *Luther's Rhetoric: Strategies and Style from the Invocavit Sermons.* St. Louis, 2002.

The summons of death comes to us all, and no one can die for another. Everyone must fight his own battle with death by himself alone. We can shout into one another's ears, but everyone must himself be prepared for the time of death, for I will not be with you nor will you be with me. Therefore, everyone must himself know and be armed with the chief things which concern a Christian. And these are what you, my friends, have heard from me many days ago.

In the first place, we must know that we are the children of wrath, and all our works, intentions, and thoughts are nothing at all. Here we need a clear, strong text to bear out this point. Such is the saying of St. Paul in Eph. 2. Note this well; and though there are many such in the Bible, I do not wish to overwhelm you with many texts. "We are all the children of wrath." And please do not to say: I have built an altar, given a foundation for masses, etc.

Secondly, God has sent us his only begotten Son that we may believe in Him and that whoever trusts in Him shall be free from sin and a child of God, as John declares in his first chapter, "To all who believed in His name, He gave power to become children of God" [John 1: 12]. Here we should all be well versed in the Bible and ready to confront the devil with many passages. With respect

---

8. John W. Doberstein, ed., *Luther's Works.* Vol. 51, *Sermons I.* Philadelphia, 1959, pp. 70–78.

to these two points I do not feel that there has been anything wrong or lacking. They have been rightly preached to you, and I should be sorry if it were otherwise. Indeed, I am well aware and I dare say that you are more learned than I, and that there are only one, two, three, or four, if perhaps ten or more, who have this knowledge and insight.

Thirdly, we must also have love and through love we must do to one another as God has done to us through faith. For without love, faith is nothing, as St. Paul says I Cor. 2: If I had the tongues of angels and could speak of the highest things in faith, and have not love, I am nothing. And here, dear friends, have you not grievously failed? I see no signs of love among you, and I observe very well that you have not been grateful to God for his rich gifts and treasures.

Let us beware lest Wittenberg become Capernaum. I notice that you have a great deal to say of the doctrine of faith and love which is preached to you, and this is no wonder; an ass can also intone the lessons, and why should you not be able to repeat the doctrines and formulas? Dear friends, the kingdom of God, and we are that kingdom, does not consist in talk or words but in activity, in deeds, works, and exercises. God does not want hearers and repeaters of words but followers and doers, and this occurs in faith through love. For faith without love is not enough, rather it is not faith at all, but a counterfeit faith, just as the face seen in a mirror is not the real face but merely the reflection of a face.

Fourthly, we need patience. For whoever has faith, trusts in God, and shows love to his neighbor, practicing it day by day, must needs suffer persecution. For the devil never sleeps but constantly gives him plenty of trouble. But patience works and produces hope which freely yields itself to God and vanishes away in Him. Thus faith, by much affliction and persecution, ever increases, and is strengthened day by day. A heart thus blessed can never rest or restrain itself but rather pours itself out again for the benefit and service of others, just as God has done.

And here, dear friends, one must not insist upon his rights but must see what may be useful and helpful to his brother, as Paul says, "All things are lawful to me but not all things are helpful" [I Cor. 6: 12]. For we are not all equally strong in faith; some of you have a stronger faith than I. Therefore, we must not look upon ourselves or our strength, or our prestige, but upon our neighbor, for God has said it so through Moses: I have borne and reared you, as a mother does her child. What does a mother do to her child? First she gives it milk, and then gruel, then eggs and soft food, whereas if she turned about and gave it solid food, the child would never thrive. So we should also deal with our brother, have patience with him for a time, have patience with his weakness and help him bear it; we should also give him milk food, too, as was done with us, until he, too, grows stronger, and thus we do not travel heavenward alone but bring our brethren, who are not now our friends, with us. If all mothers were to abandon their children, where would we have been? Dear brother, if you have suckled long enough, do not at once cut off the breast, but let your brother be suckled as you were suckled. I would not have gone so far as you have done if I had been here. The cause is good, but there has been too much haste. For there are still brothers and sisters on the other side who belong to us and must still be won...

Therefore, dear friends, follow me; I have never been a destroyer. And I was also the very first when God called me to this work. I cannot run away but will remain as long as God allows. I was also the one to whom God first revealed that His word should be preached to you. I'm also sure that you have the pure word of God.

Let us, therefore, act with fear and humility, cast ourselves at one another's feet, join hands with one another, and help one another. I will do my part, which is no more than my duty for I love you even as I have loved my own soul. For here we battle not against pope or bishop but against the devil, and do you imagine he is asleep? He sleeps not but sees the true light rising, and to keep it from shining into his eyes he would like to make a flank attack—and he will succeed if we are not on our guard. I know him well, and I hope, too, that with the help of God I am his master. But if we yield him but an inch, we must soon look to it how we may be rid of him. Therefore, all those have erred who have helped and consented to abolish the mass; not that it was not a good thing, but that it was not done in an orderly way. You say it was right according to the Scriptures. I agree, but what becomes of order? For it was done in wantonness, with no regard for proper order and with the offense to your neighbor. If beforehand you had called upon God in earnest prayer and obtained the aid of the authorities, one could be certain that it had come from God. I, too, would have taken steps toward the same end if it had been a good thing to do; and if the mass were not such an evil thing, I would introduce it again. For I cannot defend your action, as I have just said . . .

Not that I would reestablish the mass; I let it lie in God's name. Faith must not be chained and imprisoned, nor bound by an ordinance to any work. This is the principle by which you must be governed. For I am sure you will not be able to carry out your plans. And if you should carry them out with such general laws, then I will recant everything that I have written and preached and I will not support you. This I am telling you now. What harm can it do you? You still have your faith in God, pure and strong so that this thing cannot hurt you.

Love, therefore, demands that you have compassion on the weak, as all the apostles had. Once, when Paul came to Athens (Acts 17 [: 16–32]), a mighty city, he found in the temple many ancient altars, and he went from one to the other and looked at them all, but he did not kick down a single one of them with his foot. Rather he stood up in the middle of the marketplace and said they were nothing but idolatrous things and begged the people to forsake them; yet he did not destroy one of them by force. When the word took hold of their hearts, they forsook them of their own accord, and in consequence the thing fell of itself. Likewise, if I had seen them holding mass, I would have preached to them and admonished them. Had they heeded my admonition, I would have won them; if not, I would nevertheless not have torn them from it by the hair or employed any force, but simply allowed the word to act and prayed for them. For the Word created heaven and earth and all things [Ps. 33: 6]; the Word must do this thing, and not we poor sinners.

In short, I will preach it, teach it, write it, but I will constrain no man by force, for faith must come freely without compulsion. Take myself as an example. I opposed indulgences and all the papists, but never with force. I simply taught, preached, and wrote God's word; otherwise I did nothing. And while I slept or drank Wittenberg beer with my friends Philipp Melanchthon and Amsdorf, the word so greatly weakened the papacy that no prince or emperor ever inflicted such losses upon it. I did nothing; the word did everything. Had I desired to foment trouble, I could have brought great bloodshed upon Germany; indeed, I could have started such a game that even the emperor would not have been safe. But what would it have been? Mere fool's play. I did nothing; I let the word do its work. What do you suppose is Satan's thought when one tries to do the thing by kicking up a row? He sits back in hell and thinks: Oh, what a fine game the poor fools are up to now! But when we spread the word alone and let it alone do the work, that distresses him. For it is almighty and takes captive the hearts, and when the hearts are captured, the work will fall of itself. Let me cite a simple instance. In former times there were sects, too, Jewish and Gentile Christians, differing on the Law of Moses with respect to circumcision. The former wanted to keep it, the latter not. Then came Paul and preached that it might be kept or not, for it was of no consequence; and also that they should not make a "must" of it, but leave it to the choice of the individual; to keep it or not was immaterial, 1 Cor. 7[: 18–24]; Gal. 5[: 1]. So it was up to the time of Jerome, who came and wanted to make a "must" out of it, desiring to make it an ordinance and a law that it be prohibited. Then came St. Augustine and he was of the same opinion as St. Paul: It might be kept or not, as one wished. St. Jerome was a hundred miles away from St. Paul's opinion. The two doctors bumped heads rather hard, but when St. Augustine died, St. Jerome was successful in having it prohibited. After that came the popes, who also wanted to add something, and they, too, made laws. Thus out of the making of one law grew a thousand laws, until they have completely buried us under laws. And this is what will happen here, too; one law will soon make two, two will increase to three, and so forth.

9

Martin Luther: *Preface to the German Translation of the New Testament.* [1522]

Martin Luther's insistence that only the Scriptures were to serve as the guide for the Christian faith, together with his conscious effort to challenge the common people with his program of ecclesiastical transformation, made it inevitable that he turn to the task of making the Scriptures available in German so that people could read them for themselves. His involuntary stay on the Wartburg from May 1521 to March 1522 gave him the opportunity to begin the translation of the New Testament, which he completed in a surprisingly short time. Published in September 1522, it became known as the September Bible. It was a stylistic masterpiece and a superb translation of the words of the gospel writers into the idiom of sixteenth-century Saxony.

The September Bible was important in another way. It contained a number of explanatory notes in which Luther formulated his hermeneutical principle for the interpretation of Scripture. The controversy with Catholic theologians had made him aware that his opponents, too, quoted Scripture in support of their position; thus, Catholics were fond of quoting the Epistle of James, with its assertion that humans are saved by works, to counter Luther's stress upon justification by faith. Clearly, it was not sufficient to demand a simple recourse to Scripture. Catholics took this scriptural heterogeneity to underscore the need for an interpreting agent, the church. Luther, on the other hand, argued the need of distinguishing between various levels of Scriptures. Luther discussed this distinction, and the principles underlying it, in a preface, a portion of which is reprinted here.[9]

LITERATURE

H. Blum, *Luther, Translator of Paul: Studies in Romans and Galatians.* New York, 1984.

Just as the Old Testament is a book in which are written God's laws and commandments, together with the history of those who kept and of those who did not keep them, so the New Testament is a book in which are written the gospel and the promises of God, together with the history of those who believe and of those who do not believe. For "gospel" [*Euangelium*] is a Greek word and means in Greek a good message, good tidings, good news, a good report, which one sings and takes with gladness. For example, when David overcame the great Goliath, there came among the Jewish people the good report and encouraging news that their terrible enemy had been struck down and that they had been rescued and given joy and peace; and they sang and danced and were glad for it.

Thus this gospel of God, or New Testament, is a good story and report, sounded forth into all the world by the apostles, telling of a true David who strove with sin, death, and the devil, and overcame them all, and thereby rescued all those who were captive in sin, afflicted with death, and overpowered by the devil. Without any merit of their own, He made them righteous, gave them life, and saved them, so that they were given peace and brought back to

---

9. E. T. Bachmann, ed., *Luther's Works.* Vol. 35, *Word and Sacrament I.* Philadelphia, 1960, pp. 358–62.

God. For this they sing, and thank and praise God, and are glad forever, if only they believe firmly and remain steadfast in faith.

This report and comforting tidings, or evangelical and divine news, is also called a New Testament. For it is a testament when a dying man bequeaths his property, after his death, to his legally defined heirs. And Christ, before His death, commanded and ordained that this gospel be preached after His death in the entire world [Luke 24: 44–47]. Thereby He gave to all who believe, as their possession, everything that He had. This included His life, in which He swallowed up death; His righteousness, by which He blotted out sin; and His salvation, with which He overcame everlasting damnation. A poor man, dead in sin and consigned to hell, can hear nothing more comforting than this precious and tender message about Christ; from the bottom of his heart he must laugh and be glad over it, if he believes it true. Now to strengthen this faith, God has promised this gospel and testament in many ways, by the prophets in the Old Testament, as St. Paul says in Rom. 1 [: 1], "I am set apart to preach the gospel of God, which He promised beforehand through His prophets in the holy Scripture, concerning His Son, who was descended from David," etc.

To mention some of these places: God gave the first promise when He said to the serpent, in Gen. 3 [: 15], "I will put enmity between you and the woman, and between your seed and her seed; he shall bruise your head, and you shall bruise his heel! Christ is this woman's seed, who has bruised the devil's head, that is, sin, death, hell, and all his power. For without this seed, no man can escape sin." Or again, in Gen. 22 [: 18], God promised Abraham, "Through your descendant shall all the nations of the earth be blessed." Christ is that descendant .of Abraham, says St. Paul in Gal. 3 [: 16]; He has blessed the entire world, through the gospel [Gal. 3: 8]. For where Christ is not, there is still the curse that fell upon Adam and his children when he had sinned, so that they all are necessarily guilty and subject to sin, death, and hell. Over against this curse, the gospel blesses the entire world by publicly announcing, "Whoever believes in this descendant of Abraham shall be blessed." That is, he shall be rid of sin, death, and hell, and shall remain righteous, alive, and saved forever, as Christ Himself says in John 11[: 26], "Whoever believes in me shall never die."

Again God made this promise to David in 2 Sam. 7 [: 12–14] when He said, "I will raise up your son after you, who shall build a house for my name, and I will establish the throne of his kingdom forever. I will be his father, and he shall be my son," etc. This is the kingdom of Christ, of which the gospel speaks: an everlasting kingdom, a kingdom of life, salvation, and righteousness, where all those who believe enter in from out of the prison of sin and death. There are many more such promises of the gospel in the other prophets as well, for example, Micah 5 [: 2], "But you, O Bethlehem Ephrathah, who are little to be among the clans of Judah, from you shall come forth for me one who is to be ruler in Israel"; and again, Hos. 13 [: 14], "I shall ransom them from the power of hell and redeem them from death. O death, I will be your plague; O hell, I will be your destruction."

The gospel, then, is nothing but the preaching about Christ, Son of God and of David, true God and man, who by His death and resurrection has overcome for us the sin, death, and hell of all who believe in Him. Thus the gospel can be either a brief or a lengthy message; one person can write of it briefly, another at length. He writes of it at length, who writes about many words and works of Christ, as do the four evangelists. He writes of it briefly, however, who does not tell of Christ's works but indicates briefly how by His death and resurrection He has overcome sin, death, and hell for those who believe in Him, as do St. Peter and St. Paul. See to it, therefore, that you do not make a Moses out of Christ, or a book of laws and doctrines out of the gospel, as has been done heretofore and as certain prefaces put it, even those of St. Jerome. For the gospel does not expressly demand works of our own by which we become righteous and are saved; indeed it condemns such works. Rather the gospel demands faith in Christ: that He has overcome for us sin, death, and hell, and thus gives us righteousness, life, and salvation not through our works but through His own works, death, and suffering, in order that we may avail ourselves of His death and victory as though we had done it ourselves.

To be sure, Christ in the gospel, and St. Peter and St. Paul besides, do give many commandments and doctrines, and expound the Law. But these are to be counted like all Christ's other works and good deeds. To know His works and the things that happened to Him is not yet to know the true gospel, for you do not yet thereby know that He has overcome sin, death, and the devil. So, too, it is not yet knowledge of the gospel when you know these doctrines and commandments but only when the voice comes that says, "Christ is your own, with His life, teaching, works, death, resurrection, and all that He is, has, does, and can do." Thus we see also that He does not compel us but invites us kindly and says, "Blessed are the poor," etc. [Matt. 5: 3]. And the apostles use the words, "I exhort," "I entreat," "I beg," so that one sees on every hand that the gospel is not a book of law but really a preaching of the benefits of Christ, shown to us and given to us for own possession, if we believe. But Moses, in his books, drives, compels, threatens, strikes, and rebukes terribly, for he is a lawgiver and taskmaster.

Hence it comes that to believers no law is given by which they become righteous before God, as St. Paul says in Tim. 1 [: 9], because they are alive and righteous and saved by faith, and they need nothing further except to prove their faith by works. Truly, if faith is there, they cannot hold back; they prove themselves, break out into good works, confess, and teach this gospel before the people, and stake their life on it. Everything that they live and do is directed to their neighbor's profit, in order to help them—not only to the attainment of this grace but also in body, property, and honor. Seeing that Christ has done this for them, they thus follows Christ's example.

That is what Christ meant when at the last He gave no other commandment than love, by which people were to know who were His disciples [John 13: 34–35] and true believers. For where works and love do not break forth, there faith is not right, the gospel does not yet take hold, and Christ is not rightly known. See, then, that you so approach the books of the New Testament as to learn to read them in this way.

Which are the true and noblest books of the New Testament?

From all this you can now judge all the books and decide among them which are the best. John's Gospel and St. Paul's Epistles, especially Romans, and St. Peter's first Epistle are the true kernel and marrow of all the books. They ought properly to be the foremost books, and it would be advisable for every Christian to read them first and most, and by daily reading to make them as much his own as his daily bread. For in them you do not find many works and miracles of Christ described, but you do find depicted in masterly fashion how faith in Christ overcomes sin, death, and hell, and gives life, righteousness, and salvation. This is the real nature of the gospel, as you have heard.

If I had to do without one or the other, either the works or the preaching of Christ, I would rather do without the works than without His preaching. For the works do not help me, but His words give life, as He Himself says [John 6: 63]. Now John writes little about the works of Christ but very much about His preaching, while the other evangelists write much about His works and little about His preaching. Therefore John's Gospel is the one, fine, true, and chief gospel, and is far, far to be preferred over the other three and placed high above them. So, too, the Epistles of St. Paul and St. Peter far surpass the other three Gospels, Matthew, Mark, and Luke.

In a word, St. John's Gospel and his first Epistle, St. Paul's Epistles, especially Romans, Galatians, and Ephesians, and St. Peter's first Epistle are the books that show you Christ and teach you all that is necessary and salvatory for you to know, even if you were never to see or hear any other book or doctrine. Therefore, St. James's Epistle is really an Epistle of straw, compared to these others, for it has nothing of the nature of the gospel about it. But more of this in the other prefaces.

10

Martin Luther: *Concerning Governmental Authority.* [1523]

The publication of this tract indicated Luther's concern to explore the political consequences of his new understanding of the nature of the Christian faith. He set out to describe the proper Christian attitude toward political authority, in light of the medieval background, where church and state had been intimately connected and the church had sought to impose its will upon the political community. Luther was persuaded that the secular preoccupation of the medieval church had been one of its major shortcomings, and he vehemently argued for a clear separation of the two "realms." He stressed that government authority was from God, even though its principles are not those of the gospel. In its own way, Luther's treatise is a classical exposition of political theory written from a Christian perspective. It destroyed the medieval understanding of a church and state and influenced subsequent development in Germany.

Sections from parts I and II of the treatise are reprinted below. (Part III deals with the attributes of a good political leader.)

LITERATURE

James D. Tracy, editor, *Luther and the Modern State in Germany* (Kirksville, Mo. 1986). W. Elert, *The Structure of Lutheranism* (St. Louis, 1962), vol. I.

To such a one we must say: Certainly it is true that Christians, so far as they themselves are concerned, are subject neither to law nor sword, and have heed of neither. But take heed and first fill the world with real Christians before you attempt to rule it in a Christian and evangelical manner. This you will never accomplish; for the world and the masses are and always will be un-Christian, even if they are all baptized and Christian in name. Christians are few and far between (as the saying is). Therefore, it is out of the question that there should be a common Christian government over the whole world, or indeed over a single country or any considerable body of people, for the wicked always outnumber the good. Hence, a man who would venture to govern an entire country or the world with the gospel would be like a shepherd who should put together in one fold wolves, lions, eagles, and sheep, and let them mingle freely with one another, saying, "Help yourselves, and be good and peaceful toward one another. The fold is open; there is plenty of food. You need have no fear of dogs and clubs." The sheep would doubtless keep the peace and allow themselves to be fed and governed peacefully, but they would not live long, nor would one beast survive another.

For this reason one must carefully distinguish between these two governments. Both must be permitted to remain; the one to produce righteousness, the other to bring about external peace and prevent evil deeds. Neither one is sufficient in the world without the other. No one can become righteous in the sight of God by means of the temporal government, without Christ's spiritual government. Christ's government does not extend over all men; rather, Christians are always a minority in the midst of non-Christians. Now where temporal government or law alone prevails, there sheer hypocrisy is inevitable, even though the commandments are God's very own. For without the Holy Spirit in the heart no one becomes truly righteous, no matter how fine the work that is done. On the other hand, where the spiritual government alone prevails over land and people, there wickedness is given free rein and the door is open for all manner of rascality, for the world as a whole cannot receive or comprehend it.

Now you see the intent of Christ's words, which we quoted above from Matt. 5, that Christians should not go to court or use the temporal sword among themselves. Actually, He says this only to His beloved Christians, those who alone accept it and act accordingly, who do not make counsels out of it as the sophists do, but in their heart are so disposed and conditioned by the Spirit that they do evil to no one and willingly endure evil at the hands of others. If now the whole world were Christian in this sense, then these words would apply to all, and all would act accordingly.

Since the world is un-Christian, however, these words do not apply to all; and all do not act accordingly but are under another government in which those who are not Christian are kept under external constraint and compelled to keep the peace and do what is good.

This is also why Christ did not wield the sword or give it a place in His kingdom. For He is a king over Christians and rules by His Holy Spirit alone, without law. Although He sanctions the sword, He did not make use of it, for it serves no purpose in His kingdom, in which there are none but the upright. Hence, David of old was not permitted to build the temple [2 Sam. 7: 4–13] because he had wielded the sword and had shed much blood. Not that he had done wrong thereby, but because he could not be a type of Christ, who without the sword was to have a kingdom of peace. It had to be built instead by Solomon, whose name in German means "Friedrich" or "peaceful."...Whoever extends the application of these and similar passages to wherever Christ's name is mentioned, would entirely pervert the Scripture; rather, they are spoken only of true Christians, who really do this among themselves.

Fifth. But you say: If Christians then do not need the temporal sword or law, why does Paul say to all Christians in Rom. 13 [: 1], "Let all souls be subject to the governing authority," and St. Peter, "Be subject to every human law" [1 Pet. 2: 13]? Answer: I have just said that Christians, among themselves and by and for themselves, need no law or sword, since it is neither necessary nor useful for them. Since true Christians live and labor on earth not for themselves alone but for their neighbor, they do by the very nature of their spirit even what they have no need of, but is needful and useful to the neighbor. Because the sword is most beneficial and necessary for the whole world in order to preserve peace, punish sin, and restrain the wicked, the Christian submits most willingly to the rule of the sword, pays his taxes, honors those in authority, serves, helps, and does all he can to assist the governing authority, that it may continue to function and be held in honor and fear. Although he has no need of these things for himself—to him they are not essential—nevertheless, he concerns himself about what is serviceable and of benefit to others, as Paul teaches in Eph. 5 [: 21] and 6 [: 6–9].

Just as he performs all other works of love which he himself does not need—he does not visit the sick in order that he himself may be made well, or feed others because he himself needs food— so he serves the governing authority not because he needs it but for the sake of others, that they may be protected and that the wicked may not become worse. He loses nothing by this; such service in no way harms him, yet it is of great benefit to the world. If he did not so serve he would be acting not as a Christian but even contrary to love; he would also be setting a bad example to others who in like manner would not submit to authority, even though they were not Christians. In this way the gospel would be brought into disrepute, as though it taught insurrection and produced self-willed people unwilling to benefit or serve others, when in fact it makes a Christian the servant of all...

Thus you observe in the words of Christ quoted above from Matt. 5 that He clearly teaches that Christians among themselves should have no temporal sword or law. He does not, however, forbid one to serve and be subject to those who do have the secular sword and law. Rather, since you do not need it and should not have it, you are to serve all the more those who have not attained to such heights as you and who therefore do still need it. Although you do not need to have your enemy punished, your afflicted neighbor does. You should help him that he may have peace and that his enemy may be curbed, but this is not possible unless the governing authority is honored and feared. Christ does not say, "You shall not serve the governing authority or be subject to it," but rather, "Do not resist evil" [Matt. 5: 39], as much as to say, "Behave in such a way that you bear everything, so that you may not need the governing authority to help you and serve you or be beneficial or essential for you, but that you in turn may help and serve it, being beneficial and essential to it. I would have you be too exalted and far too noble to have any need of it; it should rather have need of you."

Sixth. You ask whether a Christian too may bear the temporal sword and punish the wicked, since Christ's words, "Do not resist evil," are so clear and definite that the sophists have had to make of them a "counsel." Answer: You have now heard two propositions. One is that the sword can have no place among Christians;

therefore, you cannot bear it among Christians or hold it over them, for they do not need it. The question, therefore, must be referred to the other group, the non-Christians, whether you may bear it there in a Christian manner. Here the other proposition applies, that you are under obligation to serve and assist the sword by whatever means you can, with body, goods, honor, and soul. For it is something which you do not need, but which is very beneficial and essential for the whole world and for your neighbor.

Therefore, if you see that there is a need of hangmen, constables, judges, lords, or princes, and you find that you are qualified, you should offer your services and seek the position that the essential governmental authority may not be despised and become enfeebled or perish. The world cannot and dare not dispense with it.

Here is the reason why you should do this: In such a case you would be entering entirely into the service and work of others, which would be of advantage neither to yourself nor your property or honor, but only to your neighbor and to others. You would be doing it not with the purpose of avenging yourself or returning evil for evil, but for the good of your neighbor and for the maintenance of the safety and peace of others. For yourself, you would abide by the gospel and govern yourself according to Christ's word [Matt. 5: 39–40], gladly turning the other cheek and letting the cloak go with the coat when the matter concerned you and your cause.

In this way the two propositions are brought into harmony with each other: At one and the same time you satisfy God's kingdom inwardly and the kingdom of the world outwardly. You suffer evil and injustice, and yet at the same time you punish evil and injustice; you do not resist evil, and yet at the same time you do resist it. In the one case, you consider yourself and what is yours;

in the other, you consider your neighbor and what is his. In what concerns you and yours, you govern yourself by the gospel and suffer injustice toward yourself as a true Christian; in what concerns the person or property of others, you govern yourself according to love and tolerate no injustice toward your neighbor. The gospel does not forbid this; in fact, in other places it actually commands it...

Paul says in 1 Cor. 7 [: 19] and Gal. 6 [: 15] that neither uncircumcision nor circumcision counts for anything, but only a new creature in Christ. That is, it is not sin to be uncircumcised, as the Jews thought, nor is it sin to be circumcised, as the Gentiles thought. Either is right and permissible for him who does not think he will thereby become righteous or be saved. The same is true of all other parts of the Old Testament; it is not wrong to ignore them and it is not wrong to abide by them, but it is permissible and proper either to follow them or to omit them. Indeed, if it were necessary or profitable for the salvation of one's neighbor, it would be necessary to keep all of them. For everyone is under obligation to do what is for his neighbor's good, be it Old Testament or New, Jewish or Gentile, as Paul teaches in 1 Cor. 12. For love pervades all and transcends all; it considers only what is necessary and beneficial to others, and does not ask whether it is old or new. Hence, the precedents for the use of the sword also are matters of freedom, and you may follow them or not. But where you see that your neighbor needs it, there love constrains you to do as matter of necessity that which would otherwise be optional and not necessary for you either to do or to leave undone. Only do not suppose that you will thereby become righteous or be saved—as the Jews presumed to be saved by their works—but leave this to faith, which without works makes you a new creature.

To prove our position also by the New Testament, the testimony of John the Baptist in Luke 3[: 14] stands unshaken on this point. There can be no doubt that it was his task to point to Christ, witness for Him, and teach about Him; that is to say, the teaching of the man who was to lead a truly perfected people to Christ had of necessity to be purely New Testament and evangelical. John confirms the soldiers' calling, saying they should be content with their wages. Now if it had been un-Christian to bear the sword, he ought to have censured them for it and told them to abandon both wages and sword, else he would not have been teaching them Christianity aright...

Moreover, we have the clear and compelling text of St. Paul in Rom. 13 [: 1], where he says, "The governing authority has been ordained by God," and further, "The governing authority does not bear the sword in vain. It is God's servant for your good, an avenger upon him who does evil" [Rom. 13: 4]. Be not so wicked, my friend, as to say, "A Christian may not do that which is God's own peculiar work, ordinance, and creation." Else you must also say, "A Christian must not eat, drink, or be married," for these are also God's work and ordinance. If it is God's work and creation, then it is good, so good that everyone can use it in a Christian and salutary way, as Paul says in 1 Tim. 4 [: 4], "Everything created by God is good, and nothing is to be rejected by those who believe and know the truth." Under "everything created by God" you must include not simply food and drink, clothing and shoes, but also authority and subjection, protection and punishment.

In short, since Paul says here that the governing authority is God's servant, we must allow it to be exercised not only by the heathen but by all men. What can be the meaning of the phrase, "It is God's servant," except that governing authority is by its very nature such that through it one may serve God? Now it would be quite un-Christian to say that there is any service of God in which a Christian should not or must not take part, when service of God is actually more characteristic of Christians than of anyone else. It would even be fine and fitting if all princes were good, true Christians. For the sword and authority, as a particular service of God, belong more appropriately to Christians than to any other men on earth. Therefore, you should esteem the sword or governmental authority as highly as the estate of marriage, or husbandry, or any other calling which God has instituted. Just as one can serve God in the estate of marriage, or in farming or a trade, for the benefit of others—and must so serve if his neighbor needs it—so one can serve God in government, and should there serve if the needs of his neighbor demand it. For those who punish evil and protect the good are God's servants and workmen. Only, one should also be free not to do it if there is no need for it, just as we are free not to marry or farm where there is no need for them…

From all this we gain the true meaning of Christ's words in Matt. 5 [: 39], "Do not resist evil," etc. It is this: A Christian should be so disposed that he will suffer every evil and injustice without avenging himself, neither will he seek legal redress in the courts but have utterly no need of temporal authority and law for his own sake. On behalf of others, however, he may and should seek vengeance, justice, protection, and help, and do as much as he can to achieve it. Likewise, the governing authority should, on his own initiative or through the instigation of others, help and protect him too, without any complaint, application, or instigation on his own part. If it fails to do this, he should permit himself to be despoiled and slandered; he should not resist evil, as Christ's words say.

Be certain too that this teaching of Christ is not a counsel for those who would be perfect, as our sophists blasphemously and falsely say, but a universally obligatory command for all Christians. Then you will realize that all those who avenge themselves or go to law and wrangle in the courts over their property and honor are nothing but heathens masquerading under the name of Christians.

It cannot be otherwise, I tell you. Do not be dissuaded by the multitude and common practice; for there are few Christians on earth—have no doubt about it—and God's word is something very different from the common practice...

Here you inquire further, whether constables, hangmen, jurists, lawyers, and others of similar function can also be Christians and in a state of salvation. Answer: If the governing authority and its word are a divine service, as was proved above, then everything that is essential for the authority's having the sword must also be service to God. There must be those who arrest, prosecute, execute, and destroy the wicked, and who protect, acquit, defend, and save those who are law-abiding. Therefore, when they perform their duties, not with the intention of seeking their own ends, but only of helping the law and the governing authority function to coerce the wicked, there is no peril in that; they may use their office as anybody else would use his trade, as a means of livelihood. For, as has been said, love of neighbor is not concerned about its own; it considers not how great or humble, but how profitable and needful the works are for neighbor or community...

PART TWO. HOW FAR TEMPORAL AUTHORITY EXTENDS

We come now to the main part of this treatise. Having learned that there must be temporal authority on earth, and how it is to be exercised in a Christian and salutary manner, we must now learn how far its arm extends and how widely its hand stretches, lest it extend too far and encroach upon God's kingdom and government. It is essential for us to know this, for where it is given too wide a scope, intolerable and terrible injury follows; on the other hand, injury is also inevitable where it is restricted too narrowly. In the former case, the temporal authority punishes too much; in the latter case, it punishes too little. To err in this direction, however, and punish too little is more tolerable, for it is always better to let a scoundrel live than to put a godly man to death. The world has plenty of scoundrels anyway and must continue to have them, but godly men are scarce.

It is to be noted first that the two classes of Adam's children—the one in God's kingdom under Christ and the other in the kingdom of the world under the governing authority, as was said above—have two kinds of law. For every kingdom must have its own laws and statutes; without law no kingdom or government can survive, as everyday experience amply shows. The temporal government has laws which extend no further than to life and property and external affairs on earth, for God cannot and will not permit anyone but Himself to rule over the soul. Therefore, where the temporal authority presumes to prescribe laws for the soul, it encroaches upon God's government and only misleads souls and destroys them. We want to make this so clear that everyone will grasp it, and that our fine gentlemen, the princes and bishops, will see what fools they are when they seek to coerce the people with their laws and commandments into believing this or that.

When a human-made law is imposed upon the soul to make it believe this or that as its human author may prescribe, there is certainly no word of God for it. If there is no word of God for it, then we cannot be sure whether God wishes to have it so, for we cannot be certain that something which He does not command is pleasing to Him. Indeed, we are sure that it does not please Him, for He desires that our faith be based simply and entirely on His divine word alone. He says in Matt. 16 [: 18], "On this rock I will build my church"; and in John 10 [: 27, 14, 5], "My sheep hear my voice and know me; however, they will not hear the voice of a stranger, but flee from him." From this it follows that with such a wicked command the temporal power is driving souls to eternal death. For it compels them to believe as right and certainly pleasing to God that which is in fact uncertain indeed, certain to be displeasing to Him since there is no clear word of God for it. Whoever believes something to be right which is wrong or uncertain is denying the truth, which is God Himself. He believes in lies and errors, and counting as right that which is wrong.

Hence, it is the height of folly when they command that one shall believe the Church, the Fathers, and the councils, though there be no word of God for it. It is not the Church but the devil's apostles who command such things, for the Church commands nothing unless it knows for certain that it is God's word. As St. Peter puts it, "Whoever speaks, let him speak as the word of God" [1 Pet. 4: 11]. It will be a long time, however, before they can ever prove that the decrees of the councils are God's word. Still more foolish is it when they assert that kings, princes, and the mass of mankind believe thus and so. My dear individual, we are not baptized into kings, or princes, or even into the mass of mankind, but into Christ and God Himself. Neither are we called kings, princes, or common folk, but Christians. No one shall or can command the soul unless he is able to show it the way to heaven; but this no man can do, only God alone. Therefore, in matters which concern the salvation of souls, nothing but God's word shall be taught and accepted.

Again, consummate fools though they are, they must confess that they have no power over souls. For no human being can kill a soul or give it life, or conduct it to heaven or hell. If they will not take our word for it, Christ Himself will attend to it strongly enough where He says in the tenth chapter of Matthew, "Do not fear those who kill the body, and after that have nothing that they can do; rather fear him who after he has killed the body, has power to condemn to hell." I think it is clear enough here that the soul is taken out of all human hands and is placed under the authority of God alone.

Now tell me: How much wit must there be in the head of a person who imposes commands in an area where he has no authority whatsoever? Would you not judge the person insane who commanded the moon to shine whenever he wanted it to? How well would it go if the people of Leipzig were to impose laws on us Wittenbergers, or if, conversely, we in Wittenberg were to legislate for the people of Leipzig! They would certainly send the lawmakers a gift of Hellebore to purge their brains and cure their sniffles. Yet our emperor and clever princes are doing just that today. They are allowing pope, bishop, and sophists to lead them on—one blind man leading the other—to command their subjects to believe, without God's word, whatever they please. And still they would be known as Christian princes, God forbid!

Besides, we cannot conceive how an authority could or should act in a situation except where it can see, know, judge, condemn, change, and modify. What would I think of a judge who does blindly decide cases which he neither hears nor sees? Tell me then: How can a mere man see, know, judge, condemn, and change hearts? That is reserved for God alone, as Psalm 7 [: 9] says, "God tries the hearts and reins"; and [: 8], "The Lord judges the peoples." And Acts 10 says, "God knows the hearts"; and Jer. [17: 9–10], "Wicked and unsearchable is the human heart; who can understand it? I, the Lord, who searches the heart and reins." A court should and must be quite certain and clear about everything if it is to render judgment. But the thoughts and inclinations of the soul can be known to no one but God. Therefore, it is futile and impossible to command or compel anyone by force to believe this or that. The matter must be approached in a different way. Force will not accomplish it. And I am surprised at the big fools, for they themselves all say, *De occultis non iudicat Ecclesia.* The Church does not judge secret matters. If the spiritual rule of the Church governs only public matters, how dare the mad temporal authority judge and control such a secret, spiritual, hidden matter as faith?

Furthermore, every man runs his own risk in believing as he does, and he must see to it himself that he believes rightly. As nobody else can go to heaven or hell for me, so nobody else can believe or disbelieve for me; as nobody else can open or close heaven or hell to me, so nobody else can drive me to belief or unbelief. How he believes or disbelieves is a matter for the conscience of each individual, and since this takes nothing away from the temporal authority, the latter should be content to attend to its own affairs and let men believe this or that as they are able and willing, and constrain no one by force. For faith is a free act, to which no one can be forced. Indeed, it is a work of God in the Spirit, not something which outward authority should compel or create. Hence arises the common saying, found also in St. Augustine, "No one can or ought to be forced to believe."

Moreover, the blind, wretched fellows fail to see how hopeless and impossible a thing they are attempting. For no matter how harshly they lay down the law, or how violently they rage, they can do no more than force an outward compliance of the mouth and the hand; the heart they cannot compel, though they work themselves to a frazzle. For the proverb is true: Thoughts are tax-free. Why do they persist in trying to force people to believe from the heart when they see that it is impossible? In so doing they only compel weak consciences to lie, to disavow, and to utter what is not in their hearts. They thereby load themselves down with dreadful alien sins, for all the lies and false confessions which such weak consciences utter fall back upon him who compels them. Even if their subjects were in error, it would be much easier simply to let them err than to compel them to lie and to utter what is not in their hearts. In addition, it is not right to prevent evil by something even worse...

Similarly, the temporal lords are supposed to govern lands and people outwardly. This they leave undone. They can do no more than strip and fleece, heap tax upon tax and tribute upon tribute, letting loose here a bear and there a wolf. Besides this, there is no justice, integrity, or truth to be found among them. They behave worse than any thief or scoundrel, and their temporal rule has sunk quite as low as that of the spiritual tyrants. For this reason God so perverts their minds also, that they rush into the absurdity of trying to exercise a spiritual rule over souls, just as their counterparts try to establish a temporal rule. They blithely heap alien sins upon themselves and incur the hatred of God and people, until they come to ruin together with bishops, popes, and monks, one scoundrel with the other. Then they lay all the blame on the gospel, and instead of confessing their sin, they blaspheme God and say that our preaching has brought about that which their perverse wickedness has deserved—and still unceasingly deserves—just as the Romans did when they were destroyed. Here then you have God's decree concerning the high and mighty. They are not to believe it, however, lest this stern decree of God be hindered by their repentance.

But, you say: Paul said in Rom. 13 [: 1] that every soul should be subject to the governing authority; and Peter says that we should be subject to every human ordinance [1 Pet. 2: 13]. Answer: Now you are on the right track, for these passages are in my favor. St. Paul is speaking of the governing authority. Now you have just heard that no one but God can have authority over souls. Hence, St. Paul cannot possibly be speaking of any obedience except where there can be corresponding authority. From this it follows that he is not speaking of faith, to the effect that temporal authority should have the right to command faith. He is speaking rather of external things that should be ordered and governed on earth. His words too make this perfectly clear, where he prescribes limits for both authority and obedience, saying, "Pay all of them their dues, taxes to whom taxes are due, revenue to whom revenue is due, honor to whom honor is due, respect to whom respect is due" [Rom. 13: 7]. Temporal obedience and authority, you see, apply only externally to taxes, revenue, honor, and respect. Again, where he says, "The governing authority is not a terror to good conduct, but to bad" [Rom. 13: 3], he again so limits the governing authority that it is not to have the mastery over faith or the word of God, but over evil works...

Christ Himself made this distinction, and summed it all up very nicely when He said in Matt. 22 [: 21], "Render to Caesar the things that are Caesar's and to God the things that are God's." Now, if the imperial power extended into God's kingdom and authority, and were not something separate, Christ would not have made this distinction. For, as has been said, the soul is not under the authority of Caesar; he can neither teach it nor guide it, neither kill it nor give it life, neither bind it nor loose it, neither judge it nor condemn it, neither hold it fast nor release it. All this he would have to do, if he had the authority to command it and to impose laws upon it. But with respect to body, property, and honor he has indeed to do these things, for such matters are under his authority...

If your prince or temporal ruler commands you to side with the pope, to believe thus and so, or to get rid of certain books, you should say, "It is not fitting that Lucifer should sit at the side of God. Gracious sir, I owe you obedience in body and property; command me within the limits of your authority on earth, and I will obey. But if you command me to believe or to get rid of certain books, I will not obey; for then you are a tyrant and overreach yourself, commanding where you have neither the right nor the authority," etc. Should he seize your property on account of this and punish such disobedience, then blessed are you; thank God that you are worthy to suffer for the sake of the divine word. Let him rage, fool that he is; he will meet his judge. For I tell you, if you fail to withstand him, if you give in to him and let him take away your faith and your books, you have truly denied God.

Let me illustrate. In Meissen, Bavaria, the Mark, and other places, the tyrants have issued an order that all copies of the New Testament are everywhere to be turned in to the officials. This should be the response of their subjects: They should not turn in a single page, not even a letter, on pain of losing their salvation. Whoever does so is delivering Christ up into the hands of Herod, for these tyrants act as murderers of Christ just like Herod. If their homes are ordered searched and books or property taken by force, they should suffer it to be done. Outrage is not to be resisted but endured; yet we should not sanction it, or lift a little finger to conform or obey. For these tyrants are acting as worldly princes are supposed to act, and worldly princes they surely are. But the world is God's enemy; hence, they too have to do what is antagonistic to God and agreeable to the world, that they may not be bereft of honor, but remain worldly princes. Do not wonder, therefore, that they rage and mock at the gospel; they have to live up to their name and title.

You must know that since the beginning of the world a wise prince is a mighty rare bird, and an upright prince even rarer. They are generally the biggest fools or the worst scoundrels on earth; therefore, one must constantly expect the worst from them and look for little good, especially in divine matters which concern the salvation of souls. They are God's executioners and hangmen; His divine wrath uses them to punish the wicked and to maintain outward peace. Our God is a great lord and ruler; this is why He must also have such noble, highborn, and rich hangmen and con-stables. He desires that everyone shall copiously accord them riches, honor, and fear in abundance. It pleases His divine will that we call His hangmen gracious lords, fall at their feet, and be sub-ject to them in all humility, so long as they do not ply their trade too far and try to become pastors instead of hangmen. If a prince should happen to be wise, upright, or a Christian, that is one of the great miracles, the most precious token of divine grace upon that land. Ordinarily the course of events is in accordance with the pas-sage from Is. 3 [: 4], "I will make boys their princes, and gaping fools shall rule over them"; and in Hos. 13 [: 11], "I will give you a king in my anger, and take him away in my wrath." The world is too wicked, and does not deserve to have many wise and upright princes. Frogs must have their storks.

Again you say, "The temporal power is not forcing people to believe; it is simply seeing to it externally that no one deceives the people by false doctrine; how could heretics otherwise be re-strained?" Answer: This the bishops should do; it is a function en-trusted to them and not to the princes. Heresy can never be restrained by force. One will have to tackle the problem in some other way, for heresy must be opposed and dealt with other-wise than with the sword. Here God's word must do the fighting. If it does not succeed, certainly the temporal power will not suc-ceed either, even if it were to drench the world in blood. Heresy is a spiritual matter which you cannot hack to pieces with iron, consume with fire, or drown in water. God's word alone avails here.

Moreover, faith and heresy are never so strong as when men oppose them by sheer force, without God's word. For men count it certain that such force is for a wrong cause and is directed against the right, since it proceeds without God's word and knows not how to further its cause except by naked force, as brute beasts do.

Even in temporal affairs force can be used only after the wrong has been legally condemned. How much less possible it is to act with force, without justice and God's word, in these lofty spiritual matters! See, therefore, what fine, clever nobles they are! They would drive out heresy, but set about it in such a way that they only strengthen the opposition, rousing suspicion against themselves and justifying the heretics. My friend, if you wish to drive out heresy, you must find some way to tear it first of all from the heart and completely turn people's wills away from it. With force you will not stop it, but only strengthen it. What do you gain by strengthening heresy in the heart, while weakening only its outward expression and forcing the tongue to lie? God's word, however, enlightens the heart, and so all heresies and errors vanish from the heart of their own accord...

Therefore, so long as the devil is not repelled and driven from the heart, it is agreeable to him that I destroy his vessels with fire or sword; it is as if I were to fight lightning with a straw. Job bore abundant witness of this when in his forty-first chapter he said that the devil counts iron as straw, and fears no power on earth. We learn it also from experience, for even if all Jews and heretics were forcibly burned, no one ever has been or will be convinced or converted thereby...

But you might say, "Since there is to be no temporal sword among Christians, how then are they to be ruled outwardly? There certainly must be authority even among Christians." Answer: Among Christians there shall and can be no authority; rather all are alike subject to one another, as Paul says in Rom. 12: "Each shall consider the other his superior"; and Peter says in 1 Pet. 5 [: 5], "All of you be subject to one another." This is also what Christ means in Luke 14 [: 10], "When you are invited to a wedding, go and sit in the lowest place." Among Christians there is no superior but Christ Himself and Him alone. What kind of authority can there be where all are equal and have the same right, power, possession, and honor, and where no one deserves to be the other's superior, but each the other's subordinate? Where there are such people, one could not establish authority even if he wanted to, since in the nature of things it is impossible to have superiors where no one is able or willing to be a superior. Where there are no such people, however, there are no real Christians either.

II

The Twelve Articles of the
Swabian Peasants. [1525]

The German peasant uprising of 1524–1525 had an intriguing relationship to the Protestant Reformation, since the real causes of the peasants' discontent reached back into the preceding century, where they found expression in periodic uprisings and restlessness. But the Protestant Reformation and its slogans—the freedom of the Christian, the priesthood of all believers, the repudiation of human laws and regulations—seemed to be tailor-made for the peasants, and it was natural that they would embrace the tenets of the incipient Reformation, which provided a theological rationale for their concerns.

When the peasants rose in southwest Germany in the fall of 1524, their pronouncements seemed to express a Lutheran orientation. The Twelve Articles, the most famous of a large number of similar but unprinted peasant documents, serves as an excellent illustration. Note, for example, the abundant scriptural references, or the stipulation that if any demand was contrary to Scripture it would be withdrawn.[10]

---

10. Hans J. Hillerbrand, *The Reformation. A Narrative History*. New York, 1965, pp. 89–91.

LITERATURE

Peter Blickle, *The Revolution of 1525: The German Peasants' War from a New Perspective*. Baltimore, 1985.

To the Christian Reader Peace and the Grace of God Through Christ.

There are many Antichrists who on account of the assembling of the peasants, cast scorn upon the gospel, and say: Is this the fruit of the new teaching, that no one obeys but all everywhere rise in revolt, and band together to reform, extinguish, indeed kill the temporal and spiritual authorities. The following article will answer these godless and blaspheming fault-finders. They will first of all remove the reproach from the word of God and secondly give a Christian excuse for the disobedience or even the revolt of the entire peasantry... Therefore, Christian reader, read the following articles with care, and then judge. Here follow the articles:

The First Article

First, it is our humble petition and desire, indeed our will and resolution, that in the future we shall have power and authority so that the entire community should choose and appoint a minister, and that we should have the right to depose him should he conduct himself improperly. The minister thus chosen should teach us the holy gospel pure and simple, without any human addition, doctrine, or ordinance. For to teach us continually the true faith will lead us to pray God that through His grace His faith may increase within us and be confirmed in us. For if His grace is not within us, we always remain flesh and blood, which avails nothing; since the Scripture clearly teaches that only through true faith can we come to God. Only through His mercy can we become holy.

The Second Article

Since the proper tithe is established in the Old Testament and fulfilled in the New, we are ready and willing to pay the fair tithe of the harvest. Nonetheless it should be done properly. The Word of God plainly provides that it should be given to God and passed on to His own. If it is to be given to a minister, we will in the future collect the tithe through our church elders, appointed by the congregation, and distribute from it, to the sufficient livelihood of the minister and his family elected by the entire congregation, according to the judgment of the whole congregation. The remainder shall be given to the poor, as circumstances and the general opinion demand.

The Third Article

It has been the custom heretofore for men to hold us as their own property, which is pitiable enough considering that Christ has redeemed and purchased us without exception by the shedding of His precious blood, the lowly as well as the great. Accordingly, it is consistent with Scripture that we should be free and we wish to be so. Not that we want to be absolutely free and under no authority. God does not teach us that we should lead a disorderly life according to the lusts of the flesh, but that we should live by the commandments, love the Lord our God and our neighbor.

The Fourth Article

In the fourth place, it has been the custom heretofore that no poor person was allowed to catch venison or wild fowl, or fish in flowing water, which seems to us quite unseemly and unbrotherly, as well as selfish and not according to the Word of God... Accordingly, it is our desire if a man holds possession of waters that he should prove from satisfactory documents that his right has been wittingly acquired by purchase. We do not wish to take it from him by force, but his rights should be exercised in a Christian and brotherly fashion.

The Fifth Article

In the fifth place, we are aggrieved in the matter of woodcutting, for our nobility have appropriated all the woods to themselves alone...It should be free to every one of the community to help himself to such firewood as he needs in his home. Also, if a person requires wood for carpenter's purposes, he should have it free but with the approval of a person appointed by the community for that purpose.

The Sixth Article

Our sixth complaint is in regard to the excessive services demanded of us, which increase from day to day.

We ask that this matter be properly looked into, so that we shall not continue to be oppressed in this way, and that some gracious consideration be given us, since our forefathers served only according to the Word of God.

The Seventh Article

Seventh, we will not hereafter allow ourselves to be further oppressed by our lords. What the lords possess is to be held according to the agreement between the lord and the peasant.

The Eighth Article

In the eighth place, we are greatly burdened by holdings which cannot support the rent exacted from them. The peasants suffer loss in this way and are ruined. We ask that the lords may appoint persons of honor to inspect these holdings and fix a rent in accordance with justice, so that the peasant shall not work for nothing, since the laborer is worthy of his hire.

The Ninth Article

In the ninth place, we are burdened with the great evil of the constant making of new laws. We are not judged according to the offense but sometimes with great ill will, sometimes much too leniently. In our opinion we should be judged according to the old written law, so that the case shall be decided according to its merits and not according to favors.

The Tenth Article

In the tenth place, we are aggrieved that certain individuals have appropriated meadows and fields which at one time belonged to the community. These we will take again into our own hands unless they were rightfully purchased.

The Eleventh Article

In the eleventh place, we will entirely abolish the tax called *Todfall* [heriot] and will no longer endure it, nor allow widows and orphans to be thus shamefully robbed against God's will.

Conclusion

In the twelfth place, it is our conclusion and final judgment that if any one or more of these articles should not be in agreement with the Word of God, which we do not think, we will willingly recede from such article when it is proved to be against the word of God by a clear explanation of the Scripture. For this we shall pray God, since He can grant all this and He alone. The peace of Christ abide with us all.

12

Martin Luther: *Friendly Admonition to Peace Concerning the Twelve Articles of the Swabian Peasants.* [1525]

This tract was Luther's response to the *Twelve Articles*, which had implicated him because of the "evangelical" character of their demands. From the insistence that a congregation elect its own minister to the willingness to be corrected by the Scriptures, the *Twelve Articles* seemed to be pages out of Luther's book. Luther responded with this tract, published in April 1525. Above all, it was meant as an appeal to peace, as a plea that the grievances of the peasants be duly considered and bloodshed avoided. At the same time, Luther left little doubt that he disapproved of the peasants' marshaling of scriptural arguments in support of their economic or social goals, and in this tract he expounded his understanding of the relationship of Christianity to social change. No matter how well justified certain social or economic demands may be, the gospel cannot be adduced in their support. Luther rejected the use of the gospel to sustain secular demands and insisted that the laws of society must provide the answer for social amelioration.

A condensed version of the tract is reprinted below.[11]

---

11. *Works of Martin Luther.* The Philadelphia Edition. Vol. IV. Philadelphia, 1931, pp. 219–44.

LITERATURE

Peter Blickle, *The Revolution of 1525*. Baltimore, 1985.

The peasants who have banded together in Swabia have put their intolerable grievances against the rulers into twelve articles, and undertaken to support them with certain passages of Scripture, and have published them in printed form. The thing about them that pleases me best is that, in the twelfth article, they offer to accept instruction gladly and willingly, if there is need or necessity for it, and are willing to be corrected, insofar as that can be done by clear, plain, undeniable passages of Scripture, since it is right and proper that no one's conscience should be instructed or corrected, except by divine Scripture.

Now, if that is their serious and sincere meaning—and it would not be right for me to interpret it otherwise, because in these articles they come out boldly into the open and show no desire to shun the light—then there is good reason to hope that things will be well. As one who is counted among those who now deal with the divine Scriptures here on earth, and especially as one whom they mention and call upon by name in the second document, it gives me the greater courage and confidence in openly publishing my instruction, which I do in a friendly and Christian spirit, as a duty of brotherly love, in order that, if any misfortune or disaster shall come out of this matter, it may not be attributed to me or blamed on me because of my silence. But if this offer of theirs is only pretense and show (and without doubt there are some of that kind of people among them; for it is not possible that so great a crowd should all be true Christians and have good intentions, but a large part of them must be using the good intentions of the rest for their own selfish purposes and seeking their own advantage), then without doubt, it will accomplish very little and contribute, in fact, to their great injury and eternal ruin.

Because this matter, then, is great and perilous, concerning, as it does, both the kingdom of God and the kingdom of the world (for if this rebellion were to proceed and get the upper hand, both kingdoms would be destroyed and there would be neither worldly government nor word of God, but it would result in the permanent destruction of all Germany), therefore it is necessary to speak boldly and to give advice without regard to anyone...

To the Princes and Lords. We have no one on earth to thank for this mischievous rebellion except you princes and lords; and especially you blind bishops and mad priests and monks, whose hearts are hardened, even to the present day, and who do not cease to rage and rave against the holy gospel, although you know that it is true, and that you cannot refute it. Besides, in your temporal government, you do nothing but flay and rob your subjects, in order that you may lead a life of splendor and pride, until the poor common people can bear it no longer. The sword is at your throats, but you think yourselves so firm in the saddle that no one can unhorse you. This false security and stubborn perversity will break your necks, as you will discover. I have often told you before to beware of the saying, in Psalm 107 [40], "He pours contempt upon princes." You are striving after it, and want to be smitten over the head, and no warning or exhorting will help you to avoid it.

Well, then, since you are the cause of this wrath of God, it will undoubtedly come upon you, if you do not mend your ways in time. The signs in heaven and the wonders on earth are meant for you, dear lords; they bode no good for you, and no good will come to you. A great part of God's wrath has already come, and God is sending so many false teachers and prophets among us so that through error and blasphemy we may richly deserve hell and everlasting damnation. The rest of it is now here, for the peasants are mustering, and this must result in the ruin, destruction, and desolation of Germany by cruel murder and bloodshed, unless God shall be moved by our repentance to prevent it.

For you ought to know, dear lords, that God is doing this because this raging of yours cannot and will not and ought not to be endured for long. You must become different men and yield to God's word. If you do not do this amicably and willingly, then you will be compelled to it by force and destruction. If these peasants do not do it for you, others will. Even though you were to beat them all, they would still be unbeaten, for God will raise up others. It is His will to beat you, and you will be beaten. It is not the peasants, dear lords, who are resisting you; it is God Himself who is resisting you in order to visit your raging upon you. There are some of you who have said that they will stake land and people on the extirpation of Lutheran teaching. What would you think, if you were to turn out to be your own prophets, and your land and people were already staked? Do not jest with God, dear lords! The Jews, too, said, "We have no king," and it became so serious that they had to be without a king forever.

To make your sin still greater and ensure your merciless destruction, some of you are beginning to blame this affair on the gospel and say it is the fruit of my teaching. Well, well! Slander away, dear lords. You did not want to know what I taught, and what the gospel is; now there is one at the door who will soon teach you, unless you amend your ways. You, and everyone else, must bear me witness that I have taught with all quietness, have striven earnestly against rebellion, and have diligently held and exhorted subjects to obedience and reverence toward even your tyrannous and ravenous rule. This rebellion cannot be coming from me. But the murder-prophets, who hate me as much as they hate you, have come among these people and have gone about among them for more than three years, and no one has resisted them save me alone. If, therefore, God is minded to punish you and allows the devil, through his false prophets, to stir up the people against you, and if it is, perhaps, His will that I shall not be able to prevent it any longer; what can I or my gospel do? Not only has it suffered your persecution and murdering and raging; it has also prayed for you and helped protect and maintain your rule over the common people. If I had any desire to be revenged on you, I could laugh in my sleeve and become a mere onlooker at the doings of the peasants, or even join in with them and help make matters worse; but from this may my God preserve me, as He has done hitherto.

Therefore, my dear lords, enemies or friends, I beg submissively that you will not despise my faithfulness, though I am a poor man. I beg that you will not make light of this rebellion. Not that I believe or fear that they will be too strong for you, or that I would have you be afraid of them on that account. But fear God and have respect for His wrath! If it be His will to punish you as you have deserved (and I am afraid that it is), then He would punish you, even though the peasants were a hundred times fewer than they are. He can make peasants out of stones and slay a hundred of you by one peasant, so that all your armor and your strength will be too little.

If it is still possible to give you advice, my lords, give a little place to the will and wrath of God...Do not begin a struggle with them, for you do not know what the end of it will be. Try kindness first; for you do not know what God wills to do, and do not strike a spark that will kindle all Germany and that no one can quench. Our sins are before God; therefore we have to fear his wrath when even a leaf rustles, let alone when such a multitude sets itself in motion. You lose nothing by kindness; and even though you were to lose something, it can afterward come back to you ten times over in peace, while in conflict you may, perhaps, lose both life and goods. Why run into danger, when you can get more by another and a good way?

The peasants have put forth twelve articles, some of which are so fair and just as to take away your reputation in the eyes of God and the world and fulfill what the psalm says about pouring contempt upon princes. Nevertheless, almost all of them are framed in their own interest and for their own good, though not for their best good. I should, indeed, have put forth other articles against you that would have dealt with all Germany and its government...

The first article, in which they ask the right to hear the gospel and choose their pastors, you cannot reject with any propriety, though, to be sure, it contains some selfishness, since they allege that these pastors are to be supported by the tithes, and these do not belong to them. Nevertheless, the sense of the article is that permission should be given for the preaching of the gospel, and this no ruler can or ought oppose. Indeed no ruler ought to prevent anyone from teaching or believing what he pleases, whether gospel or lies. It is enough if he prevents the teaching of sedition and rebellion.

The other articles recite physical grievances, and they, too, are fair and just. For rulers are not instituted in order that they may seek their own profit and self-will, but in order to provide for the best interests of their subjects. Flaying and extortion are, in the long run, intolerable.

To the Peasants. So far, dear friends, you have learned only that I admit it to be (sad to say!) all too true and certain that the princes and lords, who forbid the preaching of the gospel and oppress the people so unbearably, are worthy, and have well deserved that God put them down from their seats, as men who have sinned deeply against God and man. And they have no excuse. Nevertheless, you, too, must have a care that you take up your cause with a good conscience and with justice. If you have a good conscience, you have the comforting advantage that God will be with you and will help you through. Even though you were worsted for a while, and though you suffered death, you would win in the end, and would preserve your soul eternally with all the saints. But if you have not justice and a good conscience, you will be worsted; and even though you were to win for a while, and were to slay all the princes, yet in the end you would be lost eternally, body and soul. This is, therefore, no joking matter for you; it concerns your body and soul eternally. The thing that is most necessary to consider and that must be most seriously regarded, is not how strong you are and how completely wrong they are, but whether you have justice and a good conscience on your side.

Therefore, dear brethren, I beg you, in a kindly and brotherly way, to look diligently at what you do, and not to believe all kinds of spirits and preachers, now that Satan has raised up many evil spirits of disorder and of murder and filled the world with them. Only listen and give ear, as you offer many times to do. I will not spare you the earnest warning that I owe you, even though some of you, poisoned by the murderous spirits, will hate me for it and call me a hypocrite. That does not worry me; it is enough for me if I save some of the goodhearted and upright men among you from the danger of God's wrath. The rest I fear as little, as they despise me much; and they shall not harm me. I know one who is greater and mightier than they are, and He teaches me in Psalm 3, "I am not afraid, though many thousands of people set themselves against me." My confidence shall outlast their confidence; that I know for sure.

In the first place, dear brethren, you bear the name of God and call yourselves a "Christian covenant," or union, and allege that you want to live and act "according to the divine law." Now you know that the name, word, and titles of God are not to be assumed idly or in vain, as He says in the second commandment, "Thou shalt not bear the name of the Lord thy God in vain," and adds, "For God will not let him be guiltless who bears His name in vain." Here is a clear, plain text, which applies to you, as to all men. Without regard to your great numbers, your rights, and your terror, it threatens you, as well as us and all others, with God's wrath. He is, as you also know, mighty enough and strong enough to punish you as He here threatens, if His name is borne in vain; and so you have to expect no good fortune, but only misfortune, if you bear His name falsely. Learn from this how to judge yourselves; and accept this kindly warning. For Him who once drowned the whole world in the flood and sank Sodom with fire, it is a simple thing to slay or to defeat so many thousand peasants. He is an almighty and terrible God.

In the second place, it is easy to prove that you are bearing God's name in vain and putting it to shame; nor is it to be doubted that you will, in the end, encounter all misfortune unless God is untrue. For here stands God's word, and says through the mouth of Christ, "He who takes the sword shall perish by the sword." That means nothing else than that no one, by his own violence, shall arrogate authority to himself; but as Paul says, "Let every soul be subject to the higher powers with fear and reverence."

How can you get over these sayings and laws of God, when you boast that you are acting according to divine law, and yet take the sword in your own hands and revolt against the "higher powers" that are ordained of God? Do you not think that Paul's judgment in Rom. 13 will strike you, "He that disobeys the ordinance of God shall receive condemnation"? That is bearing God's name in vain: alleging God's law and disobeying God's law, under His name. Oh, have care, dear sirs! It will not turn out that way in the end.

In the third place, you say that the rulers are wicked and intolerable, for they will not allow the gospel, and they oppress us too hard by the burdens they lay on our temporal goods, and they are ruining us body and soul. I answer: The fact that the rulers are wicked and unjust does not excuse tumult and rebellion, for to punish wickedness does not belong to everybody, but to the worldly rulers who bear the sword. Thus Paul says in Rom. 13, and Peter, in 1 Pet. 3, that they are ordained of God for the punishment of the wicked. Then, too, there is the natural law for the entire world, which says that no one may be judge in his own cause or take his own revenge. The proverb is true, "He who resists is wrong," and the other proverb, "He who resists makes strife." The divine law agrees with this, and says, in Deut. 32, "Vengeance is mine, I will repay, says the Lord." Now you cannot deny that your rebellion proceeds in such a way that you make yourselves your own judges, and avenge yourselves, and are unwilling to suffer any wrong. That is contrary not only to Christian law and the gospel but also to natural law and all equity...

On the contrary, because you boast of the divine law and yet act against it, He will let you fall and be punished terribly, as people who dishonor His name; and then He will condemn you eternally, as was said above. For the word of Christ in Matt. 7, applies to you; you see the mote in the eye of the rulers, and see not the beam in your own eye. Also the saying of Paul in Rom. 3, "Let us do evil that good may come; whose damnation is just and right." It is true that the rulers do wrong when they suppress the gospel and oppress you in temporal things; but you do much more wrong when you not only suppress God's word but tread it underfoot, and invade His authority and His law, and put yourselves above God. Besides, you take from the rulers their authority and right; nay, all that they have. For what have they left, when they have lost their authority?...

Can you not imagine it, or figure it out, dear friends? If your enterprise were right, then any man might become judge over another, and there would remain in the world neither authority, nor government, nor order, nor land, but there would be only murder and bloodshed; for as soon as anyone saw that someone was wronging him, he would turn to and judge him and punish him. Now, if that is unjust and intolerable when done by an individual, neither can it be endured when done by a band or a crowd. But if it can be endured from a band or a crowd, it cannot be prevented with right and justice when individuals attempt it; for in both cases the cause is the same, namely, a wrong. And what would you do yourselves, if disorder broke out in your band, and one man set himself against another and took his own vengeance on him? Would you put up with that? Would you not say that he must let others, whom you appointed, do the judging and avenging? How, then, do you expect to stand with God and the world, when you do your own judging and avenging upon those who have injured you; nay, upon your rulers, whom God has ordained.

Now, all this has been said concerning the common, divine, and natural law which even heathen, Turks, and Jews have to keep, if there is to be any peace or order in the world. Even though you were to keep this whole law, you would do no better and no more than heathen and Turks. For not to be one's own judge and avenger, but to leave this to the authorities and the rulers, makes nobody a Christian; it is a thing that must eventually be done whether willingly or not. But because you are acting against this law, you see plainly that you are worse than heathen or Turks, to say nothing of the fact that you are not Christians. But what do you think that Christ will say to this? You bear His name and call yourselves a "Christian Assembly," and yet you are so far from being Christian, and your actions and lives are so horribly contrary to His law, that you are not worthy to be called even heathen or Turks, but are much worse than these, because you rage and struggle against the divine and natural law, which all the heathen keep...

If, now, it is really your will to keep the divine law, as you boast, then do it. There it stands! God says, "Vengeance is mine; I will repay," and again, "Be subject not only to good lords, but also to the wicked." If you do this, well and good; if not, you may, indeed, cause a calamity, but it will finally come upon yourselves. Let no one be in doubt about this! God is just and will not endure it. Be careful, therefore, with your liberty that you do not run from the rain and fall in the water, and thinking to gain freedom of body, lose body and goods and soul eternally. God's wrath is there; fear it, I advise you! The devil has sent false prophets among you; beware of them!

And now we would go on, and speak of the law of Christ and of the gospel, which is not binding on the heathen, as the other law is. For if you boast that you are Christians and are glad when you are called Christians, and want to be known as Christians, then you must allow your law to be held up before you rightly. Listen, then, dear Christians, to your Christian law! Your supreme Lord Christ, whose name you bear, says, in Matt. 5 [: 39–41], "Ye shall not resist evil, but if anyone compels you to go one mile, go with him two miles, and if anyone takes your cloak, let him have your coat, too; and if anyone smites you on one cheek, offer him the other also." Do you hear, "Christian Assembly"? How does your undertaking agree with this law? You will not endure it when anyone does you ill or wrong, but will be free, and suffer nothing but good and right; and Christ says that we are not to resist any evil or wrong, but always yield, suffer it, and let things be taken from us. If you will not bear this law, then put off the name of Christian, and boast of another name that accords with your actions, or

Christ Himself will tear His name from off you, and that will be too hard for you.

Thus says Paul, too, in Rom. 12, "Avenge not yourselves, dearly beloved, but give place to the wrath of God." Again, he praises the Corinthians, in 2 Cor. 11, because they suffer it gladly if a man smite or rob them; and in 1 Cor. 6, he rebukes them because they went to law about property and did not endure the wrong. Nay, our Leader, Jesus Christ, says, in Matt. 7, that we are to wish good to those who wrong us, and pray for our persecutors, and do good to those who do evil to us. These are our Christian laws, dear friends! Now see how far the false prophets have led you away from them, and yet they call you Christians, though they have made you worse than heathen. For from these sayings, a child easily grasps that it is Christian law not to strive against wrongs, not to grasp after the sword, not to protect oneself, not to avenge oneself, but to give up life and property, and let who takes it take it; we have enough in our Lord, who will not leave us, as He has promised. Suffering, suffering; cross, cross! This and nothing else is the Christian law! But now you battle for temporal goods, and will not let the coat go after the cloak but want to recover the cloak. How, then, will you die, and give up your life, or love your enemies, or do good to them? Oh, worthless Christians! Dear friends, Christians are not so common that so many of them can get together in one crowd. A true Christian is a rare bird! Would to God that the majority of us were good, pious heathen, who kept the natural law, not to mention the Christian law!

I will also give you some illustrations of Christian law so that you may see whither the mad prophets have led you. Look at St. Peter in the garden. He wanted to defend his Lord Christ with the sword and cut off Malchus's ear. Tell me, had not Peter great right on his side? Was it not an intolerable wrong that they were going to take from Christ, not only His property but also His life? Nay, they not only took from Him life and property; but in so doing they suppressed the gospel by which they were to be saved, and thus robbed heaven. Such a wrong you have not yet suffered, dear friends. But see what Christ does and teaches in this case. However great the wrong was, nevertheless He stopped St. Peter, bade him put up his sword, and would not allow him to avenge or prevent this wrong. In addition, He passed a judgment of death upon him, as though upon a murderer, and said, "He that takes the sword shall perish by the sword." From this we must understand that it is not enough that anyone has done us wrong, and that we have a good case and have the law on our side, but we must also have the right and power committed to us by God to use the sword and punish wrong. Moreover, a Christian must also endure it if anyone desires to keep the gospel away from him; if, indeed, it is possible to keep the gospel from anyone, as we shall hear.

A second example is Christ Himself. What did He do when they took His life on the cross and thereby took away from Him the work of preaching for which He had been sent by God Himself for the blessing of the souls of men? He did just what St. Peter says. He committed the whole matter to Him who judges righteously, and He endured this intolerable wrong. More than that, He prayed for His persecutors and said, "Father, forgive them, for they know not what they do." ...

I must also give you an illustration from this present time. Pope and emperor have set themselves against me and have raged. Now how have I brought it about that the more pope and emperor have raged, the more my gospel spread? I have never drawn the sword or desired revenge. I have begun no division and no rebellion, but, so far as I was able, I have helped the worldly rulers, even those who persecuted the gospel and me to maintain their power and honor. But I have stopped with committing the matter to God and relying confidently at all times upon His hand. Therefore, He has not only preserved my life in spite of the pope and all the tyrants (and this many really consider a great miracle; as I myself must also confess that it is), but He has caused my gospel always to increase and spread. Now you interfere with me. You want to help the gospel and do not see that by what you are doing you are hindering it and holding it down in the highest degree.

I say all this, dear friends, as a faithful warning. In this case you should rid yourselves of the name of Christians and cease to boast of Christian law. For no matter how right you are, it is not for a Christian to appeal to law, or to fight, but rather to suffer wrong and endure evil; and there is no other way (1 Cor. 6). You yourselves confess in your preface that all who believe in Christ become kindly, peaceful, patient, and united; but in your deeds you are displaying nothing but impatience, turbulence, strife, and violence; thus you contradict your own words. You want to be known as patient people, who will endure neither wrong nor evil, but will endure what is right and good. That is fine patience! Any knave can practice it! It does not take a Christian to do that! Therefore I say again, however good and right your cause may be, nevertheless, because you would defend yourselves, and suffer neither violence nor wrong, you may do anything that God does not prevent, but leave the name of Christian out of it; leave out, I say, the name Christian and do not make it a cloak for your impatient, disorderly, un-Christian undertaking. I shall not let you have that name, but as long as there is a heartbeat in my body, I shall do all I can to take that name from you. You will not succeed or will succeed only in ruining your bodies and souls.

In saying this, it is not my intention to justify or defend the rulers in the intolerable wrongs which you suffer from them. They are wrong and do you cruel wrongs; that I admit. But what I hope is that, if neither party will allow itself to be instructed, and the one party attacks and comes to blows with the other (which God forbid!), neither shall be called Christians, but that, as is usual when one people fights with another, God will punish one knave with another, as the saying goes. If it comes to a conflict (which God may graciously avert!), I hope that you will be counted as people of such a kind and such a name that the rulers may know that they are fighting not against Christians but against heathen; and that you, too, may know that you are fighting the rulers not as Christians but as heathen. For Christians fight for themselves not with sword and gun, but with the cross and with suffering, just as Christ, our leader, does not bear a sword, but hangs on the cross...

If you were Christians, you would stop defying and threatening, and stay inside the Lord's Prayer, and advance your cause with God by praying, and say, "Thy will be done," and "Deliver us from evil. Amen." You see in the Psalter that the true saints take their necessities to God, and lament them, and seek aid from Him, and do not defend themselves or resist evil. Such prayer would have done more to help you, in all your needs, than if the world were full of you, especially if, besides that, you had a good conscience and a comforting assurance that your prayers were heard, as His promises declare; such as 1 Tim. 4, "He is the helper of all people, especially of the believers," and Psalm 50 [: 15], "Call upon me in trouble, and I will help thee"; and Psalm 90, "He called upon me in trouble, therefore will I deliver him." See! That is the Christian way to get rid of misfortune and evil, namely, endure it and call upon God. But because you do neither—neither call nor endure—but aid yourselves with your own might and make yourselves your own God and Savior, therefore God cannot and must not be your God or Savior. By God's permission (which, we pray, may not be given!), you might accomplish something as heathen and blasphemers, though only for your eternal and temporal ruin; but as

Christians, or evangelicals, you will win nothing; I would wager a thousand necks in it!

On the basis of what has been said, all your articles are easily answered; for even though all of them are right and proper according to the law of nature, nevertheless you have forgotten the Christian law, since you have not put them through by means of patience and prayer to God, as Christian people ought, but have undertaken, with impatience and violence, to wrest them from the rulers and extort them by force; and this is against the law of the land and against natural justice. The man who framed your articles is no pious and honest man, for he has indicated on the margin many chapters of Scripture, on which the articles are supposed to rest, but keeps the porridge in his mouth and leaves out the passages by which he would show his own wickedness and that of your enterprise. He has done this to deceive you and urge you on and bring you into danger. For the chapters he adduces, when they are read through, say very little in favor of your undertaking, but rather the opposite; viz., that men shall live and act as Christians. He is some prophet of turbulence, who seeks, through you, to work his will upon the gospel. May God prevent, and guard you against him!

In the preface you are conciliatory and allege that you will not be seditious, and make the excuse that you desire to teach and live according to the gospel. There your own mouth and your own works rebuke you, for you confess that you create disturbances and rise up in revolt, and you want to adorn such conduct by means of the gospel. You have heard that the gospel teaches that Christians ought to endure and suffer wrong and pray to God in all their necessities, yet you are not willing to suffer but like heathen force the rulers to conform to your impatient will. You adduce the children of Israel as an example, saying that God heard their crying and delivered them. Why then do you not follow the example that you bring forward? Call upon God and wait until He sends you a Moses, who will prove by signs and wonders that he is sent from God. The children of Israel did not riot against Pharaoh or help themselves as you propose to do. This illustration, therefore, is dead against you and condemns you. You boast of it, and yet you do the opposite.

Again, it is not true when you declare that you teach and live according to the gospel. There is not one of the articles which teaches a single point of the gospel, but everything is directed to one purpose; namely, that your bodies and your properties may be free. In a word, they all deal with worldly and temporal matters. You would have power and wealth, so as not to suffer wrong; and yet the gospel does not take worldly matters into account, and makes the external life consist only in suffering, wrong, cross, patience, and contempt for temporal wealth and life. How, then, does the gospel agree with you; except that you are seeking to give your unevangelical and un-Christian enterprise an evangelical appearance, and do not see that you are thereby bringing shame on the holy gospel of Christ and making it a cloak for wickedness? Therefore you must take a different attitude and either drop this matter entirely and decide to suffer these wrongs, if you would be Christians and have the name of Christian; or else, if you are going on with it, make use of another name and not be called and considered Christians. There is no third course and no other way.

True enough, you are right in desiring the gospel, if you are really in earnest about it. Indeed, I am willing to make this article even sharper than you do, and say it is intolerable that anyone should be shut out of heaven and driven by force into hell. No one should suffer that; he ought to rather lose his neck a hundred times. But he who keeps the gospel from me, shuts heaven against me and drives me by force into hell; for the gospel is the only way and means for the soul's salvation, and on peril of losing my soul, I should not suffer this. Tell me, is that not stated sharply enough? And yet it does not follow that I must set myself with full fist against the rulers who do me this wrong. "But," you say, "how am I at the same time to suffer it and not suffer it?" The answer is easy. It is impossible that anyone shall have the gospel kept from him. There is no power in heaven or on earth that can do this, for it is a public teaching that moves freely about under the heavens and is bound to no one place. In this it is like the star, running through the air, which showed Christ's birth to the wise men from the East.

It is true, indeed, that the rulers may suppress the gospel in cities or places where the gospel is, or where there are preachers; but you can leave these cities or places and follow the gospel to some other place. It is not necessary that, for the gospel's sake, you should capture or hold the city or place; but let the lord have his city, and do you follow the gospel. Thus you suffer men to do you wrong and drive you away; and yet, at the same time you do not suffer men to take the gospel from you or keep it from you. Thus the two things, suffering and not suffering, come to one. If you will hold the city for the sake of the gospel, you rob the lord of the city, of what is his, and pretend that you are doing it for the gospel's sake. Dear friend, the gospel does not teach robbing or the taking of things, even though the lord of the property abuses it by using it against God, wrongfully and to your injury. The gospel needs no bodily place or city to dwell in; it will and must dwell in hearts. This is what Christ taught in Matt. 10, "If they drive you out of one city, flee to another."

He does not say, "If they drive you out of one city, stay there; and capture the city, to the praise of the gospel, and make a riot against the lord of the city," though that is what men now want to do, and what they are teaching. But He says, "Flee, flee straightway into another, until the Son of Man shall come." Thus He says, too, in Matt. 23, that the godless shall drive His evangelists from one city to another; and Paul also says, in 2 Cor. 4, "We are in no certain place." If it so happen that a Christian must be moving constantly from one place to another, and leaving the place where he is and everything that he has, or if he sit in uncertainty, expecting this to happen any hour, then it is well with him; it is as it should be with a Christian. For because he will not suffer the gospel to be taken from him or kept from him, he has to suffer city, place, property, and everything that he is and has to be taken and kept from him. Now how does this agree with your undertaking? You capture and hold cities and places that are not yours and will not suffer them to be taken or kept from you; though you take and keep them from their natural lords. What kind of Christians are these, who, for the gospel's sake, become robbers, thieves, and scoundrels, and then say they are adherents of the new evangelical faith?

On the First Article

"An entire community shall have the power to choose and depose a pastor." This article is right if only it were understood in a Christian sense, though the chapters indicated on the margin do not help it. If the goods of the parish come from the rulers and not from the community, then the community cannot apply these goods to the use of him whom they choose, for that would be robbery and theft. If they desire a pastor, let them first humbly ask one from the rulers. If the rulers are unwilling, then let them choose their own pastor and support him with their own property, and let the rulers have their property or else secure it from them in a lawful way. But if the rulers will not tolerate the pastor whom they chose and support, then let him flee to another city, and let any flee with him who will, as Christ teaches. That is a Christian and evangelical way to choose and have one's own pastor. Whoever does otherwise, acts in an un-Christian manner, as a robber and brawler.

On the Second Article

"The tithes shall be divided to the pastor and the poor, and the balance kept for needs of the land, etc." This article is nothing but theft and highway robbery. They would appropriate for themselves the tithes, which are not theirs but the rulers', and would do with them what they please. Not so, dear friends! That is the same thing as deposing the rulers altogether, when your preface expressly says that no one is to be deprived of what is his.

If you would make gifts and do good, do it out of your own property, as the wise man says, for God says through Isaiah, "I hate the sacrifice that is gotten by robbery." You speak in this article as though you were already lords in the land and had taken all the property of the rulers for your own and would be no one's subjects and would give nothing. From this one grasps what you have in mind. Stop it, dear sirs, stop it! It will not be you who end it! The chapters of Scripture that your lying preacher and false prophet has smeared on the margin, do not help you at all; they are against you.

On the Third Article

"There shall be no serfs, for Christ has made all people free." That is making Christian freedom an utterly carnal thing. Did not Abraham and other patriarchs and prophets have slaves? Read what St. Paul teaches about servants, who, at that time, were all slaves. Therefore this article is dead against the gospel. It is a piece of robbery by which every man takes from his lord the body, which has become his lord's property. For a slave can be a Christian and have Christian liberty, in the same way that a prisoner or a sick man is a Christian, and yet not free. This article would make all men equal and turn the spiritual kingdom of Christ into a worldly, external kingdom; and that is impossible. For a worldly kingdom cannot stand unless there is in it an inequality of persons, so that some are free, some imprisoned, some lords, some subjects, etc.; and St. Paul says in Gal. 5, that in Christ master and servant are one thing...

The other articles, about freedom of game, birds, fish, wood, forests; about services, tithe, imposts, excises, *Todfall*, etc., these I leave to the lawyers, for it is not fitting that I, a preacher of the gospel, should judge or decide them. It is for me to instruct and teach people's consciences in things that concern divine and Christian matters; there are books enough about the other things in imperial law. I have said above that these things do not concern Christians, and that they care nothing about them. They let anyone else rob, take, skin, scrape, devour, and rage, for they are martyrs on earth. Therefore the peasants ought rightly leave the name of Christian alone and act in some other name, as men who want human and natural rights, not as those who seek Christian rights. This means that on all these points they should keep still, suffer, and make their complaints to God alone.

See, dear friends, this is the instruction that you asked of me in the second document. I beg that you will remember that you suffer willingly to be instructed by the Scriptures. Now when this reaches you, do not cry out at me, "Luther flatters the princes and speaks contrary to the gospel." First read and see my arguments from Scripture; for this is your affair; I am excused in the sight of God and the world. I know well the false prophets that are among you. Do not listen to them. They are surely deceiving you. They do not think of your consciences but would make Galatians of you, so that by means of you they might come to wealth and honor, and must afterward, with you, be damned eternally in hell.

Admonition to Both Rulers and Peasants. Therefore, dear sirs, since there is nothing Christian on either side and nothing Christian is an issue between you, but both lords and peasants are dealing with heathenish, or worldly, right and wrong, and with temporal goods; since, moreover, both parties are acting against God and are under His wrath, as you have heard; therefore, for God's sake, let yourselves be advised, and approach these matters as such matters are to be approached, that is, with justice and not with force or with strife, and do not start endless bloodshed in Germany. For because both of you are wrong and both of you would avenge and defend yourselves, both of you will destroy yourselves and God will use one knave to flog another.

You lords have both Scripture and history against you, for both tell how tyrants are punished. Even the heathen poets say that tyrants seldom die a dry death, but usually have been slain and have perished in blood. Because, then, it is an assured fact that you rule tyrannically and with rage, prohibit the gospel, and slay and oppress the poor, you have no reason for confidence or hope that you will perish otherwise than your kind have perished. Look at all the kingdoms that have come to their end by the sword—Assyria, Persia, Greece, Rome. They have all been destroyed at last in the same way that they destroyed others. Thus, God shows that He is judge upon earth and leaves no wrong unpunished. Therefore nothing is more certain than that this same judgment is close to you, whether it comes now or later, unless you reform.

You peasants also have Scripture and experience against you. They teach that turbulence has never had a good end, and God has always held strictly to the word, "He that takes the sword shall perish by the sword." Because, then, you are doing wrong by judging yourselves and avenging yourselves and are bearing the name of Christian unworthily besides, you are certainly under the wrath of God; and even though you win and destroy all the lords, in the end you would have to tear the flesh from one another's bones, like wild beasts. For because not spirit, but flesh and blood, rules among you, God will shortly send an evil spirit among you, as He did to the men of Shechem and to Abimelech. See the end that finally comes to turbulence in the story of Korah, Num. 16, and of Absalom, Sheba, Samri, and their like. Briefly, God hates both tyrants and rebels; therefore He sets them on one another, so that both parties perish shamefully, and His wrath and judgment upon the godless are fulfilled.

To me the saddest and the truly pitiful thing—which I would willingly buy off with my own life and death—is that on both sides two inevitable injuries must follow. For because neither party strives with a good conscience but both fight for the upholding of wrong, it must follow, in the first place, that those who are slain are lost eternally, body and soul, as men who die in their sins, without penitence and without grace, in the wrath of God. There is nothing to be done for them. The lords would be fighting for the strengthening and maintaining of their tyranny, their persecution of the gospel, and their unjust oppression of the poor, or else for the aiding of that kind of ruler. That is a terrible wrong and is against God. He who commits such a sin must be lost eternally. The peasants, on the other hand, would fight to defend their turbulence and their abuse of the name of Christian. Both these things are greatly against God, and he who dies in them or for them must also be lost eternally, and there is no help for it.

The second injury is that Germany will be laid waste, and if this bloodshed once starts, it will scarcely cease until everything is destroyed. It is easy to start a fight, but to stop it when we will is not in our power. What have they ever done to you—all these innocent children, women, and old people, whom you fools are drawing with you into such danger—that you should fill the land with blood and robbery, widows and orphans? Oh, the devil's mind is wicked enough! And God is angry and threatens to let him loose upon us and cool his rage in our blood and souls. Beware, dear sirs, and be wise! It concerns both of you! What good will it do you to condemn yourselves eternally and willfully and leave behind you, for your descendants, a desolate and devastated and bloody land besides, when you could arrange things better, while there is still time, by penitence toward God and friendly agreement or by suffering in the sight of men? With defiance and strife, you will do nothing.

It would, therefore, be my faithful counsel to choose from among the nobles certain counts and lords, and from the cities certain councilmen, and have these matters dealt with in a friendly way and settled; that you lords give up your stubbornness—as you must do in the end, whether you will or will not—and give up a little of your tyranny and oppression; so that poor people get air and room to live; that the peasants for their part let themselves be instructed and give over and let go some of the articles that grasp too far and too high, so that the case may be settled by human law and agreement, even though it cannot be dealt with in a Christian way.

If you shall not follow this advice (and God forbid that you do not follow it!), I must let you face reality, but I am guiltless as regards your souls, your blood, and your property; you will bear the guilt yourselves. I have told you that you are both wrong and that your fighting is wrong. You lords are not fighting against Christians—for Christians do nothing against you but prefer to suffer all things—but against open robbers and defamers of the Christian name. Those of them who die are already condemned eternally. On the other hand, you peasants are not fighting against Christians but against tyrants and persecutors of God and man, and murderers of the holy Christ. Those of them who die are also condemned eternally. There you have God's sure verdict upon both parties; that I know. Do what you please to keep your bodies and souls, if you will not follow this verdict.

13

Martin Luther: *Commentary on St. Paul's Epistle to the Galatians.* [1535]

A bove all, Luther was an expositor of Scripture, and his commentaries on biblical books which grew out of his professorial responsibilities at Wittenberg show him at his best. In 1519, and again in 1535, he lectured on the Epistle to the Galatians and published his lectures in the form of a commentary. The commentary of 1535 ranks high as an expression of Luther's theology, for here he expounded in classical form his thoughts about the heart of his religion—justification by faith. Reprinted here is a section from the introduction and also part of the exposition of Galatians 1: 16.

Most of Luther's treatises were polemical, written against specific opponents, such as Eck, Carlstadt, Zwingli, and Erasmus, or dealing with specific issues such as the Lord's Supper or free will. His biblical commentaries, from his first lectures of 1513 on the Psalms to his lectures on the Book of Genesis that occupied him during the last decade of his life, expressed his thought in a different form, neither polemical nor systematic but in an exegetical exposition whose framework was the argument of the biblical text.[12]

---

12. Jaroslav Pelikan, ed., *Luther's Works.* Vol. 26, *Lectures on Galatians (1535).* St. Louis, 1963, pp 4–12, 122–36.

LITERATURE

Jaroslav J. Pelikan, *Luther the Expositor.* St. Louis, 1959.

First of all, we must speak of the argument, that is, of the issue with which Paul deals in this Epistle. The argument is this: Paul wants to establish the doctrine of faith, grace, the forgiveness of sins or Christian righteousness, so that we may have a perfect knowledge and know the difference between Christian righteousness and all other kinds of righteousness. For righteousness is of many kinds. There is a political righteousness, which the emperor, the princes of the world, philosophers, and lawyers consider. There is also a ceremonial righteousness, which human traditions teach, as, for example, the traditions of the pope and other traditions. Parents and teachers may teach this righteousness without danger because they do not attribute to it any power to make satisfaction for sin, to placate God, and to earn grace; but they teach that these ceremonies are necessary only for moral discipline and for certain observances. There is, in addition to these, yet another righteousness, the righteousness of the law or of the Decalogue which Moses teaches. We, too, teach this, but after the doctrine of faith.

Over and above all these there is the righteousness of faith or Christian righteousness, which is to be distinguished most carefully from all the others. For they are all contrary to this righteousness, both because they proceed from the laws of emperors, the traditions of the pope, and the commandments of God, and because they consist in our works and can be achieved by us with "purely natural endowments," as the Scholastics teach, or from a gift of God. For these kinds of the righteousness of works, too, are gifts of God, as are all the things we have. But this most excellent righteousness, the righteousness of faith, which God imputes to us through Christ without works, is neither political nor ceremonial nor legal nor work-righteousness but is quite the opposite; it is a merely passive righteousness, while all the others, listed above, are active. For here we work nothing, render nothing to God; we only receive and permit someone else to work in us, namely, God. Therefore it is appropriate to call the righteousness of faith or Christian righteousness "passive." This is a righteousness hidden in a mystery, which the world does not understand. In fact, Christians themselves do not adequately understand it or grasp it in the midst of their temptations. Therefore it must always be taught and continually exercised. And anyone who does not grasp or take hold of it in afflictions and terrors of conscience cannot stand. For there is no comfort of conscience so solid and certain as is this passive righteousness.

But such is human weakness and misery that in the terrors of conscience and in the danger of death we look at nothing except our own works, our worthiness, and the law. When the law shows us our sin, our past life immediately comes to our mind. Then the sinner, in his great anguish of mind, groans and says to himself: "Oh, how damnably I have lived! If only I could live longer! Then I will amend my life." Thus human reason cannot refrain from looking at active righteousness, that is, its own righteousness; nor can it shift its gaze to passive, that is, Christian righteousness, but it simply rests in the active righteousness. So deeply is this evil rooted in us, and so completely have we acquired this unhappy habit! Taking advantage of the weakness of our nature, Satan increases and aggravates these thoughts in us. Then it is impossible for the conscience to avoid being more seriously troubled, confounded, and frightened. For it is impossible for the human mind to conceive any comfort of itself, or to look only at grace amid its consciousness and terror of sin, or consistently to reject all discussion of works. To do this is beyond human power and thought. Indeed, it is even beyond the law of God. For although the law is the best of all things in the world, it still cannot bring peace to a terrified conscience but makes it even sadder and drives it to despair. For by the law sin becomes exceedingly sinful (Rom. 7: 13).

Therefore the afflicted conscience has no remedy against despair and eternal death except to take hold of the promise of grace offered in Christ, that is, this righteousness of faith, this passive or Christian righteousness, which says with confidence: "I do not seek active righteousness. I ought to have and perform it; but I declare that even if I did have it and perform it, I cannot trust in it or stand up before the judgment of God on the basis of it. Thus I put myself beyond all active righteousness, all righteousness of my own or of the divine law, and I embrace only that passive righteousness which is the righteousness of grace, mercy, and the forgiveness of sins." In other words, this is the righteousness of Christ and of the Holy Spirit, which we do not perform but receive, which we do not have but accept, when God the Father grants it to us through Jesus Christ.

As the earth itself does not produce rain and is unable to acquire it by its own strength, worship, and power but receives it only by a heavenly gift from above, so this heavenly righteousness is given to us by God without our work or merit. As much as the dry earth of itself is able to accomplish in obtaining the right and blessed rain, that much can we men accomplish by our own strength and works to obtain that divine, heavenly, and eternal righteousness. Thus we can obtain it only through the free imputation and indescribable gift of God. Therefore the highest art and wisdom of Christians is not to know the law, to ignore works and all active righteousness, just as outside the people of God the highest wisdom is to know and study the law, works, and active righteousness.

It is a marvelous thing and unknown to the world to teach Christians to ignore the law and to live before God as though there were no law whatever. For if you do not ignore the law and thus direct your thoughts to grace as though there were no law but as though there were nothing but grace, you cannot be saved. "For through the law comes knowledge of sin" (Rom. 3: 20). On the other hand, works and the performance of the law must be demanded in the world as though there were no promise or grace. This is because of the stubborn, proud, and hardhearted, before whose eyes nothing must be set except the law, in order that they may be terrified and humbled. For the law was given to terrify and kill the stubborn and to exercise the old man. Both words must be correctly divided, according to the Apostle (2 Tim. 2: 25 ff.).

This calls for a wise and faithful father who can moderate the law in such a way that it stays within its limits. For if I were to teach men the law in such a way that they suppose themselves to be justified by it before God, I would be going beyond the limit of the law, confusing these two kinds of righteousness, the active and the passive, and would be a bad dialectician who does not properly distinguish. But when I go beyond the old man, I also go beyond the law. For the flesh or the old man, the law and works, are all joined together. In the same way the spirit or the new man is joined to the promise and to grace. Therefore when I see that a man is sufficiently contrite, oppressed by the law, terrified by sin, and thirsting for comfort, then it is time for me to take the law and active righteousness from his sight and to set forth before him, through the gospel, the passive righteousness which excludes Moses and the law and shows the promise of Christ, who came for the afflicted and for sinners. Here a man is raised up again and gains hope. Nor is he any longer under the law; he is under grace, as the Apostle says (Rom. 6: 14): "You are not under law but under grace." How not under law? According to the new man, to whom the law does not apply. For the law had its limits until Christ, as Paul says (Gal. 3: 24): "The Law, until Christ." When He came, Moses and the law stopped. So did circumcision, sacrifices, and the Sabbath. So did all the prophets.

This is our theology, by which we teach a precise distinction between these two kinds of righteousness, the active and the passive, so that morality and faith, works and grace, secular society and religion may not be confused. Both are necessary, but both must be kept within their limits. Christian righteousness applies to the new man, and the righteousness of the law applies to the old man, who is born of flesh and blood. Upon this latter, as upon an ass, a burden must be put that will oppress him. He must not enjoy the freedom of the spirit or of grace unless he has first put on the new man by faith in Christ, but this does not happen fully in this life. Then he may enjoy the kingdom and the ineffable gift of grace. I am saying this in order that no one may suppose that we reject or prohibit good works, as the papists falsely accuse us because they understand neither what they themselves are saying nor what we are teaching. They know nothing except the righteousness of the law; and yet they claim the right to judge a doctrine that is far above and beyond the law, a doctrine on which the carnal man is unable to pass judgment. Therefore it is inevitable that they be offended, for they cannot see any higher than the law. Therefore whatever is above the law is the greatest possible offense to them.

We set forth two worlds, as it were, one of them heavenly and the other earthly. Into these we place these two kinds of righteousness, which are distinct and separated from each other. The righteousness of the law is earthly and deals with earthly things; by it we perform good works. But as the earth does not bring forth fruit unless it has first been watered and made fruitful from above, for the earth cannot judge, renew, and rule the heavens, but the heavens judge, renew, rule, and fructify the earth, so that it may do what the Lord has commanded—so also by the righteousness of the law we do nothing even when we do much; we do not fulfill the law even when we fulfill it. Without any merit or work of our own, we must first be justified by Christian righteousness, which has nothing to do with the righteousness of the law or with earthly and active righteousness. But this righteousness is heavenly and passive. We do not have it of ourselves; we receive it from heaven. We do not perform it; we accept it by faith, through which we ascend beyond all laws and works. "As, therefore, we have borne the image of the earthly Adam," as Paul says, "let us bear the image of the heavenly one" (1 Cor. 15: 49), who is a new man in a new world, where there is no law, no sin, no conscience, no death, but perfect joy, righteousness, grace, peace, life, salvation, and glory.

Then do we do nothing and work nothing in order to obtain this righteousness? I reply: Nothing at all. For this righteousness means to do nothing, to hear nothing, and to know nothing about the law or about works but to know and believe only this: that Christ has gone to the Father and is now invisible; that He sits in heaven at the right hand of the Father, not as a Judge but as one who has been made for us wisdom, righteousness, sanctification, and redemption from God (1 Cor. 1: 30); in short, that He is our High Priest, interceding for us and reigning over us and in us through grace. Here one notices no sin and feels no terror or remorse of conscience. Sin cannot happen in this Christian righteousness; for where there is no law, there cannot be any transgression (Rom: 4: 15). If, therefore, sin does not have a place here, there is no conscience, no terror, no sadness. Therefore John says: "No one born of God commits sin" (1 John 3: 9). But if there is any conscience or fear present, this is a sign that this righteousness has been withdrawn, that grace has been lost sight of, and that Christ is hidden and out of sight. But where Christ is truly seen, then there must be full and perfect joy in the Lord and peace of heart, where the heart declares: "Although I am a sinner according to the law, judged by the righteousness of the law, nevertheless I do not despair. I do not die, because Christ lives who is my righteousness and my eternal and heavenly life. In that righteousness and life I have no sin, conscience, and death. I am indeed a sinner according to the present life and its righteousness, as a son of Adam where the law accuses me, death reigns and devours me. But above this life I have another righteousness, another life, which is Christ, the Son of God, who does not know sin and death but is righteousness and eternal life. For His sake this body of mine will be raised from the dead and delivered from the slavery of the law and sin, and will be sanctified together with the spirit."

Thus as long as we live here, both remain. The flesh is accused, exercised, saddened, and crushed by the active righteousness of the law. But the spirit rules, rejoices, and is saved by passive righteousness, because it knows that it has a Lord sitting in heaven at the right hand of the Father, who has abolished the law, sin, and death, and has trodden all evils underfoot, has led them captive and triumphed over them in Himself (Col. 2: 15). In this Epistle, therefore, Paul is concerned to instruct, comfort, and sustain us diligently in a perfect knowledge of this most excellent and Christian righteousness. For if the doctrine of justification is lost, the whole of Christian doctrine is lost. And those in the world who do not teach it are either Jews or Turks or papists or sectarians. For between these two kinds of righteousness, the active righteousness of the law and the passive righteousness of Christ, there is no middle ground. Therefore he who has strayed away from this Christian righteousness will necessarily relapse into the active righteousness; that is, when he has lost Christ, he must fall into a trust in his own works.

We see this today in the fanatical spirits and sectarians, who neither teach nor can teach anything correctly about this righteousness of grace. They have taken the words out of our mouth and out of our writings, and these only they speak and write. But the substance itself they cannot discuss, deal with, and urge because they neither understand it nor can understand it. They cling only to the righteousness of the law. Therefore they are and remain disciplinarians of works; nor can they rise beyond the active righteousness. Thus they remain exactly what they were under the pope. To be sure, they invent new names and new works; but the content remains the same. So it is that the Turks perform different works from the papists, and the papists perform different works from the Jews, and so forth. But although some do works that are more splendid, great, and difficult than others, the content remains the same, and only the quality is different. That is, the works vary only in appearance and in name. For they are still works. And those who do them are not Christians; they are hirelings, whether they are called Jews, Mohammedans, papists, or sectarians.

Therefore we always repeat, urge, and inculcate this doctrine of faith or Christian righteousness, so that it may be observed by continuous use and may be precisely distinguished from the active righteousness of the law. (For by this doctrine alone and through it alone is the church built, and in this it consists.) Otherwise we shall not be able to observe true theology but shall immediately become lawyers, ceremonialists, legalists, and papists. Christ will be so darkened that no one in the church will be correctly taught or comforted. Therefore if we want to be preachers and teachers of others, we must take great care in these issues and hold to this distinction between the righteousness of the law and that of Christ. This distinction is easy to speak of; but in experience and practice it is the most difficult of all, even if you exercise and practice it diligently. For in the hour of death or in other conflicts of conscience these two kinds of righteousness come together more closely than you would wish or ask...

Therefore, let us learn diligently this art of distinguishing between these two kinds of righteousness, in order that we may know how far we should obey the law. We have said above that in a Christian the law must not exceed its limits but should have its dominion only over the flesh, which is subjected to it and remains under it. When this is the case, the law remains within its limits. But if it wants to ascend into the conscience and exert its rule there, see to it that you are a good dialectician and that you make the correct distinction. Give no more to the law than it has coming, and say to it: "Law, you want to ascend into the realm of conscience and rule there. You want to denounce its sin and take away the joy of my heart, which I have through faith in Christ. You want to plunge me into despair, in order that I may perish. You are exceeding your jurisdiction. Stay within your limits, and exercise your dominion over the flesh. You shall not touch my conscience. For I am baptized; and through the gospel I have been called to a fellowship of righteousness and eternal life, to the kingdom of Christ, in which my conscience is at peace, where there is no law but only the forgiveness of sins, peace, quiet, happiness, salvation, and eternal life. Do not disturb me in these matters. In my conscience not the law will reign, that hard tyrant and cruel disciplinarian, but Christ, the Son of God, the King of Peace and Righteousness, the sweet Savior and Mediator. He will preserve my conscience happy and peaceful in the sound and pure doctrine of the gospel and in the knowledge of this passive righteousness."

When I have this righteousness within me, I descend from heaven like the rain that makes the earth fertile. That is, I come forth into another kingdom, and I perform good works whenever the opportunity arises. If I am a minister of the word, I preach, I comfort the saddened, I administer the sacraments. If I am a father, I rule my household and family, I train my children in piety and honesty. If I am a magistrate, I perform the office which I have received by divine command. If I am a servant, I faithfully tend to my master's affairs. In short, whoever knows for sure that Christ is his righteousness not only cheerfully and gladly works in his calling but also submits himself for the sake of love to magistrates, also to their wicked laws, and to everything else in this present life—even, if need be, to burden and danger...

Such is the theology of the anti-Christian kingdom. I am recounting it here to make Paul's argument more intelligible; for when two opposites are placed side by side, they become more evident. In addition, I want everyone to see how far these "blind guides of the blind" have strayed. By this wicked and blasphemous teaching they have not only obscured the gospel but removed it altogether and have buried Christ completely.

Such dreadful monstrosities and horrible blasphemies ought to be propounded to Turks and Jews, not to the church of Christ. This whole business clearly shows that the pope with his bishops, theologians, monks, and all the rest has neither knowledge nor concern about sacred things; nor do they care anything about the health of the flock, which is so deserted and so miserably scattered. For if they had seen, though only through a cloud, what Paul calls sin and what he calls grace, they would not have imposed such abominations and wicked lies on Christian people. They take mortal sin to be only the external work committed against the law, such as murder, adultery, theft, etc. They did not see that ignorance, hatred, and contempt of God in the heart, ingratitude, murmuring against God, and resistance to the will of God are also mortal sin, and that the flesh cannot think, say, or do anything except what is diabolical and opposed to God. If they had seen that these huge plagues are rooted in the nature of man, they would not have dreamed so wickedly about the "merit of congruity" and the "merit of condignity."

Therefore there must be a proper and clear definition of what wicked people or mortal sinners are. They are holy hypocrites and murderers, as Paul was when he went to Damascus to persecute Jesus of Nazareth, to abolish the doctrine of Christ, to murder the faithful, and to overthrow the church of Christ altogether. Those were certainly extremely great and horrible sins against God, but Paul was unable to recognize them as such. For he was so completely blinded by a wicked zeal for God that he regarded these unspeakable crimes of his as the height of righteousness and an act of worship and obedience most pleasing to God. Can such saints, who defend such horrible sins as the height of righteousness, be supposed to merit grace? ...

Now the true meaning of Christianity is this: that a man first acknowledge, through the law, that he is a sinner, for whom it is impossible to perform any good work. For the law says: "You are an evil tree. Therefore everything you think, speak, or do is opposed to God. Hence you cannot deserve grace by your works. But if you try to do so, you make the bad even worse; for since you are an evil tree, you cannot produce anything except evil fruits, that is, sins. 'For whatever does not proceed from faith is sin' (Rom. 14: 23)." Trying to merit grace by preceding works, therefore, is trying to placate God with sins, which is nothing but heaping sins upon sins, making fun of God, and provoking His wrath. When a man is taught this way by the law, he is frightened and humbled. Then he really sees the greatness of his sin and finds in himself not one spark of the love of God; thus he justifies God in His word and confesses that he deserves death and eternal damnation. Thus the first step in Christianity is the preaching of repentance and the knowledge of oneself.

The second step is this: If you want to be saved, your salvation does not come by works; but God has sent His only Son into the world that we might live through Him. He was crucified and died for you and bore your sins in His own body (1 Pet. 2: 24). Here there is no "congruity" or work performed before grace, but only wrath, sin, terror, and death. Therefore the law only shows sin, terrifies, and humbles; thus it prepares us for justification and drives us to Christ. For by His word God has revealed to us that He wants to be a merciful Father to us. Without our merit—since, after all, we cannot merit anything—He wants to give us forgiveness of sins, righteousness, and eternal life for the sake of Christ. For God is He who dispenses His gifts freely to all, and this is the praise of His deity...

In opposition to these trifles and empty dreams, as we have noted briefly above, we teach faith and the true meaning of Christianity. First, a man must be taught by the law to know himself, so that he may learn to sing: "All have sinned and fall short of the glory of God" (Rom. 3: 23); again: "None is righteous, no, not one; no one understands, no one seeks for God. All have turned aside" (Rom. 3: 10–12); again: "Against Thee only have I sinned" (Ps. 51: 4). By this opposition of ours we drive men away from the merit of congruity and of condignity. Now once a man has thus been humbled by the law and brought to the knowledge of himself, then he becomes truly repentant; for true repentance begins with fear and with the judgment of God. He sees that he is such a great sinner that he cannot find any means to be delivered from his sin by his own strength, effort, or works. Then he understands correctly what Paul means when he says that man is the slave and captive of sin, that God has consigned all men to sin, and that the whole world is guilty in the sight of God...

14

Martin Luther: *Concerning the Jews and Their Lies.* [1543]

Martin Luther devoted several of his writings to the Jewish people and their religion. An early one, written in 1523, *That Jesus Christ Was Born a Jew*, acknowledged that Christians had mistreated Jews, apologized for such mistreatment, and expressed hope that Jews would convert to the Christian faith. The tract bespeaks the atmosphere of the early years of the Reformation, when there was boundless exuberance about the victory of the gospel. Some twenty years later, no such conversions had taken place, and when Luther received word of Christian conversions to Judaism, he published a new book, *Concerning the Jews and Their Lies*. Here the full force of traditional Christian theological anti-Judaic sentiment again came to the fore, as did the traditional cultural argument. It is, perhaps, for this reason that the treatise is most noteworthy: Luther appropriated the traditional popular anti-Judaic polemic that had little to do with theology but a great deal with fear of "the other." A portion of the middle section of the lengthy tract is printed below.[13]

---

13. *Martin Luther. American Edition.* Vol. 47. Philadelphia, 1971, pp. 290–301.

LITERATURE

Hans J. Hillerbrand, "Martin Luther and the Jews," in James H. Charlesworth, ed., *Jews and Christians: Exploring the Past, Present, and Future*. New York, 1990.

Neither Jew nor devil will in any way be able to prove that our belief that the one eternal godhead is composed of three persons implies that we believe in more than one God. If the Jews maintain that they cannot understand how three persons can be one God, why then must their blasphemous, accursed, lying mouth deny, condemn, and curse what it does not understand? Such a mouth should be punished for two reasons. In the first place, because it acknowledges that it does not understand this; in the second place, because it nevertheless blasphemes something which it does not understand. Why do they not ask first? Indeed, why have they heard it for fifteen hundred years and yet have refused to learn or understand it? Therefore such lack of understanding cannot help excuse them, nor us Christians if we tolerate this any longer from them. As already said, we must force them to prove their lies about us or to suffer the consequences. For those who slander and malign us as being idolatrous in this respect, slander and malign Christ, that is, God Himself, as an idol. For it was from Him that we learned and received this as His eternal word and truth, confirmed mightily by signs and confessed and taught now for nearly fifteen hundred years.

No person has yet been born, or will ever be born, who can grasp or comprehend how foliage can sprout from wood or a tree or how grass can grow forth from stone or earth, or how any creature can be begotten. Yet these filthy, blind, hardened liars presume to understand and to know what is happening outside and beyond the creature in God's hidden, incomprehensible, inscrutable, and eternal essence. Though we ourselves can grasp only with difficulty and with weak faith what has been revealed to us about this in veiled words, they give vent to such terrible blasphemy over it as to call our faith idolatrous, which is to reproach and defame God Himself as an idol. We are convinced of our faith and doctrine; and they, too, ought to understand it, having heard for fifteen hundred years that it is by God and from God through Jesus Christ.

If these vulgar people had expressed themselves more mildly and said, "The Christians worship one God and not many gods, and we are lying and doing the Christians an injustice when we claim that they are worshipping more than one God, though they do believe that there are three persons in the godhead; we cannot understand this but are willing to let the Christians follow their convictions," etc., that would have been sensible. But they proceed, driven by the devil, to fall into this like filthy sows fall into the trough, defaming and reviling what they refuse to acknowledge and to understand. Without further ado they declare: "We Jews do not understand this and do not want to understand it; therefore it follows that it is wrong and idolatrous."

These are the people to whom God has never been God but a liar in the person of all the prophets and apostles, no matter how much God had these preach to them. The result is that they cannot be God's people, no matter how much they teach, clamor, and pray. They do not hear God; so He, in turn, does not hear them, as Psalm 18 [: 26] says: "With the crooked thou dost show thyself perverse." The wrath of God has overtaken them. I am loath to think of this, and it has not been a pleasant task for me to write this book, being obliged to resort now to anger, now to satire, in order to avert my eyes from the terrible picture which they present. It has pained me to mention their horrible blasphemy concerning our Lord and his dear mother, which we Christians are grieved to hear. I can well understand what Paul means in Rom. 10 [9: 2] when he says that he is saddened as he considers them. I think that all Christians experience this when they reflect seriously, not on the temporal misfortunes and exile which the Jews bemoan, but on the fact that they are condemned to blaspheme, curse, and vilify God Himself and all that is God's, to their eternal damnation, and that they refuse to hear and acknowledge this but regard all of their doings as zeal for God. O God, heavenly Father, relent and let your wrath over them be sufficient and come to an end, for the sake of your dear Son! Amen.

I wish and I ask that our rulers who have Jewish subjects exercise sharp mercy toward these wretched people, as suggested above, to see whether this might not help (though it is doubtful). They must act like a good physician who, when gangrene has set in, proceeds without mercy to cut, saw, and burn flesh, veins, bone, and marrow. Such a procedure must also be followed in this instance. Burn down their synagogues, forbid all that I enumerated earlier, force them to work, and deal harshly with them, as Moses did in the wilderness, slaying three thousand lest the whole people perish. They surely do not know what they are doing; moreover, as people possessed, they do not wish to know it, hear it, or learn it. Therefore it would be wrong to be merciful and confirm them in their conduct. If this does not help, we must drive them out like mad dogs so that we do not become partakers of their abominable blasphemy and all their other vices and thus merit God's wrath and be damned with them. I have done my duty. Now let everyone see to his. I am exonerated.

Finally, I wish to say this for myself: If God were to give me no other Messiah than such as the Jews wish and hope for, I would much rather be a sow than a human being. I will give you a good reason for this. The Jews ask no more of their Messiah than that he be a worldly king who will slay us Christians and divide the world among the Jews and make them lords, and who finally will die like other kings, and his children after him. For thus declares a rabbi: You must not suppose that it will be different at the time of the Messiah than it has been since the creation of the world, etc.; that is, there will be days and nights, years and months, summer and winter, seedtime and harvest, begetting and dying, eating and drinking, sleeping, growing, digesting, eliminating—all will take its course as it does now; only the Jews will be the masters and will possess all the world's gold, goods, joys, and delights, while we Christians will be their servants. This agrees with Muhammad's thoughts and teachings. He kills us Christians as the Jews would like to do, occupies our land, and usurps our property, our joys and pleasures. If he were a Jew and not an Ishmaelite, the Jews would have accepted him as the Messiah long ago.

Even if I had all of that, or if I could become the ruler of Turkey or the Messiah whom the Jews await, I would still prefer being a sow. For what would all of this benefit me if I could not be secure in its possession for a single hour? Death, that horrible burden and plague of all mankind, would still threaten me. I would not be safe from him; I would have to fear him every moment. I would still have to quake and tremble before hell and the wrath of God. And I would know no end of all this but would have to expect it forever. The tyrant Dionysius illustrated this well when he placed a person who praised his good fortune at the head of a richly laden table. Over his head he suspended an unsheathed sword attached to a silk thread, and below him he put a red-hot fire, saying: Eat and be merry, etc. That is joy such a Messiah would dispense. I know that anyone who has ever tasted of death's terror or burden would rather be a sow than bear this forever and ever.

For a sow lies down on her featherbed, on the street, or on a dung-heap; she rests securely, snores gently, sleeps sweetly, fears neither king nor Lord, neither death nor hell, neither the devil nor God's wrath, and lives entirely without care so long as she has her bran. And if the emperor of Turkey were to draw near with all his might and wrath, she in her pride would not move a bristle for his sake. If someone were to rouse her, she would grunt and say, if she could talk, You fool, why are you raving? You are not one-tenth as well off as I am. Not for an hour do you live as securely, as peacefully and tranquilly as I do constantly, nor would you even if you were ten times as great or rich. In short, no thought of death occurs to her, for her life is secure and serene.

And if the butcher performs his job with her, she probably imagines that a stone or piece of wood is pinching her. She never thinks of death, and in a moment she is dead. Neither before, during, or in death did she feel death. She feels nothing but life, nothing but everlasting life! No king, not even the Jews' Messiah, will be able to emulate her, nor will any person, however great, rich, holy, or mighty he might be. She never ate of the apple which taught us wretched men in Paradise the difference between good and evil.

What good would the Jews' Messiah do me if he were unable to help a poor man like me in face of this great and horrible grief and make my life one-tenth as pleasant as that of a sow? I would say: Dear God, keep your Messiah, or give him to whoever will have him. Instead, make me a sow. For it is better to be a live sow than a man who is eternally dying. Yea, as Christ says: "It would have been better for that man if he had not been born" [Matt. 26: 24]. However, if I had a Messiah who could remedy this grief, so that I would no longer have to fear death but would be always and eternally sure of life, and able to play a trick on the devil and death and no longer have to tremble before the wrath of

God, then my heart would leap for joy and be intoxicated with sheer delight; then would a fire of love for God be enkindled, and my praise and thanks would never cease. Even if He would not in addition give me gold, silver, and other riches, all the world would nonetheless be a genuine paradise for me, though I lived in a dungeon.

That is the kind of Messiah we Christians have, and we thank God, the Father of all mercy, with the full, overflowing joy of our hearts, gladly and readily forgetting all the sorrow and harm which the devil wrought for us in Paradise. For our loss has been richly compensated for, and all has been restored to us through this Messiah. Filled with such joy, the apostles sang and rejoiced in dungeons and amid all misfortunes, as did even young girls, such as Agatha, Lucia, etc. The wretched Jews, on the other hand, who rejected this Messiah, have languished and perished since that time in anguish of heart, in trouble, trembling, wrath, impatience, malice, blasphemy, and cursing, as we read in Isa. 65 [: 14 f.]: "Behold, my servants shall sing for gladness of heart, but you shall cry out for pain of heart, and shall wail for anguish of spirit. You shall leave your name to my chosen for a curse, and the Lord God will slay you; but his servants he will call by a different name." And in the same chapter we read [: 1 f.], "I was ready to be sought by those who did not ask for me; I was ready to be found by those who did not seek me. I said, 'Here am I, here am I,' to a nation that did not call on my name (that is, who were not my people). I spread out my hands all the day to a rebellious people."

We, indeed, have such a Messiah, who says to us, "I am the resurrection and the life; he who believes in me, though he die, yet shall he live, and whoever lives and believes in me shall never die." And John 8 [: 51]: "Truly, truly, I say to you, if any one keeps my word, he will never see death." The Jews and the Turks care nothing for such a Messiah. And why should they? They must have a Messiah from the fool's paradise, who will satisfy their stinking belly, and who will die together with them like a cow or dog.

Nor do they need him in the face of death, for they themselves are holy enough with their penitence and piety to step before God and attain this and everything. Only the Christians are such fools and timid cowards who stand in such awe of God, who regard their sin and His wrath so highly that they do not venture to appear before the eyes of His divine majesty without a mediator or Messiah to represent them and to sacrifice Himself for them. The Jews, however, are holy and valiant heroes and knights who dare to approach God themselves without mediator or Messiah, and ask for and receive all they desire...

Furthermore, not only do we foolish, craven Christians and accursed Goyim regard our Messiah as indispensable for delivering us from death without our holiness, but we wretched people are also afflicted with such great and terrible blindness as to believe that He needs no sword or worldly power to accomplish this. For we cannot comprehend how God's wrath, sin, death, and hell can be banished with the sword, since we observe that from the beginning of the world to the present day death has not cared a fig for the sword; it has overcome all emperors, kings, and whoever wields a sword as easily as it overcomes the weakest infant in the cradle.

In this respect, the great seducers Isaiah, Jeremiah, and all the other prophets do us great harm. They beguile us mad Goyim with their false doctrine, saying that the kingdom of the Messiah will not bear the sword. Oh, that the holy rabbis and the chivalrous, bold heroes of the Jews would come to our rescue here and extricate us from these abominable errors! For when Isa. 2 [: 2 f.] prophesies concerning the Messiah that the Gentiles shall come to the house and mountain of the Lord and let themselves be taught (for undoubtedly they do not expect to be murdered with the sword; in this case they would surely not approach but would stay away), he says [: 4]: "He (the Messiah) shall judge between the nations, and shall decide for many peoples; and they shall beat their swords into plowshares, and their spears into pruning hooks; nation shall not lift up sword against nation, neither shall they learn war anymore."

Similar sorcery is also practiced upon us poor Goyim in Isa. 11 [: 9]: "They shall not hurt or destroy in my entire holy mountain; for the earth shall be full of the knowledge of the Lord." We poor blind Goyim cannot conceive of this "knowledge of the Lord" as a sword but as the instruction by which one learns to know God; our understanding agrees with Isaiah 2, cited above, which also speaks of the knowledge which the Gentiles shall pursue. For knowledge does not come by the sword but by teaching and hearing, as we stupid Goyim assume. Likewise Isa. 53 [: 11]: "By his knowledge shall the righteous one, my servant, make many to be accounted righteous"; that is, by teaching them and by their hearing Him and believing in Him.

The proof of this is before your eyes, namely, that the apostles used neither spear nor sword but solely their speech. Their example has been followed in the entire world for fifteen hundred years by all the bishops, pastors, and preachers, and is still being followed. Just see whether a pastor wields sword or spear when he enters the church, preaches, baptizes, administers the sacrament, when he retains and remits sin, restrains evildoers, comforts the godly, and teaches, helps, and nurtures everyone's soul. Does he not do all of this exclusively with the tongue or with words? And the congregation, likewise, brings no sword or spear to such a ministry but only its ears...

To speak first of the saying of Jacob in Genesis 49, we heard before what idle and senseless foolishness the Jews have invented regarding it, yet without hitting upon any definite meaning. But if we confess our Lord Jesus and let him be the "Shiloh" or Messiah, all agrees, coincides, rhymes, and harmonizes beautifully and delightfully. For He appeared promptly on the scene at the time of Herod, after the scepter had departed from Judah. He initiated His rule of peace without a sword, as Isaiah and Zechariah had prophesied, and all the nations gathered about Him—both Jews and Gentiles—so that on one day in Jerusalem three thousand souls became believers, and many members of the priesthood and of the princes of the people also flocked to Him, as Luke records in Acts 3 and 4.

For more than one hundred years after Jesus' resurrection—that is, from the eighteenth year of the reign of Emperor Tiberius until the eighteenth year of the reign of Emperor Hadrian, who inflicted the second and last bloodbath of the Jews, who defeated Kokhba and drove the Jews utterly and completely from their country—there were always bishops in Jerusalem from the tribe of the children of Israel, all whom Eusebius mentions by name. He begins with St. James the Apostle and enumerates about fifteen of them, all of whom preached the gospel with great diligence, performed miracles, and lived a holy life, converting many thousands of Jews and children of Israel to their promised Messiah who had now appeared, Jesus of Nazareth; apart from these there were the Jews living in the Diaspora who were converted together with the Gentiles by St. Paul, other apostles, and their disciples. This was accomplished despite the fact that the other faction, the blind, impenitent Jews—the fathers of the present-day Jews—raved, raged, and ranted against it without letup and without ceasing, and shed much blood of members of their own race both within their own country and abroad among the Gentiles, as was related earlier also of Kochba....

The Gentiles all over the world now also gathered about these pious, converted children of Israel. This they did in great numbers and with such zeal that they gave up not only their idols and their own wisdom but also forsook wife and child, friends, goods and honor, life and limb for the sake of it. They suffered everything that the devil and all the other Gentiles, as well as the mad Jews, could contrive. For all of that, they did not seek a Kochba, or the Gentiles' gold, silver, possessions, dominion, land, or people: They sought eternal life, a life other than this temporal one. They were poor and wretched voluntarily and yet were happy and content. They were not embittered or vindictive but kind and merciful. They prayed for their enemies and, in addition, performed many and great miracles. That has lasted uninterruptedly from that time on down to the present day, and it will endure to the end of the world.

It is a great, extraordinary, and wonderful thing that the Gentiles in all the world accepted, without sword or coercion, with no temporal benefits accruing to them, gladly and freely, a poor man of the Jews as the true Messiah, one whom his own people had crucified, condemned, cursed, and persecuted without end....

Whoever is not moved by this miraculous spectacle quite deserves to remain blind or to become an accursed Jew. We Christians perceive that these events are in agreement with the statement of Jacob found in Gen. 49: "To the Messiah (after the scepter has dropped from the hands of Judah) shall be the obedience of the peoples." We have the fulfillment of this before our eyes: The peoples—that is, not only the Jews but also the Gentiles—are in perfect accord in their obedience to this Shiloh; they have become one people: that is, Christians. One cannot mention or think of anyone to whom this verse of Jacob applies and refers so fittingly as to our dear Lord Jesus. It would have had to be someone who appeared just after the loss of the scepter, or else the Holy Spirit lied through the mouth of the holy patriarch Jacob, and God forgot his promise. May the devil say that, or anyone who wishes to be an accursed Jew! ...

That they have now died and lie buried does not matter; they are nonetheless His kingdom and His people before Him. They are dead to us and to the world, but to Him they are alive and not dead. It is natural that the blind Jews are unaware of this; for he who is blind sees nothing at all. We Christians, however, know that He says in John 8 [: 56] and in Matt. 22 [: 32]: "Abraham lives." Also in John 11 [: 25]: "He who believes in me, though he die, yet shall he live." Thus David's house and throne are firmly established. There is a Son occupying it eternally, who never dies, nor does He ever let die those who are of His kingdom or who accept Him in true faith as King. That marks the true fulfillment of this verse which declares that David's throne shall be eternal. Now let all the devils and Jews, Turks, and whoever wants to concern himself with it also name one or more sons of David to whom this verse regarding the house of David applies so precisely and beautifully, since the time of Herod, and we shall be ready to praise them.

To such kingdom and throne of David we Gentiles belong, along with all who have accepted this Messiah and Son of David as King with the same faith, and who continue to accept Him to the end of the world and in eternity. Jacob's saying in Gen. 49 [: 10] states: "To him shall be the obedience of the peoples." This means not only one nation, such as the children of Israel but also whatever others are called nations. And later we read in Gen. 22 [: 18]: "In thy seed shall all the nations of the earth bless themselves." In this verse we find the term "Goyim," which in the Bible commonly means the Gentiles, except where the prophets also call the Jews this in a strong tone of contempt. To summarize, the blessing of God through the seed of Abraham shall not be confined to his physical descendants but shall be disseminated among all the Gentiles. That is why God Himself calls Abraham "father of a multitude of nations" [Gen. 17: 5].

15

Argula von Grumbach:
Account of a Christian Woman. [1523]

In the early years of the reform movement in Germany, which subsequently coalesced into the Reformation, a large number of laypersons took to the pen and published pamphlets on a variety of religious, theological, and social topics. Among these writers were several women. Argula von Grumbach, one of these female authors, is noteworthy because her writings reveal a stunning conversancy with the Bible and a keen theological mind. The following is an excerpt from her *Account of a Christian Woman*, which was addressed to the University of Ingolstadt for declaring a reformer by the name of Seehofer to be a heretic.[14]

LITERATURE

Peter Matheson, ed., *Argula von Grumbach: A Woman's Voice in the Reformation.* Edinburgh, 1995.

---

14. The German text is found at http://sophie.byu.edu/literature/index. An English translation is Peter Matheson, ed., *Argula von Grumbach: A Woman's Voice in the Reformation*. Edinburgh, 1995, pp. 75–90. The original title is *Account of a Christian Woman of the Bavarian Nobility whose open letter, with arguments based on divine Scripture, criticizes the University of Ingolstadt for compelling a young follower of the gospels to contradict the word of God.* Ingolstadt, Germany, 1523.

There is a passage in Matthew 10: "Whoever confesses me before another I will confess before my heavenly Father." And Luke 9: "Whoever is ashamed of me and of my words, I will be ashamed of when I come into my majesty," etc. Words like these, coming from the very mouth of God, are always before my eyes. For they apply to women and men.

This is why as a Christian I am compelled to write to you. For Ezekiel 33 says: "If you see your brother sin, reprove him, or I will require his blood at your hands." In Matthew 12, the Lord says: "All sins will be forgiven; but the sin against the Holy Spirit will never be forgiven, neither here nor in eternity." And in John 6 the Lord says: "My words are spirit and life."

How in God's name can you and your university expect to prevail, when you use foolish violence against the Word of God? When you force someone to hold the holy gospel in his hands for the purpose of denying it, as you did in the case of Arsacius Seehofer? When you confront him and make use of imprisonment and even the threat of fire to force him to deny Christ and His word?

Indeed, when I reflect on this, my heart and my limbs tremble. What do Luther or Melanchthon teach other than the Word of God? You condemn them without having refuted them. Did Christ teach you to do so, did his apostles, prophets, or evangelists? Show me where it is written! You lofty experts, nowhere in the Bible do I find that Christ, or his apostles, or his prophets, put people in prison, burned or murdered them, or sent them into exile. Do you not know what the Lord says in Matthew 10? "Have no fear of him who can take your body but then his power is at an end. But fear him who has power to dispatch soul and body into the depths of hell."

1. To the University of Ingolstadt concerning Arsacius Seehofer.

How do you obey the imperial mandate which was just issued on March 6 and which states clearly that the gospel is to be preached, as God commanded, and this be done by teachers approved by the Christian churches. The mandate says nothing of the Roman church, however, concerning which I cannot find a single word in the Bible. I would be pleased to be shown by you what God has said about the Roman church. I have read in the history of saints that they were put to martyrdom mostly by that church. I find little good in it; may God improve matters. Are you not ashamed that Seehofer had to deny all of Martin Luther's writings? He simply translated the New Testament according to the sources. Therefore, the holy Gospels and the epistles and the history of the apostles are considered heresy by you. One cannot discuss matters with you. And the five books of Moses have also been printed—does that not mean anything? It is easier to have a discussion with a Jew. I have not heard that any article of his has been disproved in writing. I was pleased to hear that a learned lawyer approached him and asked why he was weeping and if he was still a heretic? But jurisprudence helps little here.

I had thought that in line with the imperial mandate you would desist from academic disputations and refer matters to a council of the church. This was read straight from the pulpit. I do not know the reason; Luther does not tempt many here. Our clergy raise few questions, finally some can read the Psalms, which is good indeed. . . . I plead with you for the sake of God and admonish you through God's judgment and righteousness that you point out to me in writing those articles written by Martin or Melanchthon which you consider to be heretical. I do not find any article written in German which to my mind is heretical. Much has been published in German and I have read it. Spalatin sent me a list of titles because I wanted to learn the truth. Even though I have not read anything for a long time, I read the Bible even as it has been Luther's foremost concern that it be read. My dear father of blessed memory earnestly asked me to read, giving me a copy when I was ten years old. Regrettably, I did not follow his advice because I was misled by the priests. But how splendidly does the Spirit of God provide understanding, leading from one point to the other. God may be praised that I have been enlightened by the right, true light. I do not want to bury my talent; the Lord give me grace. Christ says in Luke 9 that the gospel will be preached to the poor and blessed are those who are not annoyed with him. Paul says in I Corinthians 9: "I am not ashamed of the gospel and will not misuse my authority." I truly say to you that light that is shining is now in the world. Psalm 118: "The opening of your word provides illumination and understanding." Psalm 36: "You are the fountain of life and in your light will we see light." John 16: "The Spirit will lead you into all truth." John 14: "I am the Way, the truth, and the life. No one comes to the father then through me."

2. Argula's Letter to the Magistracy of the Town of Regensburg, June 1524.

To my good friends, the honorable, thoughtful, and wise mayor and council of the town of Regensburg.

May God's grace and peace increase among you, my dear lords and brothers in Christ.

I have learned that recently a mandate contrary to the word of God was issued, surely because of the doings of Satan, who is always busy and takes no rest, as we read in the first epistle of Peter in the fifth chapter: "Be alert! Your enemy the devil roams like a roaring lion looking for someone to devour. Be firm in your faith and resist him." May God grant that you take to heart what the Lord says in Matthew 24, that you will not have to flee in the winter or on a Sabbath, when it will be too late. He says we should look at the abomination which has placed itself onto the holy city. Open your eyes; truly the time has come and it has become evident that he surely can be recognized: the pope with all of his courtiers, under whose power you are. May the Lord come to help you and enlighten us all! For he says further in the same chapter that the coming of the Lord will be like a lightning flashing across the whole firmament from the east to the west. Note this chapter; it is awesome.

I also regret not a little that you have agreed to be the first of all imperial cities to oppose God. Truly, nothing will come of it. For He is a Lord above all Lords, as we read in Psalm 144: "The Lord is mighty and greatly to be praised, and to his power there is no end." Deuteronomy 10: "God is God of all gods, and Lord over all lords, a great God, mighty, and no respecter of persons."

Therefore, my dear brothers, I cannot keep from writing to you as a fellow member of the body of Christ, even though I am myself most unworthy. But I am not ashamed of the gospel, as my mind allows me to understand it, for it is the power of God for those who believe. Romans 1. I must confess God, like all the others who want to be Christians, as the Lord says in Matthew 10: "Whoever confesses me publicly, I will also confess before my father. But whoever does not confess me publicly, I will not confess before my heavenly father." And in Romans 10 we read that if one confesses with one's mouth one will be saved.

For the sake of God, do not be offended by me, a poor and weak woman. I know very well indeed that according to worldly custom I am not your equal, but God loves those who are despised. Whatever others are doing, I do not want to bury my talents; others can do what they want. Ezekiel 33: "If you do not punish him who sins, I will demand his soul from your hands." I see that you are in error; therefore I must admonish you. Even so it is clear that I will be ridiculed by those who are wise in the ways of the world. But God has made foolish the wisdom of the world. I Corinthians 1. If I were out to please people, says Paul in Galatians, I would not be a servant of the Lord. We must not seek for ourselves, but for God and his praise and glory. Therefore, Paul says in Ephesians 4 that we should cease being children, allowing ourselves to be tossed about by old and erroneous human teachings, blown about by every shifting wind and the teachings of deceitful men, who are leading others into error.

Oh, my dear brothers, watch out for the oppressive wolves! Acts 20. They are close at hand; may God keep you from those who serve only their bellies so that you will not fall into the pit with the blind and are eternally condemned with them. God says to you: "How often have I wanted to gather you as a hen gathers its chicks under its wings, but you did not want to be gathered." And he wept over you when he said in Luke 19, "If you recognized the day of your temptation you would weep with me."

Dear brothers, remember that God appointed you guardians and supervisors. Consider that the souls entrusted to you were not purchased with expensive gold or silver but with the crimson blood of the Lord Jesus. I Peter 1: "It is time to arise from sleep and to look to the Lord, for our salvation is closer at hand than when we first believed." Romans 13: "Be not misled by tradition and old customs." The Lord says, "I am the way, the truth, and the life." John 14 does not say "I am the customary." Jeremiah 17: "Lord, all those who have forsaken the fountain of living water, they will be put to shame." Listen, how kindly he summons us! Isaiah 55: "All who are thirsty, come to the water; you who have nothing and buy without silver and gold or anything else." Likewise in John 7 the Lord cries out his "If anyone thirsts, let him come to me." Never did he point to human decrees or to the pope. John 1. "As many as accepted him he gave power to become children of God." And when he came to his own, they did not recognize him. I pray to God that it will be otherwise. We must fight nobly against the enemies of God, and he will slay them with the breath of his mouth. The word of God will be our weapon; we will not be defeated with other weapons but will conquer with love of neighbor and peace, as the Lord says in John 13: "Thereby will they know that you are my disciples that you love one another." And in Isaiah 33 the Lord says that the word will not leave his mouth without bringing forth fruit.

That is the reason why I as emboldened to write to you and admonish you. Now is the time that the stones themselves cry out. Luke 19. Even though it will be reckoned as foolishness on my part, for Paul says in I Corinthians 4, "I know that the God has placed us lowest, deserving of death. We are a mirror to all people." May you remain eternally in the grace of God who rules according to his pleasure.

The Lord says in the Gospel of John, chapter 12, "I am the light that came into this world so that all who believe in me will not stay in darkness." I truly wish us all that this light may live among us and enlighten all hardened and blinded hearts. Amen.

I find a sentence in the Gospel of Matthew which reads as follows: "Whoever confesses me publicly, I will I also confess before my heavenly father." And Luke 9: "If anyone is ashamed of me and of my teaching, I will also be ashamed of them when I come to my glory, etc." These words, spoken by God himself, are always before me, for neither women nor men are here excluded.

For this reason I am compelled as a Christian to write to you, for Ezekiel 33 says, "If you see your brother in sin, reprove him or I will demand his blood from your hands." In Matthew 12 the Lord says that all sins will be forgiven but the sin against the Holy Spirit will not be forgiven, neither now nor then. And in John 6 the Lord says, "My words are spirit and life."

Oh, my God, how do you expect to prevail when you act so foolishly and vehemently against the Word of God and compel someone with force to keep the holy gospel in one's hands only to deny it as you did with Arsacius Seehofer. With the threat of fire and imprisonment you demanded that he deny Christ and his Word. Indeed, when I consider this my heart trembles as do all my limbs. After all, what do Luther and Melanchthon teach you other than the word of God? You condemn them without having refuted them—is that what Christ taught at you or his apostles, prophets or evangelists? Show me were this is written. You learned experts, I do not find any passage in the Bible where Christ or his apostles or prophets imprisoned, burned, murdered, or even exiled. Do you not know that the Lord says in Matthew 10: "Do not fear to not fear him who takes your body and cannot do more." But you should fear him who has power to send both soul and body to hell.

It is well known that we should be obedient to governmental authorities. But government has no power over the word of God, neither do pope, emperor, or rulers, as we find in Acts 4 and 5. I confess, however, in the name of God and the salvation of my soul that if I were to deny the writings of Luther and Melanchthon, I would deny God and his Word, for God is eternal. Amen.

Did you not read in Jeremiah, the first chapter, that the Lord says to him, "What do you see?" "I see a vigilant rod." Says the Lord: "You see well, I always guard my word with vigilance." He asks a second time: "What else do you see?" "I see a burning pot and the face of God comes from midnight." The Lord says to you, "You saw well, for at midnight all evil will be revealed to all inhabitants of the earth."

The pot is burning, and you will not extinguish it with your university and papal decretals nor with Aristotle, who never was a Christian. You are mistaken if you think that you can defy God, expel his prophets and apostles from heaven and remove them from the earth. This will not happen. I beg you, dear Lords, not to touch his body, for you must not doubt that God will keep his holy and blessed word as he has done to this day in the Old and New Testaments.

From now on God will come to you as the prophet Hosea says in the thirteenth chapter: "They lifted up their hearts and forgot me." . . .

Hosea 6: "I smote them with the words of my mouth. Woe unto you, for you made your counsel without listening to me." Isaiah 30 and Ezekiel 13: "Woe unto the foolish prophets who follow their own spirit as they see unprofitable things and teach." They say "the Lord says," when I have not spoken this way nor have sent them. For a piece of bread they kill the souls which will not die and claim that souls are living which do not live. . . .

What does God say further in Ezekiel 33? "The threat of the Lord was like cheerful music until punishment came, for they did not know that a prophet was among them." And Jeremiah 48: "God became to them an empty chatter, as if they had found him among thieves." Avarice has consumed you, for otherwise you would be ready to suffer God's word. What did you accomplish with the decretals? The gospel does not yield much money to its interpreters. I saw how my father had to give twenty guilders to receive four lines of counsel, and it was not worth one penny. But what does David say in Psalm 36? "I was young and have become old, and yet see the children of righteousness beg for bread." I beg you, trust in God; he will not desert us for he has numbered every hair on our heads, as Matthew 10 tells us. I have often listened to your decretal preachers in the Church of St. Mary's yell "Heretic, heretic" even though it was poor Latin as even I who never went to a university knew. But more is needed if they want to prove their case. I have always intended to write him to show me the heretical proposition which that faithful worker of the gospel, Martin Luther, has taught, but I suppressed my inclination and with a heavy heart I failed to do anything. The reason was what Paul says in I Timothy 2, that women should be silent in the churches. But in as much as I now see that in this matter no man who wishes (or is allowed) to speak is doing so, I am compelled by the insistence of the passage that says "whoever confesses me . . ." as I mentioned above. I claim for myself Isaiah 3: "I will send children and women to the rulers or they will rule in a womanly fashion." And Isaiah 29: "Those who are in error will have spiritual knowledge and those who murmur will teach the law." Ezekiel 20: "I lifted my hand against them to scatter. They never followed my judgments, rejected my commandments and their eyes were after the idols of their fathers. Therefore, I gave them commandments and judgments according to which they could not live." Psalm 8: "You have received praise out of the mouths of children and suckling infants, on account of your enemies. And Luke 10: Jesus rejoiced in the spirit and said: "Father, I thank you that you have hidden these things from the wise and have revealed them to the humble." Jeremiah 3. They will all acknowledge God from the lowest to the highest. John 6. And Isaiah 54: They will all learn from God. Paul says, I Corinthians 12, that no one can speak about Jesus without the Spirit of God, even as our Lord in Matthew 16 says about the confession of Peter: "Flesh and blood did not reveal this to you but my heavenly father." Listen, this is an understanding that only God can give us. As Paul says in I Corinthians 2: "Your faith shall not be in the wisdom of men, etc." You will not control us with people, laws, and statutes for we have sufficient testimony of Scripture that they did not have power and authority without God's command to make laws. Jeremiah 23. Whatever is found in the Bible, which is based in its content on God's law, we will happily accept. But whatever is not, we will not accept, though I must be concerned about being instructed. For God says that we shall not add to his word nor take from it. And Proverbs 30: "Do not add to the words of God that you will not punish and found to be a liar," even as immediately preceding we read that the word of God is a fiery shield for all to be comforted and to be found in him. This is the word that I challenge you to proclaim. How can those who make laws, and their representatives, maintain what they claim, when in fact they make law with their own hands and not with the counsel and word of God. I think that the Lord will label them as we read in Matthew 15: "You hypocrites, you have made the word and command of God to nothing."

PART II

THE DIVISION OF THE REFORMATION

16

Conrad Grebel and Others:
Letter to Thomas Müntzer. [1524]

mong the earliest evidence that the impulses for reform associated with the name of Martin Luther were variously interpreted is Thomas Müntzer. He had been one of the numerous followers of Luther and had settled for tumultuous stays in Zwickau and Prague in the Saxon town of Alstedt. Müntzer published several vehemently anti-Lutheran tracts in early 1524, in which he outlined, with a vitriolic and eloquent pen, a vision of reform quite different from that of Luther. At the same time, a group of followers of Huldrych Zwingli in Zurich had become dissatisfied with the slow and seemingly compromising progress of ecclesiastical reform in Zurich. They set out to delineate the proper faith, as they understood it. Among their tenets was the notion of a church composed only of true believers and baptism as a public testimony of one's faith. Their stress on baptism soon gave them the label "Anabaptists."

The relationship between Luther, Müntzer, and Zwingli and the emerging Anabaptist movement has been variously interpreted in scholarship. Lutheran scholars have tended to argue that the Zurich Anabaptists owe their origin to Thomas Müntzer, while other scholars have argued the essential independence of the Zurich group from Müntzer. More recently, scholars have pointed to a matrix of social and political concerns as instrumental in the rise of Anabaptism in Zurich. The following letter, written in September 1524 by the Zurich dissidents to Müntzer, shows the areas of both agreement and disagreement. It is thus an important document for understanding the self-consciousness of the emerging Anabaptist movement and the temper of dissent at that particular time. The main body of the letter is reprinted here, without the lengthy postscript.[15]

LITERATURE

Leland Harder, ed., *The Sources of Swiss Anabaptism: The Grebel Letters and Related Documents*. Scottdale, PA, 1985.

Hans J. Goertz, *The Anabaptists*. London, 1996.

Dear Brother Thomas: For God's sake do not marvel that we address you without title, and request you like a brother to communicate with us by writing, and that we have ventured, unasked and unknown to you, to open communications between us. God's Son, Jesus Christ, who offers Himself as the one master and head of all who would be saved, and bids us be brethren by the one common word given to all brethren and believers, has moved us and compelled us to make friendship and brotherhood and to bring the following points to thy attention. Thy writing of two tracts on fictitious faith has further prompted us. Therefore, we ask that you will take it blindly for the sake of Christ our Savior. If God wins, it shall serve and work to our good. Amen.

Just as our forebears fell away from the true God and from the one true, common, divine word, from the divine institutions, from

---

15. J. C. Wenger, ed., *Conrad Grebel's Programmatic Letters of 1524*. Scottdale, PA, 1970.

Christian love and life, and lived without God's law and gospel in human, useless, un-Christian customs and ceremonies, and expected to attain salvation therein, yet fell far short of it, as the evangelical preachers have declared, and to some extent are still declaring, so today too every man wants to be saved by superficial faith, without fruits of faith, without baptism of trial and probation, without love and hope, without right Christian practices, and wants to persist in all the old manner of personal vices, and in the common ritualistic and anti-Christian customs of baptism and of the Lord's Supper, in disrespect for the divine word and in respect for the word of the pope and of the anti-papal preachers, which yet is not equal to the divine word nor in harmony with it. In respecting persons and in manifold seduction there exists grosser and more pernicious error now than ever has been since the beginning of the world. In the same error, we too lingered as long as we heard and read only the evangelical preachers who are to blame for all this, in punishment for our sins. But after we took Scripture in hand, and consulted it on many points, we were instructed somewhat and discovered the great and harmful error of the shepherds, of ours too, namely, that we do not daily beseech God earnestly with constant groaning to be brought out of this destruction of all godly life and out of human abominations, to attain to the true faith and divine practice. The cause of all this is false forbearance, the hiding of the divine word, and the mixing of it with the human. Yes, we say it harms all and frustrates all things divine. There is no need of specifying and reciting.

While we were marking and deploring these facts, your book against false faith and baptism was brought to us, and we were more fully informed and confirmed, and we rejoiced that we found someone who was of the same Christian mind with us and dared to show the evangelical preachers their shortcomings, how in all the chief points they falsely forbear and act and set their own opinions, and even those of Antichrist, above God and against God, as befits not the ambassadors of God to act and preach. Therefore, we beg and admonish you as a brother by the name, power, word, spirit, and salvation that has come to all Christians through Jesus Christ our Master and Savior that you will earnestly heed to preach only the divine word without fear, set up and defend only divine institutions, esteem as good and right only what may be found in pure and clear Scripture, reject, hate, and curse all human designs, words, customs, and opinions, including your own.

(1) We understand and have seen that you have translated the mass into German and have introduced new German hymns. That cannot be for the good, since we find nothing taught in the New Testament about singing, no example of it. Paul scolds the learned among the Corinthians more than he praises them, because they mumbled in meeting as if they sang, just as the Jews and the Italians chant their words. (2) Since singing in Latin developed without divine instruction and apostolic example and custom, without producing good or edification, it will still less edify in German and will create a faith of outward appearance only. (3) Paul clearly forbids singing in Eph. 5: 19 and Col. 3: 16 since he says and teaches that they are to speak to one another and teach one another with Psalms and spiritual songs, and if anyone would sing, he should sing and give thanks in his heart. (4) Whatever we are not taught by clear passages or examples must be regarded as forbidden, just as if it were written: "This do not; sing not." (5) Christ bids his messengers in the Old and especially in the New Testament simply proclaim the word. Paul too says that the word of Christ profits us, not the song. Whoever sings poorly gets vexation by it; whoever sings well gets conceit. (6) We must not follow our notions; we must add nothing to the word and take nothing from it. (7) If you will abolish the mass, it cannot be accomplished with German chants, which is thy suggestion perhaps, or comes from

Luther. (8) It must be rooted up by the word and command of Christ. (9) For it is not planted by God. (10) The Supper of fellowship Christ did institute and plant. (11) The words found in Matt. 26, Mark 14, Luke 22, and 1 Cor. 1, alone are to be used, no more, no less. (12) The server, a member of the congregation, should pronounce them from one of the evangelists or from Paul. (13) They are the words of the instituted meal of fellowship, not words of consecration. (14) Ordinary bread ought to be used, without idols and additions. (15) For [the latter] creates an external reverence and veneration of the bread, and a turning away from the inward. An ordinary drinking vessel too ought to be used. (16) This would do away with the adoration and bring true understanding and appreciation of the Supper, since the bread is nothing but bread. In faith, it is the body of Christ and the incorporation with Christ and the brethren. But one must eat and drink in the Spirit and love, as John shows in chapter 6 and the other passages, Paul in 1 Cor. 10 and 11, and as is clearly learned in Acts 2. (17) Although it is simply bread, yet if faith and brotherly love precede it, it is to be received with joy, since, when it is used in the church, it is to show us that we are truly one bread and one body, and that we are and wish to be true brethren with one another, etc. (18) But if one is found who will not live the brotherly life, he eats unto condemnation, since he eats it without discerning, like any other meal, and dishonors love, which is the inner bond, and the bread, which is the outer bond. (19) For also it does not call to his mind Christ's body and blood, the covenant of the cross, or that he should be willing to live and suffer for the sake of Christ and the brethren, of the head and the members. (20) Also it ought not to be administered by you. That was the beginning of the mass that only a few would partake, for the Supper is an expression of fellowship, not a mass and sacrament. Therefore, none is to receive it alone, neither on his deathbed or otherwise. Nor is the bread to be locked away, etc., for the use of a single person, since no one should take for himself alone the bread of those in unity, unless he is not one with himself—which no one is, etc. (21) Neither is it to be used in "temples" according to all Scripture and example, since that creates a false reverence. (22) It should be used much and often. (23) It should not be used without the rule of Christ in Matt. 18: 15–18, otherwise it is not the Lord's Supper, for without that rule every man will run after the externals. The inner matter, love, is passed by, if brethren and false brethren approach or eat it together. (24) If ever you desire to serve it, we should wish that it would be done without priestly garment and vestment of the mass, without singing, without addition. (25) As for the time, we know that Christ gave it to the apostles at supper and that the Corinthians had the same usage. We fix no definite time, etc.

Let this suffice, since you are much better instructed about the Lord's Supper, and we only state things as we understand them. If we are not in the right, teach us better. And do you drop singing and the mass, and act in all things only according to the word, and bring forth and establish by the word the usages of the apostles. If that cannot be done, it would be better to leave all things in Latin and unaltered and mediated [by a priest]. If the right cannot be established, do not then administer according to thy own or the priestly usage of Antichrist. And at least teach how it ought to be, as Christ does in John 6, and teaches how we must eat and drink His flesh and blood, and takes no heed of backsliding and anti-Christian caution, of which the most learned and foremost evangelical preachers have made a veritable idol and propagated it in the entire world. It is much better that a few be rightly taught through the word of God, believing and walking aright in virtues and practices, than that many believe falsely and deceitfully through adulterated doctrine. Though we admonish and beseech you, we hope that you will do it of thy own accord; and we admonish the more willingly, because you have so kindly listened to our brother and confessed that you too have yielded too much, and because you and Carlstadt are esteemed by us the purest proclaimers and preachers of the purest word of God. And if ye two rebuke, and justly, those who mingle the words and customs of men with those of God, ye must by rights cut yourselves loose and be completely purged of popery, benefices, and all new and ancient customs, and of your own and ancient notions. If your benefices, as with us, are supported by interest and tithes, which are both true usury and it is not the whole congregation which supports you, we beg that ye free yourselves of your benefices. You know well how a shepherd should be sustained...

Go forward with the word and establish a Christian church with the help of Christ and His rule, as we find it instituted in Matt. 18: 15–18 and elaborated in the Epistles. Use determination and common prayer and decision according to faith and love, without command or compulsion. Then God will help you and your little sheep to all sincerity, and the singing and the tablets will cease. There are more than enough of wisdom and counsel in Scripture, how all classes and all people may be taught, governed, instructed, and turned to piety. Whoever will not mend and believe, but resists the word and action of God and thus persists, such a person, after Christ and His word and rule have been declared to him and he has been admonished in the presence of the three witnesses and the church, such a man, we say, taught by God's word, shall not be killed, but regarded as a heathen and publican and let alone.

Moreover, the gospel and its adherents are not to be protected by the sword, nor are they thus to protect themselves, which, as we learn from our brother, is thy opinion and practice. True Christian believers are sheep among wolves, sheep for the slaughter; they must be baptized in anguish and affliction, tribulation, persecution, suffering, and death; they must be tried with fire, and must reach the fatherland of eternal rest, not by killing their bodily, but by mortifying their spiritual, enemies. Neither do they use worldly sword nor war, since all killing has ceased with them—unless, indeed, we would still be of the old law. And even there [in the Old Testament], as far as we recall, war was a misfortune after they had once conquered the Promised Land. No more of this.

On the matter of baptism, your book pleases us well, and we desire to be further instructed by you. We understand that even an adult is not to be baptized without Christ's rule of binding and loosing. The Scripture describes baptism for us thus, that it signifies that, by faith and the blood of Christ, sins have been washed away for him who is baptized, changes his mind, and believes before and after; that it signifies that a man is dead and ought to be dead to sin and walks in newness of life and spirit, and that he shall certainly be saved if, according to this meaning, by inner baptism he lives his faith; so that the water does not confirm or increase faith, as the scholars at Wittenberg say, and [does not] give very great comfort [nor] is it the final refuge on the deathbed. Also baptism does not save, as Augustine, Tertullian, Theophylact, and Cyprian have taught, dishonoring faith and the suffering of Christ in the case of the old and adult, and dishonoring the suffering of Christ in the case of the unbaptized infants. We hold (according to the following passages: Gen. 8: 21; Deut. 1: 39; 30: 6; 31: 13; and 1 Cor. 14: 20; Wisdom of Solomon 12: 19; 1 Peter 2: 2; Rom. 1; 2: 7; 10; Matt. 18: 1–6; 19: 13–15; Mark 9: 33–47; 10: 13–16; Luke 18: 15–17, etc.) that all children who have not yet come to the discernment of the knowledge of good and evil, and have not yet eaten of the tree of knowledge, that they are surely saved by the suffering of Christ, the new Adam, who has restored their vitiated life, because they would have been subject to death and condemnation only if Christ had not suffered; but they're not yet grown up to the infirmity of our broken nature—unless, indeed, it can be proved that Christ did not suffer for children. But as to the objection that faith is demanded of all who are to be saved, we exclude children from this and hold that they are saved without faith, and we do not believe from the above passages [that children must be baptized], and we conclude from the description of baptism and from the accounts of it (according to which no child was baptized), also from the above passages (which alone apply to the question of children, and all other Scriptures do not refer to children), that infant baptism is a senseless, blasphemous abomination, contrary to all Scripture, contrary even to the papacy; since we find, from Cyprian and Augustine, that for many years after apostolic times believers and unbelievers were baptized together for six hundred years, etc. Since you know this ten times better and have published thy protests against infant baptism, we hope that you are not acting against the eternal word, wisdom, and commandment of God, according to which only believers are to be baptized, and are not baptizing children.

The Schleitheim Confession of Faith. [1527]

The Schleitheim Confession, named after a small town on the Swiss-German border, was drafted in conjunction with a meeting of South German and Swiss Anabaptists in 1527. Its purpose was to clarify the theological heterogeneity of the Anabaptist movement, which had expanded rapidly and become a catchall for all sorts of radical dissent. While the emphasis upon believer's baptism was shared by Anabaptists everywhere, other tenets were by no means universally accepted. The Schleitheim Confession, acknowledging that not all Anabaptists concurred with its affirmations, expressed a consensus in several other areas and showed that the ramifications of Anabaptist thought went beyond the issue of baptism.

Though Anabaptism was never a heterogeneous movement and soon split into three major groupings—the Swiss and South German Anabaptists, the Mennonites in North Germany and Holland, and the Hutterites in Moravia—the Schleitheim Confession can be taken as a generally normative statement of Anabaptist belief in the sixteenth century. Reprinted here is a condensed version of the entire Confession.[16]

---

16. John C. Wenger, "The Schleitheim Confession of Faith," *Mennonite Quarterly Review* 19 (1945), 243 ff.

LITERATURE

G. H. Williams, *The Radical Reformation.* Kirksville, MO, 1992.

John Howard Yoder, ed., *The Legacy of Michael Sattler.* Scottdale, PA, 1973.

Beloved brethren and sisters in the Lord: First and foremostly we are always concerned about your consolation and the assurance of your conscience (which had been previously misled) so that you may not always remain strangers to us and by right almost completely excluded, but that you may turn again to the true implanted members of Christ, who have been armed with patience and self-knowledge, and accordingly have been reunited with us in the strength of a godly Christian spirit and zeal for God.

It is also apparent with what cunning the devil has turned us aside, so that he might destroy and bring to an end the work of God, which in mercy and grace has been partly begun in us. But Christ, the true Shepherd of our souls, who has begun this in us, will certainly direct the same and teach us to His honor and our salvation, Amen.

Dear brethren and sisters, we who have been assembled at Schleitheim on the border, make known in points and articles to all who love God that as concerns us we are of one mind to abide in the Lord as God's obedient children, His sons and daughters, we who have been and shall be separated from the world in everything, and completely at peace. To God alone be praise and glory without the contradiction of any brethren. In this, we have perceived the oneness of the Spirit, of our Father, and of our common Christ with us. For the Lord is the Lord of peace and not of quarreling, as Paul points out. That you may understand in what articles this has been formulated you should observe and note the following.

A very great offense has been introduced by certain false brethren among us, so that some have turned aside from the faith, in the way they intend to practice and observe the freedom of the Spirit and of Christ. But such have missed the truth and to their condemnation are given over to the lasciviousness and self-indulgence of the flesh. They think faith and love may do and permit everything, and nothing will harm them nor condemn them, since they are believers...

But you are not that way. For they that are Christ's have crucified the flesh with its passions and lusts. You understand me well and know the brethren whom we mean. Separate yourselves from them for they are perverted. Petition the Lord that they may have the knowledge which leads to repentance, and pray for us that we may have constancy to persevere in the way which we have espoused, for the honor of God and of Christ, His Son. Amen.

The articles which we discussed and on which we were of one mind are these (1) Baptism; (2) The Ban [Excommunication]; (3) Breaking of Bread; (4) Separation from the Abomination; (5) Pastors in the Church; (6) The Sword; and (7) The Oath.

First. We observe concerning baptism: Baptism shall be administered to those who have learned repentance and amendment of life, and who believe truly that their sins are taken away by Christ, and to all those who walk in the resurrection of Jesus Christ, and wish to be buried with Him in death, so that they may be resurrected with Him, and to all those who with this significance request baptism of us and demand it for themselves. This excludes all infant baptism, the highest and chief abomination of the pope. In this, you have the foundation and testimony of the apostles. Matt. 28, Mark 16, Acts 2, 8, 16, 19. This we wish to hold simply, yet firmly and with assurance.

Second. We are agreed as follows on the ban: The ban shall be employed with all those who have given themselves to the Lord, to walk in His commandments, and with all those who are baptized into the one body of Christ and who are called brethren or sisters, and yet who slip sometimes and fall into error and sin, being inadvertently overtaken. The same shall be admonished twice in secret and the third time openly disciplined or banned according to the command of Christ. Matt. 18. But this shall be done according to the regulation of the Spirit (Matt. 5) before the breaking of bread, so that we may break and eat one bread, with one mind and in one love, and may drink of one cup.

Third. In the breaking of bread we are of one mind and are agreed as follows: All those who wish to break one bread in remembrance of the broken body of Christ, and all who wish to drink of one drink as a remembrance of the shed blood of Christ, shall be united beforehand by baptism in one body of Christ which is the church of God and whose head is Christ. For as Paul points out we cannot at the same time be partakers of the Lord's Table and the table of devils; we cannot at the same time drink the cup of the Lord and the cup of the devil. That is, all those who have fellowship with the dead works of darkness have no part in the light. Therefore, all who follow the devil and the world have no part with those who are called unto God out of the world. All who live in evil have no part in the good.

Therefore it is and must be thus: Whoever has not been called by one God to one faith, to one baptism, to one Spirit, to one body, with all the children of God's church, cannot be made [into] one bread with them, as indeed must be done if one is truly to break bread according to the command of Christ.

Fourth. We are agreed as follows on separation: A separation shall be made from the evil and from the wickedness which the devil planted in the world; in this manner, simply that we shall not have fellowship with them, the wicked, and not run with them in the multitude of their abominations. This is the way it is: Since all who do not walk in the obedience of faith, and have not united themselves with God so that they wish to do His will, are a great abomination before God, it is not possible for anything to grow or issue from them except abominable things. For truly all creatures are in but two classes, good and bad, believing and unbelieving, darkness and light, the world and those who have come out of the world, God's temple and idols, Christ and Belial; and none can have part with the other.

To us then the command of the Lord is clear when He calls upon us to be separate from the evil and thus He will be our God and we shall be His sons and daughters.

He further admonishes us to withdraw from Babylon and the earthly Egypt that we may not be partakers of the pain and suffering which the Lord will bring upon them.

From all this we should learn that everything which is not united with our God and Christ cannot be other than an abomination which we should shun and flee from. By this is meant all popish and anti-popish works and church services, meetings and church attendance, drinking houses, civic affairs, the commitments made in unbelief and other things of that kind, which are highly regarded by the world and yet are carried on in flat contradiction to the command of God, in accordance with all the unrighteousness which is in the world. From all these things we shall be separated and have no part with them for they are nothing but an abomination, and they are the cause of our being hated before our Christ Jesus, who has set us free from the slavery of the flesh and fitted us for the service of God through the Spirit whom He has given us.

Therefore, there will also unquestionably fall from us the un-Christian, devilish weapons of force—such as sword, armor, and the like, and all their use either for friends or against one's ene-mies—by virtue of the word of Christ, Resist not him that is evil.

Fifth. We are agreed as follows on pastors in the church of God: The pastor in the church of God shall, as Paul has prescribed, be one who altogether has a good report of those who are outside the faith. This office shall be to read, to admonish and teach, to warn, to disciple, to ban in the church, to lead out in prayer for the advancement of all the brethren and sisters, to lift up the bread when it is to be broken, and in all things to see to the care of the body of Christ, in order that it may be built up and developed, and the mouth of the slanderer be stopped.

This one moreover shall be supported of the church which has chosen him, wherein he may be in need, so that he who serves the gospel may live of the gospel as the Lord has ordained. But if a pastor should do something requiring discipline, he shall not be dealt with except on the testimony of two or three witnesses. And when they sin, they shall be disciplined before all in order that the others may fear.

But should it happen that through the cross this pastor should be banished or led to the Lord through martyrdom, another shall be ordained in his place in the same hour so that God's little flock and people may not be destroyed.

Sixth. We are agreed as follows concerning the sword: The sword is ordained of God outside the perfection of Christ. It pun-ishes and puts to death the wicked, and guards and protects the good. In the law, the sword was ordained for the punishment of the wicked and for their death, and the same sword is now or-dained to be used by the worldly magistrates.

In the perfection of Christ, however, only the ban is used for a warning and for the excommunication of the one who has sinned, without putting the flesh to death—simply the warning and the command to sin no more.

Now it will be asked by many who do not recognize this as the will of Christ for us, whether a Christian may or should employ the sword against the wicked for the defense and protection of the good, or for the sake of love.

Our reply is unanimously as follows: Christ teaches and commands us to learn of Him, for He is meek and lowly in heart and so shall we find rest to our souls. Also Christ says to the heathenish woman who was taken in adultery, not that one should stone her according to the law of His Father (and yet He says, As the Father has commanded me, thus I do), but in mercy and forgiveness and warning, to sin no more. Such an attitude we also ought to take completely according to the rule of the ban.

Secondly, it will be asked concerning the sword, whether a Christian shall pass sentence in worldly dispute and strife such as unbelievers have with one another. This is our united answer: Christ did not wish to decide or pass judgment between brother and brother in the case of the inheritance, but refused to do so. Therefore, we should do likewise.

Thirdly, it will be asked concerning the sword, Shall one be a magistrate if one should be chosen as such? The answer is as follows: They wished to make Christ king, but He fled and did not view it as the arrangement of His Father. Thus shall we do as He did, and follow Him, and so shall we not walk in darkness. For He Himself says, He who wishes to come after me let him deny himself, take up his cross, and follow me. In addition, He Himself forbids the employment of the force of the sword, saying, The worldly princes lord it over them, etc., but not so shall it be with you. Further, Paul says, Whom God did foreknow He also did predestinate to be conformed to the image of His Son, etc. Also Peter says, Christ has suffered (not ruled) and left us an example, that ye should follow His steps.

Finally, it will be observed that it is not appropriate for a Christian to serve as a magistrate because of these points: The government magistracy is according to the flesh, but the Christian's is according to the Spirit; their houses and dwelling remain in this world, but the Christians' are in heaven; their citizenship is in this world, but the Christians' citizenship is in heaven; the weapons of their conflict and war are carnal and against the flesh only, but the Christians' weapons are spiritual, against the fortification of the devil. The worldlings are armed with steel and iron, but the Christians are armed with the armor of God, with truth, righteousness, peace, faith, salvation, and the word of God. In brief, as is the mind of Christ toward us, so shall the mind of the members of the body of Christ be through Him in all things, that there may be no schism in the body through which it would be destroyed. For every kingdom divided against itself will be destroyed. Now since Christ is as it is written of Him, His members must also be the same, that His body may remain complete and united to its own advancement and upbuilding.

Seventh. We are agreed as follows concerning the oath: The oath is a confirmation among those who are quarreling or making promises. In the law, it is commanded to be performed in God's name, but only in truth, not falsely. Christ, who teaches the perfection of the law, prohibits all swearing to His followers, whether true or false—neither by heaven, nor by the earth, nor by Jerusalem, nor by our head,—and that for the reason which He shortly thereafter gives, For you are not able to make one hair white or black. So you see it is for this reason that all swearing is forbidden: We cannot fulfill that which we promise when we swear, for we cannot change even the very least thing on us.

Now there are some who do not give credence to the simple command of God, but object with this question: Well now, did not God swear to Abraham by Himself (since He was God) when He promised him that He would be with him and that He would be his God if he would keep His commandments—why then should I not also swear when I promise to someone? Answer: Hear what the Scripture says: God, since He wished more abundantly to show unto the heirs the immutability of His counsel, inserted an oath, that by two immutable things (in which it is impossible for God to lie) we might have a strong consolation. Observe the meaning of this Scripture: What God forbids you to do, He has power to do, for everything is possible for Him. God swore an oath to Abraham, says the Scripture, so that He might show that His counsel is immutable. That is, no one can withstand or thwart His will; therefore He can keep His oath. But we can do nothing, as is said above by Christ, to keep or perform our oaths: therefore, we shall not swear at all.

Then others further say as follows: It is not forbidden of God to swear in the New Testament, when it is actually commanded in the Old, but it is forbidden only to swear by heaven, earth, Jerusalem, and our head. Answer: Hear the Scripture: He who swears by heaven swears by God's throne and by Him who sits thereon. Observe: It is forbidden to swear by heaven, which is only the throne of God; how much more is it forbidden to swear by God Himself! Ye fools and blind, which is greater, the throne or Him that sits thereon?

Further some say: Because evil is now in the world, and because man needs God for the establishment of the truth, so did the apostles Peter and Paul also swear. Answer: Peter and Paul only testify of that which God promised to Abraham with the oath. They themselves promise nothing, as the example indicates clearly. Testifying and swearing are two different things. For when a person swears, he is in the first place promising future things, as Christ was promised to Abraham whom we a long time afterward received. But when a person bears testimony he is testifying about the present, whether it is good or evil, as Simeon spoke to Mary about Christ and testified, Behold this (child) is set for the fall and rising of many in Israel, and for a sign which shall be spoken against.

Christ also taught us along the same line when He said, Let your communication be Yea, yea; Nay, nay; for whatsoever is more than these cometh of evil. He says, Your speech or word shall be yea and nay. However, when one does not wish to understand, he remains closed to the meaning. Christ is simply Yea and Nay, and all those who seek Him simply will understand His word. Amen.

18

Augustin Würzlburger:
Proceedings of His Trial. [1528]

The suspicion of the authorities that the Anabaptists not only dissented from the officially enjoined religion of a community but were also political insurrectionists prompted an extensive system of legal suppression. Of the numerous official court documents dealing with Anabaptists, excerpts from one particular case (about half of the extant documents) are printed below. They pertain to one Augustin Würzlburger, a schoolteacher and Anabaptist from near Regensburg in South Germany. These documents reveal the various facets of the legal suppression of dissenting religious sentiment in the sixteenth century. As the excerpts show, the suppression was entirely in the hands of the political authorities.[17]

LITERATURE

J. Denny Weaver, *Becoming Anabaptist: The Origin and Significance of Sixteenth-century Anabaptism.* Scottdale, PA, 1987.

Brad Gregory, *Salvation at Stake: Christian Martyrdom in Early Modern Europe.* Cambridge, MA, 1999.

---

17. K. Schornbaum, ed., *Quellen zur Geschichte der Täufer V.* Bayern, II. Gütersloh, Germany, 1951, pp. 27–49. Translation by Hans J. Hillerbrand.

Hans Sedlmair, of Oberhaim, confesses and states that one Augustin Würzlburger, of Regensburg, had visited him last Lent; he could not recall the exact date. This Augustin had talked about the gospel and had asserted that to eat meat during Lent was not sinful. Also, our first baptism was invalid, for God Himself had said: "He who believes and is baptized, shall be saved; he who does not believe, shall be condemned."...

Hans Sedlmair further confesses and states that Augustin visited him again at his house in Oberhaim on April 14 [1528] and proclaimed from a book to him and Hans Weber, who was also arrested, the true gospel. Augustin asked him if he believed in our Lord Jesus Christ who suffered death and pain on the cross. He answered affirmatively and Würzlburger asked him if from the bottom of his heart he desired to be baptized. He answered affirmatively. Afterward Augustin brought water in a small pitcher into the stable, took some water with his hands, and baptized him in the name of the Father, Son, and Holy Spirit...After Würzlburger had baptized him, he prohibited him to attend church, unless the gospel was preached. If he went to church, he should not remove his hat...

May 20, 1528. First Interrogation

On May 20, in the year of the Lord 1528, Augustin Würzlburger was interrogated by City Councilor Stuchsen.

Augustin Würzlburger, a schoolteacher, states that he was baptized on November 17 by one Leonhart Freisleben near Prul, south of Regensburg. Two other teachers had gone there with him, but were not baptized. Prior to his baptism he had been preached the gospel of all creatures in the name of the Father, Son, and Holy Spirit and was entreated henceforth to sin no more. He should do all in power to bring others onto the right path...

During the week of April 5 a letter from the congregation at

Augsburg was sent to him through someone named Hans, who had been schoolteacher at Weiden and had since then gone to Austria. He, Augustin, or Hans, who had brought the letter, had been elected by the congregation in Augsburg to be an apostle to preach the gospel. Neither of them had wanted to accept this charge and had agreed to draw a lot to decide. They had made lines with chalk and the lot had fallen on him. He had accepted and during the Easter holidays he traveled to Sussbach, where he had several friends. There he had baptized Hans Sedlmair and a weaver. He had also baptized Sedlmair's two sons, his wife and a daughter, a shoemaker, and a stranger whose name he did not know...

Sedlmair, the weaver, and he were arrested at Sussbach by a ducal official who examined them and then released them with the charge to move away. He, Würzlburger, had instructed his brother Hans, a butcher from Landshut, to die unto the world and to serve God, but he had not baptized him. He had heard, however, that his brother had been arrested; perhaps he had talked too much about the matter. He had also preached the gospel to several people and challenged them to accept baptism according to the Word of God. His wife had been baptized by one Burkhart Praun, of Ofen, in their apartment in the house of Wisen without anyone else present.

He stated furthermore that clear scriptural testimony convinced him that he denied God if he desisted from this position. He would rather let himself be hanged. Luther could write in his Postill what he wanted; he would turn things according to his pleasure. One should not take anything away from Scripture...

There were many apostles among them and wherever one is sent, he has to go and preach, even if it should mean death. They did not mean to offend anyone. There was no special directive concerning food; he had eaten meat during Lent when it was available... He said that all this he clearly found in Scripture. If he were taught better and differently, he would desist.

May 20, 1528. Interrogation of Würzlburger's wife

Barbara, wife of Augustin Würzlburger, says that she only knows about baptism. A certain Burkhart had baptized her in her house in Regensburg in November in the name of the Father, Son, and Holy Spirit. Only her husband was present. Also, she truly knew no one whom her husband had baptized. She did not know who had baptized him. A priest came to her and told her that her husband had baptized several people in Landshut. Also, her husband said to her that he had baptized several women who thus belonged to him; he had become single again. Her husband had told two men about baptism, but they had not received it. She could not desist from this teaching and turn against the Lord, her God. She had trusted God and would remain true to Him, for His will was to be done.

May 22, 1528. Questions for the Second Interrogation of Würzlburger

1. How had he accepted this unbelief or error? How, or from whom had he heard, learned, and accepted it?

2. What innovations had he accepted and practiced after he had stained himself with rebaptism?

3. By whom was he baptized and with what words was he entreated to accept it?

4. Had he himself requested baptism?

5. Who had been baptized with him?

6. The other leaders, directors, preachers, and helpers: Who and where are they?

7. The secret assemblies or services attended by him with his fellows: What sign do they use to recognize one another?

8. Had he himself baptized and preached?

9. What were their notions and regulations concerning a community of goods?

10. Their notions concerning confession, mass, reception of the sacrament, and church attendance?

11. Why had he accepted this opinion and what had he hoped for?

12. How often and at what places, here at Landshut or elsewhere in Bavaria, had he preached? Who had been present at this preaching; also from whom had he heard this teaching?

13. What is the present whereabouts of his associate in preaching and rebaptizing at Oberhaim? Had this associate also preached in Bavaria, and whom had he rebaptized?

14. How often had his brother been present at his preaching? Was he rebaptized by him or by others?...

16. What were his intentions and why had he accepted this preaching and rebaptism? Had he accepted it for the purpose of insurrection and other evil doings? Whom had he baptized in Bavaria; what were their names and residence?

17. Did he revoke this opinion and repent?

May 25, 1528. Second Interrogation of Würzlburger

In response to the first article Augustin said that he had been told the gospel by those who recently had been expelled from Regensburg because of their baptism. He had also read himself and examined the Scriptures and he had found that this teaching alone was the divine truth. Everyone must be persecuted and suffer, for the world has no friendship with Christians. He thinks nothing of his first baptism; one must not baptize unbelievers. Only after one believes and the gospel has been preached is one to be baptized, if it is so desired...

Concerning the second question he said that he did not accept anything new except that he would live solely for God and not unto himself; for this reason he was baptized.

Concerning the third question he said that he was baptized by Leonhart Freisleben, one of those recently expelled because of baptism, at Prul. This was in November and he was baptized, according to God's command in the Gospel according to Matthew and Mark, in the name of the Father, Son, and Holy Spirit. There were four of them as well as one woman who had been expelled from Regensburg because of their baptism.

Fourth: He said yes, since he knew this to be the divine truth, he had desired baptism, and nothing else.

Fifth: He said that only he had been baptized at that time.

Sixth: He said that he did not know any, for he had remained here and had only traveled to such places in Bavaria, where there were none of them. He knew only one Burkhart Praun, of Ofen, a tall man, about thirty years of age, whom he had met at Regensburg last winter. He was a leader but had told him nothing but what the one who had baptized him had also told him. Since that time he had heard nothing from him. Also, it was true that the congregation at Augsburg had sent one called Hans to Regensburg with a letter. Over a year ago he had been a choirmaster at Regensburg and before that a schoolteacher at Weiden. The letter stated that the congregation had named him or Hans to the office of apostle to preach the gospel. They had cast lots as to who should accept the office, and the lot had fallen to him. For this office he had been given the instruction that he should proclaim the divine truth.

Seventh: That he knew of no secret assembly or gathering, nor of a sign by which they might recognize one another.

Eighth: That he had preached and baptized. First, he had baptized a cousin, at Sussbach, called Sedlmair. He had preached to him and to his household during the Easter holidays. Present had been Sedlmair, his wife, two sons and a daughter, also a weaver from Sussbach, and a miller whom he did not know...He had preached to them the gospel of all creatures, that they might recognize God and also how they were to live, and he had told them that if they followed Christ they would be persecuted. If they wanted to accept this, they should do it. Thereupon they did accept it and surrendered to the discipline of the Father and the pure Word of God to live henceforth according to the commands of God...

June 2, 1528. Communication of the Dukes of Bavaria to the Regensburg City Council

We have received the interrogation records of Augustin Würzlburger together with a letter from our officials who note your concern and eagerness...Würzlburger has been shown by his own confession to be a leader and preacher of the heretical sect of the Anabaptists, against the order of the Holy Christian Church and the imperial edict and mandate. He has also been the cause of the execution of several persons despite their recantations. Therefore, we wish that said Würzlburger be sentenced to death according to imperial law because of his confession and evil heretical misdemeanor. You are not to refuse our will or show any mercy.

June 5, 1528. Regensburg City Council to the Dukes of Bavaria

Your letter concerning Augustin Würzlburger, instructing us to sentence him to death because of his confession concerning rebaptism, has caused us great concern. We do not wish to refuse you anything in this or any other matter, and we are grieved indeed by Augustin Würzlburger's error. Since he has no other fault than that concerning rebaptism and the faith, we cannot understand why we are to put him to death. We want to make him desist from his opinion and error. If this should be unsuccessful, we would seek the counsel of other Christian and learned men on how to proceed further...

October 10, 1528. Regensburg Chronicle

On Saturday, October 10, Augustin N., a teacher and Anabaptist, was led to the front of the city hall, placed on a bench, where he was charged with having been rebaptized and afterward rebaptizing others, nine persons all in all...Even though he deserved, according to imperial law, death by burning, the Council had mercifully ruled that he was to be executed by beheading. This happened...the henchman leading him like a butcher leads a calf. He did not say a word even as no one spoke to him.

19

Peter Riedemann:
Account of Our Religion. [*c.* 1545]

The Hutterite Anabaptists in Moravia developed a unique characteristic of their own. Relatively unmolested by the authorities, they were able to establish communities and structure them in accord with their beliefs. Elsewhere Anabaptist conventicles were like small islands in a huge ocean; in Moravia they had their own communal and social life. They stressed communal living and, following what was to them a biblical precedent, practiced complete sharing of goods.

The theological justification for the practice of communal living was described in the *Account of Our Religion*, the major confessional document of sixteenth-century Hutterite Anabaptism. Its author was Peter Riedemann, leader of the Hutterites from 1542 to his death in 1556. Riedemann was also the author of other important theological writings. Reprinted here is the section on the Community of Goods.[18]

---

18. *Account of Our Religion, Doctrine and Faith, Given by Peter Riedemann of the Brothers Whom Men Call Hutterians.* London, 1950, pp. 102–21.

LITERATURE

Leonard Gross, *The Golden Years of the Hutterites: The Witness and Thought of the Communal Moravian Anabaptists*. Scottdale, PA, 1980.

Concerning Community of Goods

Now, since all the saints have fellowship in holy things, that is in God, who also has given to them all things in His Son Christ Jesus—which gift none should have for himself, but each for the other; as Christ also has naught for Himself, but has everything for us, even so all the members of His body have naught for themselves, but for the whole body, for all the members. For His gifts are not sanctified and given to one member alone, or for one member's sake, but for the whole body with its members.

Now, since all God's gifts—not only spiritual but also material things—are given to man, not that he should have them for himself alone but with all his fellows, therefore the communion of saints itself must show itself not only in spiritual but also in temporal things; that as Paul said, one might not have abundance and another suffer want, but that there may be equality. This he shows from the law touching manna, in that he who gathered much had nothing over, whereas he who gathered little had no less, since each was given what he needed according to the measure.

Furthermore, one sees in all things created, which testify to us still today, that God from the beginning ordained no private property for humans, but all things to be in common. But through wrong taking, since man took what he should not and forsook what he should take, he drew such things to himself and made them his property, and so grew and became hardened therein. Through such wrong taking and collecting of created things he has been led so far from God that he has even forgotten the Creator, and has even raised up and honored as God the created things which had been put under and made subject to him. Moreover, such is still the case if one steps out of God's order and forsakes the same.

Now, however, as has been said, created things which are too high for man to draw within his grasp and collect, such as the sun with the whole course of the heavens, day, air, and such like, show that not they alone, but all other created things are likewise made common to man. That they have thus remained and are not possessed by man is due to their being too high for him to bring under his power; otherwise—so evil had he become through wrong taking—he would have drawn them to himself as well as the rest and made them his property.

That this is so, however, and that the rest is just as little made by God for man's private possession, is shown in that man must forsake all other created things as well as this when he dies, and can carry nothing with him to use as his own. For which reason Christ also called temporal all things foreign to man's essential nature, and said, "If ye are not faithful in what is not your own, who will entrust to you what is your own?"

Now, because what is temporal doth not belong to us, but is foreign to our true nature, the law commands that none covet strange possessions, that is, set his heart upon and cleave to what is temporal and alien. Therefore whosoever will cleave to Christ and follow Him must forsake such taking of created things and property, as He Himself also said, "Whosoever forsakes not all that he has cannot be my disciple." For if a man is to be renewed again into the likeness of God, he must put off all that leads him from Him—that is, the grasping and drawing to himself of created things—for he cannot otherwise attain God's likeness. Therefore Christ says, "Whosoever shall not receive the kingdom of God as a little child shall not enter therein," or, "Except ye overcome yourselves and become as little children, ye shall not enter into the kingdom of heaven."

Now, he who thus becomes free from created things can then grasp what is true and divine; and when he grasps it, and it becomes his treasure, he turns his heart toward it, empties himself of all else and takes nothing as his, and regards it no longer as his but as of all God's children. Therefore we say that as all the saints have community in spiritual gifts, still much more should they show this in material things, and not ascribe the same to and covet them for themselves, for they are not their own; but regard them as of all God's children, that they may thereby show that they are partakers in the community of Christ and are renewed into God's likeness. For the more man yet cleaves to created things, appropriates and ascribes such to himself, the further does he show himself to be from the likeness of God and the community of Christ.

For this reason the Holy Spirit also at the beginning of the church began such community right gloriously again, so that none said that aught of the things that he possessed was his own, but they had all things in common; and it is His will that this might still be kept, as Paul says, "Let none seek his own profit but the profit of another," or, "Let none seek what benefits himself but what benefits many." Where this is not the case, it is a blemish upon the church, which ought verily to be corrected. If one should say, it was so nowhere except in Jerusalem, therefore it is now not necessary, we say, even if it were nowhere but in Jerusalem, it does not follow that it ought not to be so now. For neither apostles nor churches were lacking, but rather the opportunity, manner, and time.

Therefore, this should be no cause for us to hesitate, but rather should it move us to more and better zeal and diligence, for the Lord now gives us both time and cause so to do. That there was no lack of either apostles or churches is shown by the zeal of both. For the apostles have pointed the people thereto with all diligence and most faithfully prescribed true surrender, as all their Epistles still prove today. In addition, the people obeyed with zeal, as Paul bears witness—especially of those of Macedonia—saying, "I tell you of the grace that is given to the churches in Macedonia for their joy was the most rapturous since they had been tried by much affliction, and their poverty, though it was indeed deep, overflowed as riches in all simplicity. For I bear witness that with all their power, yea, and beyond their power, they were themselves willing, and besought us earnestly with much admonition to receive the benefit and community of help which is given to the saints; and not as we had hoped, but first gave themselves to the Lord, and then to us also, by the will of God."

Here one can well see with what inclined and willing hearts the churches were ready to keep community not only in spiritual but also in material things, for they desired to follow the master Christ, and become like Him and one with Him, who Himself went before us in such a way, and commanded us to follow Him.

20

Elizabeth, a Dutch Anabaptist Martyr: *A Letter.* [1573]

No matter where they appeared and what form they assumed, sixteenth-century religious dissenters were persecuted by governmental authorities, both Catholic and Protestant. In some instances theological deviation provided the rationale for this persecution, in others the fear that the religious dissenters intended to overthrow existing law and order. Thus, these "radicals" were rarely free to exercise their faith. Usually they were in danger of being arrested and thrown into dungeons; often they were put to the stake. The latter formed the company of the martyrs.

The documents concerning the Anabaptist martyrs were collected in the seventeenth century by the Dutchman Thieleman van Braght in an impressive volume entitled *The Bloody Theater or The Martyrs' Mirror.* Though generally an accurate historical guide to suppression and persecution, this martyrology meant to inspire rather than convey an objective historical account for the reader. Reprinted below is the letter of Elizabeth, a Dutch Anabaptist woman about whom little is known. It is written to her infant daughter just before her own execution.[19]

---

19. Thieleman van Braght, *The Bloody Theater or The Martyrs' Mirror.* Scottdale, PA, 1951, pp. 984–87.

LITERATURE

Thieleman van Braght, *The Bloody Theater or The Martyrs' Mirror*. Scottdale, PA, 1951.

Brad Gregory, *The Forgotten Writings of the Mennonite Martyrs*. Leiden, Netherlands, 2002.

[Testament] written to Janneken my own dearest daughter, while I was (unworthily) confined for the Lord's sake, in prison, at Antwerp, A.D. 1573

The true love of God and wisdom of the Father strengthen you in virtue, my dearest child; the Lord of heaven and earth, the God of Abraham, the God of Isaac, and the God of Jacob, the Lord in Israel, keep you in His virtue, and strengthen and confirm your understanding in his truth. My dear little child, I commend you to the almighty, great and terrible God, who only is wise, that He will keep you, and let you grow up in His fear, or that He will take you home in your youth, this is my heart's request of the Lord: you who are yet so young, and whom I must leave here in this wicked, evil, perverse world.

Since, then, the Lord has so ordered and foreordained it, that I must leave you here, and you are here deprived of father and mother, I will commend you to the Lord; let Him do with you according to His holy will. He will govern you, and be a Father to you, so that you shall have no lack here, if you only fear God; for He will be the Father of the orphans and the protector of the widows.

Hence, my dear lamb, I who am imprisoned and bound here for the Lord's sake, can help you in no other way; I had to leave your father for the Lord's sake, and could keep him only a short time. We were permitted to live together only half a year, after which we were apprehended, because we sought the salvation of our souls. They took him from me, not knowing my condition, and I had to remain in imprisonment, and see him go before me; and it was a great grief to him that I had to remain here in prison. And now that I have abided the time, borne you under my heart with great sorrow for nine months, and given birth to you here in prison, in great pain, they have taken you from me. Here I lie, expecting death every morning, and shall now soon follow your dear father. And I, your dear mother, write you, my dearest child, something for a remembrance, that you will thereby remember your dear father and your dear mother.

Since I am now delivered up to death, and must leave you here alone, I must through these lines cause you to remember, that when you have attained your understanding, you endeavor to fear God, and see and examine why and for whose name we both died; and be not ashamed to confess us before the world, for you must know that it is not for the sake of any evil. Hence be not ashamed of us; it is the way which the prophets and the apostles went, and the narrow way which leads into eternal life, for there shall no other way be found by which to be saved.

Hence, my young lamb, for whose sake I still have, and have had, great sorrow, seek, when you have attained your understanding, this narrow way, though there is sometimes much danger in it according to the flesh, as we may see and read, if we diligently examine and read the Scriptures, that much is said concerning the cross of Christ. And there are many in this world who are enemies of the cross, who seek to be free from it among the world, and to escape it. But, my dear child, if we would with Christ seek and inherit salvation, we must also help bear His cross; and this is the cross which He would have us bear: to follow His footsteps, and to help bear His reproach; for Christ Himself says: "Ye shall be persecuted, killed, and dispersed for my name's sake." Yea, He Himself went before us in this way of reproach, and left us an example, that we should follow His steps; for, for His sake all must be forsaken, father, mother, sister, brother, husband, child, yea, one's own life...

Thus, my dear child, it is now fulfilled in your dear father and mother. It was indeed prophesied to us beforehand, that this was awaiting us; but not everyone is chosen hereunto, nor expects it; the Lord has chosen us hereunto. Hence, when you have attained your understanding, follow this example of your father and mother. And, my dear child, this is my request of you, since you are still very little and young; I wrote this when you were but one month old. As I am soon now to offer up my sacrifice, by the help of the Lord, I leave you this: "That you fulfill my request, always uniting with them that fear God; and do not regard the pomp and boasting of the world, nor the great multitude, whose way leads to the abyss of hell, but look at the little flock of Israelites, who have no freedom anywhere, and must always flee from one land to the other, as Abraham did; that you may hereafter obtain your fatherland; for if you seek your salvation, it is easy to perceive which is the way that leads to life, or the way that leads into hell. Above all things, seek the kingdom of heaven and His righteousness; and whatever you need besides shall be added unto you." Matt. 6: 33.

Further, my dear child, I pray you, that wherever you live when you are grown up, and begin to have understanding, you conduct yourself well and honestly, so that no one need have cause to complain of you. And always be faithful, taking good heed not to wrong anyone. Learn to carry your hands always uprightly, and see that you like to work, for Paul says: "If any will not work, neither shall he eat." 2 Thess. 3: 10. And Peter says: "He that will love life, and see good days, let him refrain his tongue from evil." 1 Pet. 3: 10.

Hence, my dear Janneken, do not accustom your mouth to filthy talk, nor to ugly words that are not proper, nor to lies; for a liar has no part in the kingdom of heaven; for it is written: "The mouth that lies, slays the soul." Hence beware of this, and run not in the street as other bad children do; rather take up a book, and learn to seek there that which concerns your salvation.

And where you have your home, obey those whose bread you eat. If they speak evil, do you speak well. And learn always to love to be doing something; and do not think yourself too good for anything, nor exalt yourself, but condescend to the lowly, and always honor the aged wherever you are.

I leave you here. Oh, that it had pleased the Lord, that I might have brought you up; I should so gladly have done my best with respect to it; but it seems that it is not the Lord's will. And though it had not come thus, and I had remained with you for a time, the Lord could still take me from you, and then, too, you should have to be without me, even as it has now gone with your father and myself, that we could live together but so short a time, when we were so well joined since the Lord had so well mated us, that we would not have forsaken each other for the whole world, and yet we had to leave each other for the Lord's sake. Therefore, I must also leave you here, my dearest lamb; the Lord that created and made you now takes me from you, it is His holy will. I must now pass through this narrow way which the prophets and martyrs of Christ passed through, and many thousands who put off the mortal clothing, who died here for Christ, and now they wait under the altar till their number shall be fulfilled, of which number your dear father is one. And I am now on the point of following him, for I am delivered up to death, as it appears in the eyes of man; but if it were not the will of the Lord (though it seems that I am delivered up to death), He could yet easily deliver me out of their hands and give me back to you, my child. Even as the Lord returned to Abraham his son Isaac, so He could still easily do it; He is still the same God that delivered Daniel out of the lion's den, and the three young men out of the fiery furnace; He could still easily deliver me out of the hands of man...

If they have persecuted the Lord, they will also persecute us; if they have hated Him, they will also hate us; and this they do because they have not known my Father, nor me, says the Almighty Lord. For His kingdom was not of this world; had His kingdom been of this world, the world would have loved Him; but because His kingdom was not of this world, therefore the world hated Him. So it also is now: Since our kingdom is not of this world, the world will hate us; but it is better for us to be despised here by the world, than that we should hereafter have to mourn forever. But they that will not taste the bitter here, can hereafter not expect eternal life; for we know that Paul says, that all that will live godly in Christ Jesus shall be persecuted and be a prey to everyone.

Thus, my dear child, this way the prophets and apostles and many thousands of other Godfearing persons went before us, for an example unto us; and Christ Himself did not spare Himself for us, but delivered up Himself unto death for our sakes—how then should He not give us all things? Hence, my dearest lamb, seek to follow this way, this I pray you, as much as you value your salvation; for this is the only way which leads to eternal life, yea, there is no other way by which we can be saved than only through Jesus Christ, as Paul says: "Other foundation can no man lay than that is laid, which is Jesus Christ" (1 Cor. 3: 11)...

My dear lamb, we can merit nothing, but must through grace inherit salvation; hence always endeavor to fear God, for the fear of the Lord is the beginning of wisdom, and he that fears the Lord will do good, and it will be well with him in this world and in that which is to come. And always join those that seek to fear the Lord from the heart, and be not conformed to the world, to do as she does, nor walk in any improper course of life; for the world shall pass away, and all the nations that serve her shall perish with her. Nor have fellowship with the unfruitful works of darkness, but rather reprove them; and be transformed by the renewing of your life, that you may show forth the virtues in which God has called you.

O my dearest lamb, that you might know the truth when you have attained your understanding, and that you might follow your dear father and mother, who went before you; for your dear father demonstrated with his blood that it is the genuine truth, and I also hope to attest the same with my blood, though flesh and blood must remain on the posts and on the stake, well knowing that we shall meet hereafter. Do you also follow us, my dear lamb, that you too may come where we shall be, and that we may find one another there, where the Lord shall say: "Come, ye blessed of my Father, inherit the kingdom prepared for you from the beginning."...

I leave you here among my friends; I hope that my father, and my stepmother, and my brothers, and my sisters will do the best with you as long as they live. Be subject and obedient to them in everything, as far as it is not contrary to God. I leave you what comes from my mother's death, namely, thirty guilders and over; I do not know how much it is, since I have been long imprisoned here, and do not know what it has all cost. But I hope that Grietge, my dear sister, who has shown me so much friendship, will do her best to give you what belongs to you. And as to what may come to you from your father, I do not know, since I can learn nothing about his parents, because it is so far from here; if they should inquire after you, my friends may do the best in the matter.

And now, Janneken, my dear lamb, who are yet very little and young, I leave you this letter, together with a gold real, which I had with me in prison, and this I leave you for a perpetual adieu, and for a testament; that you may remember me by it, as also by this letter. Read it, when you have understanding, and keep it as long as you live in remembrance of me and of your father, if per-adventure you might be edified by it. And I herewith bid you adieu, my dear Janneken Munstdorp, and kiss you heartily, my dear lamb, with a perpetual kiss of peace. Follow me and your father, and be not ashamed to confess us before the world, for we were not ashamed to confess our faith before the world, and this adulterous generation; hence I pray you, that you be not ashamed to confess our faith, since it is the true evangelical faith, another than which shall never be found.

Let it be your glory that we did not die for any evil doing, and strive to do likewise, though they should also seek to kill you. And on no account cease to love God above all, for no one can prevent you from fearing God. If you follow that which is good, and seek peace, and ensue it, you shall receive the crown of eternal life; this crown I wish you and the crucified, bleeding, naked, despised, re-jected, and slain Jesus Christ for your bridegroom.

PART III

JOHN CALVIN AND HIS INFLUENCE

John Calvin: *Ecclesiastical Ordinances of Geneva.* [1541]

The adoption of a church order for Geneva was the price for Calvin's return to the city in 1541. Drafted by Calvin, subsequently slightly modified, this church order meant to fashion the Genevan church according to what Calvin understood to be the biblical paradigm. It also was to allow Calvin to put his understanding of the life of the church into practice. The *Ecclesiastical Ordinances*, approved by the Genevan citizens in November 1541, were a comprehensive summary of how the Genevan church was to function. Four church offices were established—pastor, teacher, elder, and deacon—each with its particular responsibilities and functions. Significant was the provision for the office of "elder"— "presbyter" in Greek—occupied by laymen. Other provisions of the *Ordinances* stipulated the election of the ministers, the frequency of preaching, etc.

One of the distinctive features of the *Ordinances*, and of those of other church orders in the Calvinist tradition modeled after it, was the explicit provision for the exercise of church discipline— that is, the supervision of the lives and beliefs of the people. Such church discipline was to be exercised by the institution of the consistory, whose members, consisting of the pastors and the elders, met regularly to monitor both the morals and the theology of the people of Geneva.

Reprinted here is the middle section of the *Ordinances*.[20]

LITERATURE

F. Wendel, *The Origin and Development of Calvin's Thought*. New York, 1963.

Philip Benedict, *Christ's Churches Purely Reformed: A Social History of Calvinism*. New Haven, CT, 2002.

Of the Frequency, Place, and Time of Preaching

Each Sunday, at daybreak, there shall be a sermon in St. Peter's and St. Gervaise's, also at the customary hour at St. Peter, Magdalene and St. Gervaise. At three o'clock, as well, in all three parishes, there shall be a second sermon.

For purposes of catechetical instruction and the administration of the sacraments, the boundaries of the parishes are to be observed as far as possible. St. Gervaise is to be used by those who have done so in the past; likewise Magdalene. Those who formerly attended St. Germain, Holy Cross, the new church of Our Lady, and St. Legier are to attend St. Peter's.

On work days, there shall be preaching three times each week, on Monday, Wednesday, and Friday besides the two sermons mentioned. These sermons shall be announced to take place at an early hour so that they may be finished before the day's work begins. On special days of prayer the Sunday order is to be observed.

To carry out these provisions and the other responsibilities

---

20. Corpus Reformatorum 38, 21 ff. Reprinted from Hans J. Hillerbrand, *The Reformation: A Narrative History*. New York, 1965, pp.191–94.

pertaining to the ministry, five ministers and three coadjutors will be needed. The latter will also be ministers and help and reinforce the others as the occasion arises.

Concerning the Second Order, Called Teachers

The proper duty of teachers is to instruct the faithful in sound doctrine so that the purity of the gospel is not corrupted by ignorance or evil opinions. We include here the aids and instructions necessary to preserve the doctrines and to keep the church from becoming desolate for lack of pastors and ministers. To use a more familiar expression, we shall call it the order of the schools.

The order closest to the ministry and most closely associated with the government of the church is that of lecturer in theology who teaches the Old and the New Testament.

Since it is impossible to profit by such instruction without first knowing languages and the humanities, and also since it is necessary to prepare for the future so that the church will not be neglected by the young, it will be necessary to establish a school to instruct the youth, to prepare them not only for the ministry but also for government service.

First of all, a proper place for teaching purposes must be designated, fit to accommodate children and others who wish to profit by such instruction; to secure someone who is both learned in subject matter and capable of looking after the building, who can also read. This person is to be employed and placed under contract on condition that he provide under his charge readers in the languages and in dialectics, if it be possible. He is also to secure men with bachelor degrees to teach the children. This we hope to do to further the work of God.

These teachers shall be subject to the same ecclesiastical discipline as the pastors. There shall be no other school in the city for young children; the girls shall have their school apart, as before.

No one shall be appointed unless he is approved by the ministers, who will make their selection known to the authorities, after which he shall be presented to the council with their recommendation. In any case, when he is examined, two members of the Small Council shall be present.

The Third Order Is That of Elders, Those Commissioned or Appointed to the Consistory by the Authorities

Their office is to keep watch over the lives of everyone, to admonish in love those whom they see in error and leading disorderly lives. Whenever necessary they shall make a report concerning these to the ministers who will be designated to make brotherly corrections and join with the others in making such corrections.

If the church deems it wise, it will be well to choose two from the Small Council, four from the Council of Two Hundred, honest men of good demeanor, without reproach and free from all suspicion, above all fearing God and possessed of good and spiritual judgment. It will be well to elect them from every part of the city so as to be able to maintain supervision over all. This we desire to be instituted.

This shall be the manner of their selection, inasmuch as the Small Council advises that the best men be nominated, and to call the minister so as to confer with them, after which those whom they suggest may be presented to the Council of Two Hundred for their approval. If they are found worthy, after being approved, they shall take an oath similar to that required of the ministers. At the end of the year, after the election of the council, they shall present themselves to the authorities in order that it may be decided if they are to remain in office or be replaced. It will not be expedient to replace them often without cause, or so long as they faithfully perform their duties.

The Fourth Order or the Deacons

There were two orders of deacons in the ancient church, the one concerned with receiving, distributing, and guarding the goods of the poor, their possessions, income, and pensions as well as the quarterly offerings; the other, to take heed to and care for the sick and administer the pittance for the poor. This custom we have preserved to the present. In order to avoid confusion, for we have both stewards and managers, one of the four stewards of the hospital is to act as receiver of all its goods and is to receive adequate remuneration in order that he may better exercise his office.

The number of four stewards shall remain as it is, of which number one shall be charged with the common funds, as directed, not only that there may be greater efficiency, but also that those who wish to make special gifts may be better assured that these will be distributed only as they desire. If the income which the officials assign is not sufficient, or if some emergency should arise, the authorities shall instruct him to make adjustments according to the need.

The election of the managers, as well as of the stewards, is to be conducted as that of the elders; in their election the rule is to be followed which was delivered by St. Paul respecting deacons.

Concerning the office and authority of stewards, we confirm the articles which have already been proposed, on condition that, in urgent matters, especially when the issue is no great matter and the expenditure involved is small, they not be required to assemble for every action taken, but that one or two of them may be permitted to act in the absence of the others, in a reasonable way. It will be his task to take diligent care that the public hospital is well administered and that it is open not only to the sick but also to aged persons who are unable to work, to widows, orphans, and other needy persons. Those who are sick are to be kept in a separate lodging, away from those who cannot work, old persons, widows, orphans, and other needy persons.

Also the care of the poor who are scattered throughout the city is to be conducted as the stewards may order. Also, that another hospital is established for the transients who should be helped. Separate provision is to be made for any who are worthy of special charity. To accomplish this, a room is to be set aside for those who shall be recommended by the stewards, and it is to be used for no other purpose. Above all, the families of the managers are to be well managed in an efficient and godly fashion, since they are to manage the houses dedicated to God.

The ministers and the commissioners or elders, with one of the syndics, for their part, are carefully to watch for any fault or negligence of any sort, in order to beg and admonish the authorities to set it in order. Every three months they are to cause certain of their company, with the stewards, to visit the hospital to ascertain if everything is in order.

It will be necessary, also, for the benefit of the poor in the hospital and for the poor of the city who cannot help themselves, that a doctor and a competent surgeon be secured from among those who practice in the city to have the care of the hospital and to visit the poor.

The hospital, for the pestilence in any case, is to be set apart; especially should it happen that the city is visited by this rod from God.

Moreover, to prevent begging, which is contrary to good order, it will be necessary that the authorities delegate certain officers. They are to be stationed at the doors of the churches to drive away any who try to resist and, if they act impudently or answer insolently, to take them to one of the syndics. In like manner, the heads of the precincts should always watch that the law against begging is well observed.

The Persons Whom the Elders Should Admonish, and Proper Procedure in This Regard

If there shall be anyone who lays down opinions contrary to received doctrine, he is to be summoned. If he recants, he is to be dismissed without prejudice. If he is stubborn, he is to be admonished from time to time until it shall be evident that he deserves greater severity. Then, he is to be excommunicated and this action reported to the magistrate.

If anyone is negligent in attending worship so that a noticeable offense is evident for the communion of the faithful, or if anyone shows himself contemptuous of ecclesiastical discipline, he is to be admonished. If he becomes obedient, he is to be dismissed in love. If he persists, passing from bad to worse, after having been admonished three times, he is to be excommunicated and the matter reported to the authorities. For the correction of faults, it is necessary to proceed after the ordinance of our Lord. That is, vices are to be dealt with secretly and no one is to be brought before the church for accusation if the fault is neither public nor scandalous, unless he has been found rebellious in the matter.

For the rest, those who scorn private admonitions are to be admonished again by the church. If they will not come to reason nor recognize their error, they are to be ordered to abstain from communion until they improve.

As for obvious and public evil, which the church cannot overlook: If the faults merit nothing more than admonition, the duty of the elders shall be to summon those concerned, deal with them in love in order that they may be reformed, and, if they correct the fault, to dismiss the matter. If they persevere, they are to be admonished again. If, in the end, such procedure proves unsuccessful, they are to be denounced as contemptuous of God, and ordered to abstain from communion until it is evident that they have changed their way of life.

As for crimes that merit not only admonition but punitive correction: If any fall into such error, according to the requirements of the case, it will be necessary to command them to abstain from communion so that they humble themselves before God and repent of their error.

If anyone by being contumacious or rebellious attempts that which is forbidden, the duty of the ministers shall be to reject him, since it is not proper that he receive the sacrament.

Nevertheless, let all these measures be moderate; let there not be such a degree of rigor that anyone should be cast down, for all corrections are but medicinal, to bring back sinners to the Lord.

And let all be done in such a manner as to keep from the ministers any civil jurisdiction whatever, so that they use only the spiritual sword of the word of God as St. Paul ordered them. Thus, the consistory may in no wise take from the authority of the officers or of civil justice. On the contrary, the civil power is to be kept intact. Likewise, when it shall be necessary to exercise punishment or restraint against any party, the ministers and the consistory are to hear the party concerned, deal with them, and admonish them as it may seem good, reporting all to the council, which, for its part, shall deliberate and then pass judgment according to the merits of the case.

John Calvin: *Institutes of the Christian Religion.* [1559]

John Calvin was the great theological systematician of the Reformation, and his *Institutes of the Christian Religion*, first published in 1536 and afterward substantially enlarged, remains one of the classical statements of Protestant thought. Written first when its author was only twenty-six, the *Institutes* initially showed Calvin's dependence upon Luther. Subsequent editions, however, increasingly expressed the author's own theological brilliance. Calvin's religion is found within the covers of this book.

Scholars have disagreed about the heart of Calvin's religion. The doctrine of predestination has been most often cited, and even though other doctrines might be mentioned with equal validity there can be little doubt that predestination formed an important aspect of Calvin's thought; a lengthy section in the *Institutes* is devoted to it. Calvin believed that it was a biblical doctrine, and he went to considerable lengths to argue its biblical basis. Equally noteworthy is Calvin's systematic exposition of this topic. Calvin begins his exposition by referring to the empirical reality that not all people have been exposed to the Christian gospel, nor have all those who have accepted it. The setting of Calvin's exposition is also worth noting: Predestination is not discussed in conjunction with the nature of God, as might be expected, but in the context of a description of God's redemptive work in Christ.

The sections reprinted here are from Book III, "The way in which we receive the grace of Christ. What benefits come to us from it, and what effects follow" and from Book IV, "The external means or aids by which God invites us into the society of Christ and holds us therein." (Books I and II deal with the knowledge of God the creator and God the redeemer in Christ.)[21]

LITERATURE

François Wendel, *The Origin and Development of Calvin's Thought.* New York, 1963.

Paul Helm, *John Calvin's Ideas.* Oxford, 2004.

CHAPTER XXI

Eternal Election, by Which God Has Predestined Some to Salvation, Others to Destruction

   (Importance of the doctrine of predestination excludes both presumption and reticence in speaking of it, 1–4)

1. Necessity and beneficial effect of the doctrine of election; danger of curiosity

The covenant of life is not preached equally to all, and among those to whom it is preached, it does not always meet with the same reception. This diversity displays the unsearchable depth of the divine judgment, and is without doubt subordinate to God's purpose of eternal election. But if it is plainly due to the mere pleasure of God that salvation is offered to some, while others have no

---

21. John Calvin, *The Institutes of the Christian Religion.* www.reformed.org/books/institutes.

access to it, many great and difficult questions arise, questions which are inexplicable, when proper views are not entertained concerning election and predestination. To many this seems a perplexing subject, because they deem it most incongruous that of the great throng of humankind, some should be predestined to salvation and others to destruction....

It is plain how much ignorance of this notion detracts from the glory of God and impairs true humility. But though necessary to be known, Paul declares that it cannot be known unless God, throwing works entirely aside, elects those whom he has predestined. His words are: "Even so then at this present time also, there is a remnant according to the election of grace. And if by grace, then no more of works: otherwise grace is no more grace. But if it be of works, then it is no more grace: otherwise work is no more work" [Rom. 11:6]. If to make it appear that our salvation flows entirely from the good mercy of God, we must be carried back to the origin of election, then those who would extinguish it, wickedly do as much as in them lies to obscure what they ought most loudly to extol, and pluck up humility by the very roots. Paul clearly declares that it is only when the salvation of a remnant is ascribed to gratuitous election, we arrive at the knowledge that God saves whom he wills of his mere good pleasure and does not pay a debt, a debt which never can be due. Those who prohibit access, and would not have anyone to obtain a taste of this doctrine, are equally unjust to God and to humankind, for there is no other means of humbling us as we ought, or making us feel how much we are bound to him. Nor, indeed, have we elsewhere any sure ground of confidence. This we say on the authority of Christ, who, to deliver us from all fear and render us invincible amid our many dangers, snares, and mortal conflicts, promises safety to all that the Father has taken under his protection [John 10:26]. From this we infer that all who know not that they are the peculiar people of

God must be wretched from perpetual trepidation, and that those therefore, who, by overlooking the three advantages which we have noted, would destroy the very foundation of our safety, consult ill for themselves and for all the faithful....

But before I discuss the subject, I have some remarks to address to two classes of individuals. The subject of predestination, which in itself is attended with considerable difficulty, is made complicated and dangerous by human curiosity, which cannot be restrained from wandering into forbidden paths and climbing up to the clouds, determined that none of the secret things of God shall remain unexplored. When we see many people, some in other respects not bad individuals, rushing into this audacity and wickedness, it is necessary to remind them of the course of duty in this matter. First, when they inquire about predestination, let them remember that they are penetrating into the recesses of the divine wisdom, where those who rush forward securely and confidently, instead of satisfying their curiosity, will enter into an inextricable labyrinth. For it is not right that humans should with impunity pry into things which the Lord has been pleased to conceal within himself, and scan that sublime eternal wisdom which in his pleasure we should not apprehend but adore so that his perfections may appear. Those secrets of God's will, which he has seen fit to manifest, are revealed in his word—revealed in so far as he knew would be conducive to our interest and welfare.

2. The Doctrine of Predestination sought in Scripture only

"We have come into the way of faith," says Augustine. "Let us constantly adhere to it. It leads to the royal chambers, in which are hidden all the treasures of wisdom and knowledge." For our Lord Jesus Christ did not speak resentfully to his disciples when he said, "I have yet many things to say unto you, but ye cannot bear them now" [John 16:12]. We must walk, advance, increase, that our hearts may be able to comprehend those things which they cannot now comprehend. But if the last day shall find us making progress, we shall there learn what here we could not. If we give due weight to the fact that the word of the Lord is the only way which can lead us to the investigation of whatever it is lawful for us to hold with regard to him—is the only light which can enable us to discern what we ought to see with regard to him; it will curb and restrain all presumption. For it will show us that the moment we go beyond the bounds of the Word we are off course, in darkness, and must stumble, go astray, and fall. Let it, therefore, be our first principle that to desire any other knowledge of predestination than that which is expounded by the Word of God is no less troublesome than to walk where there is no path, or to seek light in darkness. Let us not be ashamed to be ignorant in a matter in which ignorance is learning. Rather, let us abstain from the search of knowledge, to which it is foolish as well as perilous and even fatal to aspire. If an unrestrained imagination urges us, our proper course is to oppose it with these words: "It is not good to eat much honey: so for individuals to search their own glory is not glory" [Prov. 25:27]. There is good reason to fear a presumption which can only plunge us headlong into ruin.

3. The second danger: anxious silence about the doctrine of election

There are others who recommend that the subject of predestination should rarely if ever be mentioned, and tell us to avoid every question concerning it as we would a rock. Although their thinking that such mysteries should be treated with moderation is commendable, yet because they keep too far away, they have little influence over the human mind, which does not readily allow itself to be curbed. Therefore, in order to keep the proper course in this matter, we must return to the Word of God, in which we are furnished with the right rule of understanding. For Scripture is the school of the Holy Spirit, in which nothing useful and necessary has been omitted, so nothing is taught but what it is of importance to know. Everything delivered in Scripture on the subject of predestination we must not keep from the faithful, lest we seem either to deprive them maliciously of the blessing of God or to accuse and scoff at the Spirit, as having divulged what ought to be suppressed. Let us, I say, allow the Christians to unlock their minds and ears to all the words of God which are addressed to them, provided they do it with moderation—that whenever the Lord shuts his sacred mouth, they also desists from inquiry. The best rule of sobriety is not only learning to follow wherever God leads, but also, when he ends his teaching, to cease from wishing to be wise. The danger which they dread is not so great that we ought to turn away our minds from the oracles of God....

4. Alleged peril in the doctrine dismissed

I admit that worldly individuals talk about the subject of predestination to carp, or cavil, or snarl, or scoff. But if their petulance frightens us, it will be necessary to conceal also all main articles of faith, because they and their fellows leave hardly any one of them unassailed with blasphemy. A rebellious spirit will display itself no less insolently when it hears that there are three persons in the divine essence, than when it hears that God when he created man foresaw every thing that was to happen to him. Nor will they abstain from their jeers when told that little more than five thousand years have elapsed since the creation of the world. For they will ask, Why did the power of God slumber so long in idleness? In short, nothing can be stated that they will not assail with derision. To quell their blasphemies, must we say nothing concerning the divinity of the Son and Spirit? Must the creation of the world be passed over in silence? No! The truth of God is too powerful, both here and everywhere, to dread the slanders of the ungodly. For we see that the false apostles were unable, by defaming and accusing the true doctrine of Paul, to make him ashamed. There is nothing in the allegation that the whole subject is fraught with danger to pious minds, as tending to destroy exhortation, shake faith, disturb and dispirit the heart.... Only I wish it to be received as a general rule that the secrets of God are not to be scrutinized, and that those which he has revealed are not to be overlooked, lest we are, on the one hand, charged with curiosity and, on the other, with ingratitude. For it has been shrewdly observed by Augustine that we can safely follow Scripture, which walks softly, as with a mother's step, in accommodation to our weakness. Those, however, who are cautious and timid that they would bury all mention of predestination in order not to trouble weak minds, how will they hide their arrogance, when they charge God with a lack of due consideration in not having foreseen a danger? Whoever, therefore, throws disgrace on the doctrine of predestination, brings a charge against God, as having inconsiderately allowed something to escape from him which is injurious to the church.

5. *Predestination and Foreknowledge of God; Election of Israel*

The predestination by which God adopts some to the hope of life and condemns others to eternal death, no one who would be thought pious will simply deny, but it is greatly complained about, especially by those who focus on foreknowledge. We, indeed, ascribe both foreknowledge and predestination to God, but we say that it is absurd to make the latter subordinate to the former. When we attribute foreknowledge to God, we mean that all things always were, and ever continue, under his eye; that to his knowledge there is no past or future, but all things are present, and indeed so present that it is not merely their idea that is before him (as those objects are which we retain in our memory), but that he truly sees and contemplates them as actually under his immediate inspection. This foreknowledge extends to the whole circuit of the world, and to all creatures.

By predestination we mean the eternal decree of God, by which he determined with himself whatever he wished to happen with regard to every human. All are not created on equal terms, but some are preordained to eternal life, others to eternal damnation; and accordingly, as each has been created for one or other of these ends, we say that he or she has been predestinated to life or to death.

This God has testified not only in the case of single individuals; he has also given an illustration of it in the whole posterity of Abraham, to make it plain that the future state of each nation depends entirely at his determination: "When the Most High divided to the nations their inheritance, when he separated the sons of Adam, he set the bounds of the people according to the number of the children of Israel. For the Lord's portion is his people; Jacob is the lot of his inheritance" [Deut. 32:8, 9]. The separation is before the eyes of all. In Abraham, as in a withered stock, a people is specially chosen while the others are rejected, but the cause does not appear, except that Moses, to deprive posterity of any means for glorying, tells them that their superiority was owing entirely to the free love of God. The cause which he assigns for their deliverance is, "Because he loved thy fathers, therefore he chose their seed after them" [Deut. 4:37].

6. The second stage: election and reprobation of individual Israelites

We must add a second consideration of a more limited nature, or one in which the grace of God was displayed in a more special form. Of the same family of Abraham, God rejected some and by keeping others within his church showed that he retained them among his sons. At first Ishmael had obtained the same rank with his brother Isaac because the spiritual covenant was equally sealed in him by the symbol of circumcision. He is first cut off, then Esau, finally an innumerable multitude, almost the whole of Israel. In Isaac was the seed. The same calling held good in the case of Jacob. God gave a similar example in the rejection of Saul. This is also celebrated in the psalm: "Moreover he refused the tabernacle of Joseph and chose not the tribe of Ephraim, but chose the tribe of Judah" [Ps. 78:67, 68]. . . . I admit that it was by their own fault that Ishmael, Esau, and others fell from their adoption, for the stipulation was that they should faithfully keep the covenant of God, whereas they deceitfully violated it. The singular kindness of God was that he had been pleased to prefer them to other nations, as is said in the psalm: "He has not dealt so with any nation: and as for his judgments, they have not known them" [Ps. 147:20].

But I had good reason for saying that two considerations are here to be observed, for in the election of the whole nation, God had already shown that in the exercise of his mere kindness he was under no law but was free, so that he was not to be restricted to an equal division of grace; its very inequality proved it to be gratuitous. Accordingly, Malachi enlarged on the ingratitude of Israel, which, after having been not only selected from the whole human race but also set apart as a sacred household, they perfidiously and impiously spurn God, their beneficent parent. "Was not Esau Jacob's brother? says the Lord, yet I loved Jacob, and I hated Esau" [Mal. 1:2, 3]. For God takes it for granted that as both were the sons of a holy father and successors of the covenant, branches from a sacred root, the sons of Jacob were under no ordinary obligation to having been admitted to that dignity. When by the rejection of the firstborn Esau, their progenitor though inferior in birth, was made heir, God charges them with double ingratitude.

7. *The election of individuals as actual election*

Although it is sufficiently plain that God by his secret counsel chooses whom he wills while he rejects others, his gratuitous election has only been partially explained until we come to the case of single individuals, to whom God not only offers salvation but so assigns it that the certainty of the result remains not dubious or suspended. These are considered as belonging to that one seed of which Paul makes mention [Rom. 9:8; Gal. 3:16]. For although adoption was deposited in the hand of Abraham, yet as many of his posterity were cut off as rotten members; in order that election may stand and be effectual, it is necessary to ascend to the head in whom the heavenly Father has connected his elect with each other, and bound them to himself by an indissoluble tie. Thus in the adoption of the family of Abraham, God gave them a liberal display of favor which he has denied to others; but in the members of Christ there is a far more excellent display of grace because those engrafted into him as their head never fail to obtain salvation. Hence Paul skillfully argues from the passage of Malachi which I quoted [Rom. 9:13; Mal. 1:2] that when God, after making a covenant of eternal life, invites any people to himself, a special mode of election is in part understood, so that he does not with promiscuous grace effectually elect all of them....

The reason why the general election of individuals is not always firmly ratified, readily presents itself: that on those with whom God makes the covenant, he does not immediately bestow the spirit of regeneration, by whose power they persevere in the covenant even to the end. The external invitation, without the internal efficacy of grace which would have the effect of retaining them, holds a kind of middle place between the rejection of the human race and the election of a small number of believers.... But until the proper view is made clear by Scripture, I advise my readers not to prejudge the question.

We say, then, that Scripture clearly proves that God by his eternal and immutable counsel determined once for all those whom it was his pleasure one day to admit to salvation and those whom, on the other hand, it was his pleasure to doom to destruction. We maintain that this counsel, as regards the elect, is founded on his free mercy, without any respect to human worth, while those whom he dooms to destruction are excluded from access to life by a just and blameless, but at the same time incomprehensible, judgment. In regard to the elect, we regard calling as the evidence of election, and justification as another symbol of its manifestation, until it is fully accomplished by the attainment of glory. But as the Lord seals his elect by calling and justification, so by excluding the reprobate either from the knowledge of his name or the sanctification of his Spirit, he by these marks in a manner discloses the judgment which awaits them. I will here omit many of the fictions which foolish individuals have devised to overthrow predestination. There is no need of refuting objections which the moment they are produced abundantly betray their hollowness. I will dwell only on those points which either form the subject of dispute among the learned, or may occasion any difficulty to the simple, or may be employed by impiety as specious pretexts for assailing the justice of God. . . .

CHAPTER XXII

This doctrine confirmed by scriptural testimony.

1. *Election vs. foreknowledge of merits*

Many oppose all the positions which we have laid down, especially the gratuitous election of believers, which, however, cannot be overthrown. For they commonly imagine that God distinguishes between individuals according to the merits which he foresees that each individual will have, giving the adoption of sons and daughters to those whom he foreknows will not be unworthy of his grace and dooming those to destruction whose dispositions he perceives will be prone to mischief and wickedness. Thus by introducing foreknowledge as a veil, they not only obscure election but give it a different origin. Nor is this the common opinion only of the unlearned, for it has had great supporters in all ages. This I openly confess, lest any one should expect greatly to prejudice our cause by opposing it with their names. The truth of God is too certain to be shaken, too clear to be overborne by human authority.

Others who are neither versed in Scripture, nor entitled to any approbation, assail sound doctrine with a petulance and improbity which it is impossible to tolerate. Because God of his good pleasure electing some passes by others, they raise a plea against him. But if the fact is certain, what can they gain by quarreling with God? We teach nothing but what experience proves to be true: that God has always been at liberty to bestow his grace on whom he would. Not to ask in what respect the posterity of Abraham excelled others if it be not in a worth, the cause of which has no existence out of God, let them tell why individuals are better than oxen or asses. God might have made them dogs when he formed them in his own image. Will they allow the lower animals to expostulate with God, as if the inferiority of their condition were unjust? It is certainly not more equitable that individuals should enjoy the privilege which they have not acquired by any merit, than that he should variously distribute favors as seems to him meet. If they pass to the case of individuals where inequality is more offensive to them, they ought at least, in regard to the example of our savior, to be restrained by feelings of awe from talking so confidently of this sublime mystery. He is conceived a mortal human of the seed of David; what, I would ask them, are the virtues by which he deserved to become in the very womb, the head of angels the only begotten Son of God, the image and glory of the Father, the light, righteousness, and salvation of the world?.... When Paul declares that we were chosen in Christ before the foundation of the world [Eph. 1:4], he shows that no regard is had to our own worth; for it is just as if he had said that because in the whole seed of Adam our heavenly Father found nothing worthy of his election, he turned his eye upon his own anointed that he might select as members of his body those whom he was to receive into the fellowship of life....

3. Wherever this good pleasure of God reigns, no good works are taken into account. The apostle, indeed, does not follow the antithesis, as he himself explains it in another passage, "Who has called us with a holy calling, not according to our works but according to his own purpose and grace, which was given us in Christ Jesus before the world began" [1 Tim. 2:9]. We have already shown that the additional words, "that we might be holy," remove every doubt. If you say that he foresaw that they would be holy, and therefore elected them, you invert Paul's order. You may, therefore, safely infer that if he elected us that we might be holy; he did not elect us because he foresaw that we would be holy. The two things are evidently inconsistent: that the pious owe it to election that they are holy and yet attain election by means of works. There is no force in the quibble to which they are ever recurring that the Lord does not bestow election in recompense of past but in consideration of future merits. For when it is said that believers were elected that they might be holy, it is at the same time intimated that the holiness which was to be in them has its origin in election. And how can it be consistently said that things derived from election are the cause of election?

4. Romans, chapters 9–11

In the Letter to the Romans [Rom. 9:6], in which he treats this subject more reconditely and at greater length, Paul declares that "they are not all Israel which are of Israel," for though all were blessed in respect of hereditary rights, yet all did not equally obtain the succession. The whole discussion was occasioned by the pride and vain-glorying of the Jews, who, by claiming the name of the church for themselves, would have made the faith of the gospel dependent on their pleasure, just as in the present day the papists would substitute themselves in place of God under this pretext. Paul, while he concedes that with respect to the covenant they were the holy offspring of Abraham, yet contends that most of them were strangers to it, and that not only because they were degenerate, and had become bastards instead of sons, but because the principal point was the special election of God, by which alone his adoption was ratified. If the piety of some established them in the hope of salvation and the revolt of others was the sole cause of their being rejected, it would have been foolish and absurd for Paul to carry his readers back to a secret election. But if the will of God (no cause of which external to him either appears or is to be looked for) distinguishes some from others, so that all the sons of Israel are not true Israelites, it is pointless for any one to seek the origin of his condition in himself.

Paul afterwards discusses the subject at greater length, by contrasting Jacob and Esau. Both were sons of Abraham; both had been in the womb of their mother. There was something strange in the turn by which the honor of birthright was transferred to Jacob, and yet Paul declares that the change was a testimony to the election of the one and the reprobation of the other.

The question to be considered is the origin and cause of election. The advocates of foreknowledge insist that it is to be found in the virtues and vices of individuals. For they take the short and easy method of asserting that God showed in Jacob that he elects those who are worthy of his grace, and in Esau that he rejects those whom he foresees to be unworthy. Such is their confident assertion, but what does Paul say? "For the children being not yet born, neither having done any good or evil that the purpose of God according to election might stand, not of works, but of him that calleth; it was said unto her [Rebecca], The elder shall serve the younger. As it is written, Jacob have I loved, but Esau have I hated" [Rom. 9:11–13]. If foreknowledge had anything to do with this distinction of the brothers, the mention of time would have been out of place. Granted that Jacob was elected in view of future virtues, to what end did Paul say that he was not yet born? Nor would there have been any occasion for adding, since as yet he had done no good, because the answer was always ready that nothing is hid from God, and that therefore the piety of Jacob was present before him. If works lead to favor, a value ought to have been put upon them before Jacob was born, just as if he had been of ripe age....

7. *Christ's witness concerning election*

Now let the supreme judge and master decide on the whole matter. Seeing such obduracy in his hearers that his words fell upon the multitude almost without fruit, to remove this stumbling-block he exclaims, "All that the Father gives me shall come to me." And this is the Father's will which has sent me that of all which he has given me I should lose nothing" [John 6:37, 39]. Observe that the Father's donation is the first step in our delivery into the charge and protection of Christ. Some one, perhaps, will object that those only peculiarly belong to the Father who make a voluntary surrender by faith. But the only thing which Christ maintains is that though the defections of vast multitudes should shake the world, yet the counsel of God will stand firm, more stable than heaven itself; his election will never fail. The elect are said to have belonged to the Father before he bestowed them on his only begotten Son. It is asked if they were his by nature? Nay, they were aliens, but he makes them his own. The words of Christ are too clear to be rendered obscure by any of the mists of caviling. "No one can come to me except the Father which has sent me draw him." "Everyone, therefore, who has heard and learned of the Father comes unto me" [John 6:44, 45]. Did all promiscuously bend the knee to Christ, election would be common; whereas now in the small number of believers a manifest diversity appears. Accordingly our Savior, shortly after declaring that the disciples who were given to him were the common property of the Father, adds, "I pray not for the world, but for them which you hast given me; for they are thine" [John 17:9]. Hence it is that the whole world no longer belongs to its Creator, except insofar as grace rescues from malediction, divine wrath, and eternal death some, not many, who would otherwise perish, while he leaves the world to the destruction to which it is doomed. Meanwhile, though Christ interpose as a Mediator, yet he claims the right of election in common with the Father, "I speak not of you all: I know whom I have chosen" [John 13:18]. If it is asked whence he has chosen them, he answers in another passage, "Out of the world"—which he excludes from his prayers when he commits his disciples to the Father [John 15:19]. We must believe, indeed hold, when he affirms that he knows whom he has chosen, first that some individuals of the human race are denoted, and secondly that they are not distinguished by the quality of their virtues, but by a heavenly decree....

10. The universality of God's invitation and particularity of election

Some object that God would be inconsistent in inviting all without distinction while he elects only a few. According to them, the universality of the promise destroys the distinction of special grace. Some moderate individuals speak this way, not so much for the purpose of suppressing the truth as to get rid of puzzling questions and curb excessive curiosity. The intention is laudable, but the design is not to be approved, dissimulation being at no time excusable. The mode in which Scripture reconciles the two things—that through preaching all are called to faith and repentance, and that yet the spirit of faith and repentance is not given to all—I have already explained. But their point I reject as false in two respects: for he who threatens that when it shall rain on one city there will be drought in another [Amos 4:7], and declares in another passage that there will be a famine of the word [Amos 8:11], does not lay himself under a fixed obligation to call all equally. And he who, forbidding Paul to preach in Asian and leading him away from Bithynia, carries him over to Macedonia [Acts 16:6], shows that it belongs to him to distribute the treasure in what way he pleases....

But it is said, there is a mutual agreement between faith and the word. That must be wherever there is faith. But it is no new thing for the seed to fall among thorns or in stony places—not only because the majority of people appear to be rebellious against God but because all are not gifted with eyes and ears. How, then, can it consistently be said that God calls while he knows that the called will not come?...Moreover, if election is, as Paul declares, the parent of faith, I retort the argument, and maintain that faith is not general since election is special. For it is easily inferred from the series of causes and effects, when Paul says that the father "has blessed us with all spiritual blessings in heavenly places in Christ, according as he has chosen us in him before the foundation of the world" [Eph. 1:3, 4] that these riches are not common to all, because God has chosen only whom he would. And the reason why in another passage he commends the faith of the elect is to prevent anyone from supposing that they acquire faith of their own, since to God alone belongs the glory of freely illuminating those whom he had previously chosen [Tit. 1:1]....And, indeed, faith is aptly conjoined with election, provided it holds the second place. This order is clearly expressed by our Savior in these words: "This is the Father's will which has sent me that of all which he has given me I should lose nothing"; "And this is the will of him that sent me that everyone which sees the Son, and believes in him, may have everlasting life" [John 6:39, 40]. If he would have all to be saved, he would appoint his Son their guardian, and would engraft them all into his body by the sacred bond of faith....

CHAPTER XXIII

Refutation of the Accusations With Which This Doctrine Is Always Unjustly Assailed

1. Election, but no reprobation?

The human mind, when it hears this doctrine, cannot restrain its petulance, but boils and rages as if aroused by the sound of a trumpet. Many professing a desire to defend the deity from an invidious charge admit the doctrine of election but deny that any one is reprobated. This they do ignorantly and childishly since there could be no election without its opposite reprobation. God is said to set apart those whom he adopts for salvation. It were most absurd to say that he admits others fortuitously or that they by their efforts acquire what election alone confers on a few. Those, therefore, whom God passes by he reprobates, and that for no other cause but because he is pleased to exclude them from the inheritance which he predestines to his children. Nor is it possible to tolerate the petulance of individuals in refusing to be restrained by the Word of God in regard to his incomprehensible counsel, which even angels adore. We have already been told that hardening is no less under the immediate hand of God than mercy. Paul does not, after the example of those whom I have mentioned, labor anxiously to defend God, by calling in the aid of falsehood; he only reminds us that it is unlawful for the creature to quarrel with its Creator. Then how will those who refuse to admit that any are reprobated by God explain the following words of Christ? "Every plant which my heavenly Father has not planted shall be rooted up" [Mt. 15:13]. They are plainly told that all whom the heavenly Father has not been pleased to plant as sacred trees in his garden are doomed and committed to destruction. If they deny that this is a sign of reprobation, there is nothing, however clear that can be proved to them. If they will still murmur, let us in the soberness of faith rest contented with Paul's admonition that God, "willing to show his wrath and to make his power known, endured with much long suffering the vessels of wrath fitted for destruction: and that he might make known the riches of his glory on the vessels of mercy, which he had store prepared unto glory" [Rom. 9:22, 23].

Let my readers observe that Paul, to cut off all cause for murmuring and detraction, attributes supreme sovereignty to the wrath and power of God, for it were unjust that those profound judgments, which transcend our powers of discernment, should be subjected to our understanding. It is frivolous for our opponents to reply that God does not completely reject those whom he tolerates but remains in suspense with regard to them, if perhaps they may repent; as if Paul were representing God as patiently waiting for the conversion of those whom he describes as fitted for destruction.... They add also that it is not without cause the vessels of wrath are said to be fitted for destruction, and that God is said to have prepared the vessels of mercy, because in this way the praise of salvation is claimed for God, whereas the blame of perdition is thrown upon those who of their own accord bring it upon themselves.... Hence it follows that the hidden counsel of God is the cause of hardening. I hold with Augustine that when God makes sheep out of wolves, he forms them again by the powerful influence of grace that their hardness may thus be subdued, and that he does not convert the obstinate because he does not exert that more powerful grace, a grace which he has at command, if he were disposed to use it .

2. God's will is the rule of righteousness

These observations would be sufficient for the pious and modest and those who remember that they are human. But because many are the species of blasphemy which these virulent dogs utter against God, we shall give an answer to each. Foolish individuals raise many reasons of quarrel with God, as if they held him subject to their accusations. First they ask why God is offended by his creatures who have not provoked him with any previous offense, for to devote to destruction whomever he pleases resembles more the caprice of a tyrant than the sentence of a judge; therefore, there is reason to expostulate with God, if at his mere pleasure individuals are, without any desert of their own, predestined to eternal death. If at any time thoughts of this kind come to the pious, they will be sufficiently armed to repress them, by considering how sinful it is to insist on knowing the causes of the divine will, since it is itself, and justly ought to be, the cause of all that exists. For if his will has any cause, there must be something antecedent to it, and to which it is annexed; this would be impious to imagine. The will of God is the supreme rule of righteousness so that everything which he wills must be held to be righteous by the mere fact of his willing it. Therefore, when it is asked why the Lord did so, we must answer, because he pleased. But if you proceed further to ask why he pleased, you ask for something greater and more sublime than the will of God, and nothing will be found.

Let human temerity be quiet and cease to inquire after what exists not, lest it fails to find what does exist. This will be sufficient to restrain any one who would reverently contemplate the secret things of God. Against the audacity of the wicked who hesitate to blaspheme openly, God will sufficiently defend himself by his own righteousness, without our assistance, when depriving their consciences of all means of evasion, he shall hold them under conviction, and make them feel their guilt.

We, however, do not advocate the fiction of absolute power, which, as it is heathenish, so it ought justly to be held in detestation by us. We do not imagine God to be lawless. He is a law to himself because, as Plato says, individuals laboring under the influence of concupiscence need law; but the will of God is not only free from all vice but is the supreme standard of perfection, the law of all laws. But we deny that he is bound to give an account of his procedure, and we moreover deny that we are fit of our own ability to give judgment in such a case....

3. God is just toward the reprobate

God may thus quell his enemies by silence. But lest we should allow them to hold his sacred name in derision with impunity, he supplies us with weapons from his Word. Accordingly, when we are accosted in such terms as these, why did God from the first predestine some to death when, as they were not yet in existence, they could not have merited sentence of death? Let us by way of reply ask in our turn, what do you imagine that God owes to humans, if he is pleased to evaluate them by his own nature? As we are all vitiated by sin, we cannot but be hateful to God, and that not from tyrannical cruelty but the strictest justice. But if all whom the Lord predestines to death are naturally liable to be sentenced to death, of what injustice do they complain?

Should all the sons of Adam come to dispute and contend with their Creator because by his eternal providence they were before their birth doomed to perpetual destruction; when God comes to reckon with them, what will they be able to mutter against this defense? If all are taken from a corrupt mass, it is not strange that all are subject to condemnation. Let them not, therefore, charge God with injustice, if by his eternal judgment they are doomed to a death to which they themselves feel that whether they will or not they are drawn spontaneously by their own nature. Hence it appears how perverse is this murmuring when they suppress the cause of condemnation which they are compelled to recognize in themselves that they may lay the blame upon God. But though I should confess a hundred times that God is the author (and it is most certain that he is), they do not, however, thereby efface their own guilt, which, engraven on their own consciences, is ever and anon presenting itself to their view.

4. God's decree also hidden in his justice

They again object: were not individuals predestined by the ordination of God to that corruption which is now held to be the cause of condemnation? If so, when they perish in their corruptions, they do nothing else than suffer punishment for that calamity, into which, by the predestination of God, Adam fell and dragged all his posterity headlong with him. Is not he, therefore, unjust in thus cruelly mocking his creatures? I admit that by the will of God all the sons and daughters of Adam fell into that state of wretchedness in which they still find themselves; and this is just what I said at the outset that we must always return to the pleasure of the divine will, the cause of which is hidden in Himself. But it does not follow that God is guilty of this charge.... They will deny that the justice of God is truly defended, and will allege that we seek an evasion, such as those are wont to employ who have no good excuse. For what more seems to be said here than just that the power of God is such as cannot be hindered, so that he can do whatsoever he pleases? But it is far otherwise. For what stronger reason can be given than when we are ordered to reflect who God is? How could he who is the Judge of the world commit any unrighteousness? If it properly belongs to the nature of God to do judgment, he must naturally love justice and abhor injustice. Wherefore, the apostle did not, as if he had been caught in a difficulty, have recourse to evasion; he inferred that divine justice is too high to be scanned by human measure or comprehended by the feebleness of human intellect. The apostle, indeed, confesses that in the divine judgments there is a depth in which all the minds of individuals must be engulfed if they attempt to penetrate it. But he also shows how unbecoming it is to reduce the works of God to such a law as that we can presume to condemn them the moment they accord not with our reason....

5. God's hidden decree is not to be searched but obediently accepted

I say with Paul that no account of it can be given because by its magnitude it far surpasses our understanding. Is there any thing strange or absurd in this? Would we limit the power of God so as to be unable to do more than our mind can comprehend? Why he willed it is not ours to ask, as we cannot comprehend, nor can it become us even to raise a controversy as to the justice of the divine will. Whenever we speak of it, we are speaking of the supreme standard of justice. But when justice appears, why should we raise any question of injustice? Let us not, therefore, be ashamed to stop their mouths after the example of Paul. Whenever they presume to carp, let us repeat: Who are ye, miserable people that bring an accusation against God, and bring it because he does not adapt the greatness of his works to your meager capacity? As if everything must be perverse that is hidden from the flesh. The immensity of the divine judgment is known to you by experience. You know that they are called "a great deep" [Ps. 36:6]. Now, look at the narrowness of your minds and say whether they can comprehend the decrees of God. Why then should you, by infatuated inquisitiveness, plunge yourselves into an abyss which reason itself tells you will prove your destruction? Why are you not deterred, in some degree at least, by what the Book of Job, as well as the prophetic books, declares about the incomprehensible wisdom and dreadful power of God? ...

6. Second objection: The doctrine of election takes guilt and responsibility from individuals

Impiety causes another objection, which, however, seeks not so much to incriminate God as to excuse the sinner, though he who is condemned by God as a sinner cannot ultimately be acquitted without impugning the judge. This, then, is the scoffing language which profane tongues employ. Why should God blame individuals for things the necessity of which he has imposed by his own predestination? What could they do? Could they struggle with his decrees? It were in vain for them to do it since they could not possibly succeed. It is not just, therefore, to punish them for things the principal cause of which is in the predestination of God. Here I will abstain from a defense to which ecclesiastical writers usually recur that there is nothing in the foreknowledge of God to prevent him from regarding humans as sinners, since the evils which he foresees are those of humans, not his. This would not stop the quibblers, who would still insist that God might, if he had pleased, have prevented the evils which he foresaw, and not having done so, must with determined counsel have created humans for the very purpose of so acting on the earth. But if by the providence of God, humans were created on the condition of afterwards doing whatever they do, then that which they cannot escape, and which they are constrained by the will of God to do, cannot be charged upon them as a crime.

Let us see what is the proper method of solving the difficulty.

First all must admit what Solomon says, "The Lord has made all things for himself; yea, even the wicked for the day of evil" [Prov. 16:4]. Now, since the arrangement of all things is in the hand of God, since to him belongs the disposal of life and death, he arranges all things by his sovereign counsel, in such a way that individuals are born, doomed from the womb to certain death, to glorify him by their destruction. If anyone alleges that no necessity is laid upon them by the providence of God, but rather that they are created by him in that condition because he foresaw their future depravity, something, but not enough, is said. Ancient writers, indeed, occasionally employ this solution, though with hesitation. The scholastic theologians rest in it as if it could not be rejected. I, for my part, am willing to admit that mere foreknowledge lays no necessity on the creatures; though some do not assent to this, but hold that it is itself the cause of things. But [Lorenzo] Valla, otherwise not greatly skilled in sacred matters, seems to me to have taken a shrewder and more acute view, when he shows that the dispute is superfluous since life and death are acts of the divine will rather than of foreknowledge. If God merely foresaw human events, and did not also arrange and dispose of them at his pleasure, there might be room for agitating the question, how far his foreknowledge amounts to necessity; but since he foresees the things which are to happen, simply because he has decreed that they are so to happen, it is vain to debate about foreknowledge, while it is clear that all events take place by his sovereign appointment.

7. *God also predestined the fall into sin*

They deny that it is ever said in distinct terms, God decreed that Adam should perish by his revolt. As if the same God, who is declared in Scripture to do whatsoever he pleases, could have made the noblest of his creatures without any special purpose. They say that, in accordance with free-will, he was to be the architect of his own fortune, that God had decreed nothing but to treat him according to his desert. If this fiction is accepted, where will be the omnipotence of God, by which, according to his secret counsel on which everything depends, he rules over all? But whether they will allow it or not, predestination is manifest in Adam's posterity. It was not due to nature that they all lost salvation by the fault of one parent. Why should they refuse to admit with regard to one individual that which against their will they admit with regard to the whole human race? Why should they in caviling lose their labor? Scripture proclaims that all were, in the person of one, made liable to eternal death. As this cannot be ascribed to nature, it is plain that it the result of the wonderful counsel of God. It is absurd in these worthy defenders of the justice of God to strain at a gnat and swallow a camel.

I again ask how it is that the fall of Adam involves so many nations with their infant children in eternal death without remedy unless that it so seemed meet to God? Here the most loquacious tongues must be silent. The decree, I admit, is, dreadful, and yet it is impossible to deny that God foreknew what the end of man was to be before he made him, and foreknew because he had so ordained by his decree. Should any one inveigh against the foreknowledge of God, they do it rashly and unadvisedly. For why should it be made a charge against the heavenly Judge that he was not ignorant of what was to happen? Thus, if there is any just or plausible complaint, it must be directed against predestination. Nor ought it to seem absurd when I say that God not only foresaw the fall of the first human, and the ruin of his posterity, but also at his own pleasure arranged it. For as it belongs to his wisdom to foreknow all future events, so it belongs to his power to rule and govern them by his hand. This question, like others, is skillfully explained by Augustine: "Let us confess with the greatest benefit what we believe with the greatest truth that the God and Lord of all things who made all things very good, both foreknow that evil was to arise out of good, and knew that it belonged to his most omnipotent goodness to bring good out of evil, rather than not permit evil to be, and so ordained the life of angels and individuals as to show in it, first, what free will could do, and, secondly, what the benefit of his grace and his righteous judgment could do."

8. No distinction between God's will and God's permission!

Here they recur to the distinction between will and permission, the object being to prove that the wicked perish only by the permission but not by the will of God. But why do we say that he permits, but just because he wills? Nor, indeed, is there any probability in the thing itself—viz. that all brought death upon themselves merely by the permission, and not by the ordination of God; as if God had not determined what he wished the condition of the chief of his creatures to be. I will not hesitate, therefore, simply to confess with Augustine that the will of God is necessity, and that everything is necessary which he has willed, just as those things will certainly happen which he has foreseen. Now if in excuse of themselves and the ungodly, either the Pelagians, or Manichees, or Anabaptists, or Epicureans (for it is with these four sects we have to discuss this matter), should object to the necessity by which they are constrained, in consequence of divine predestination, they do nothing that is relevant to the cause. For if predestination is nothing else than a dispensation of divine justice, secret indeed but unblamable, because it is certain that those predestinated to that condition were not unworthy of it, it is equally certain that the destruction consequent upon predestination is also most just. Moreover, though their perdition depends on the predestination of God, the cause and matter of it is in themselves. The first human fell because the Lord deemed that he should: why he so deemed it, we do not know. It is certain, however, that it was just, because he saw that his own glory would thereby be displayed.

When you hear the glory of God mentioned, understand that it includes his justice. For that which deserves praise must be just. Humans fall, divine providence so ordaining, but they fall by their own fault. The Lord had declared that all the things which he had made were very good [Gen. 1:31]. Whence then human depravity, which made Adam revolt against God? Lest it should be supposed that it was from his creation, God expressly approved what proceeded from himself. Therefore, human wickedness corrupted the pure nature which they had received from God, and their ruin brought with it the destruction of all his posterity. Wherefore, let us in the corruption of human nature contemplate the evident cause of condemnation (a cause which comes more closely home to us), rather than inquire into a cause hidden and almost incomprehensible in the predestination of God. Nor let us refuse to submit our judgment to the boundless wisdom of God, so far as to confess its insufficiency to comprehend many of his secrets. Ignorance of things which we are not able, or which it is not lawful to know, is learning, while the desire to know them is a species of madness.

9. *Summary refutation of the second objection*

Someone, perhaps, will say that I have not yet stated enough to refute this blasphemous excuse. I confess that it is impossible to prevent impiety from murmuring and objecting; but I think I have said enough not only to remove the reason but also the pretext for casting blame upon God. The reprobate would excuse their sins by alleging that they are unable to escape the necessity of sinning, especially because a necessity of this nature is laid upon them by the ordination of God. We deny that they can be validly excused, since the ordination of God, by which they complain that they are doomed to destruction, is consistent with equity, an equity, indeed, unknown to us, but most certain. We conclude that every evil which they bear is inflicted by the most just judgment of God. We have shown that they act preposterously when, in seeking the origin of their condemnation, they turn their view to the hidden recesses of the divine counsel and wink at the corruption of nature, which is the true source. They cannot impute this corruption to God, because he bears testimony to the goodness of his creation. For though, by the eternal providence of God, humans were was formed for the calamity under which they lie, they took the matter of it from themselves, not from God, since the only cause of his destruction was his degenerating from the purity of his creation into a state of vice and impurity.

10. Third objection: doctrine of election leads to the view that God shows partiality

There is a third absurdity by which the adversaries of predestination defame it. As we ascribe predestination entirely to the counsel of the divine will that those whom God adopts as the heirs of his kingdom are exempted from universal destruction, they infer that he is an acceptor of persons; but Scripture uniformly denies this: therefore Scripture is either at variance with itself or there is merit involved in election. First, the sense in which Scripture declares that God is not an acceptor of persons is different from that which they suppose: since the term *person* means not *man*, but those things which, when conspicuous in humans, either produce favor, grace, and dignity, or, on the contrary, produce hatred, contempt, and disgrace. Among these are, on the one hand, riches, wealth, power, rank, office, country, beauty, etc.; and, on the other hand, poverty, want, mean birth, sordidness, contempt, and the like. Thus Peter and Paul say that the Lord is no acceptor of persons because he makes no distinction between the Jew and the Greek; does not make the mere circumstance of country the ground for rejecting one or embracing the other [Acts 10:34; Rom. 2:10, Gal. 3:28]. Thus James also uses the same words when he would declare that God has no respect to riches in his judgment [James 2:5]. Paul also says in another passage that God has no judgment about slavery or freedom [Eph. 6:9; Col. 3:25]. There is nothing inconsistent with this when we say that God, according to the good pleasure of his will, without any regard to merit, elects those whom he chooses for sons and daughters, while he rejects and reprobates others.

It is asked how it happens that of two, between whom there is no difference of merit, God in his election adopts the one and passes by the other? I, in turn, ask, Is there anything in him who is adopted to incline God towards him? If it must be confessed that there is nothing, it will follow that God looks not to the individual but is influenced by his own goodness to do him good. Therefore, when God elects one and rejects another, it is owing not to any respect to the individual but entirely to his own mercy which is free to display and exert itself when and where he pleases....

11. *God's mercy and righteousness in predestination*

Wherefore, it is false and most wicked to charge God with dispensing justice unequally because in this predestination he does not observe the same course towards all. If (say they) he finds all guilty, let him punish all alike: if he finds them innocent, let him relieve all from the severity of judgment. But they plead with God as if he were either prohibited from showing mercy, or were obliged, if he showed mercy, to renounce his judgment. What is it that they demand? That if all are guilty all shall receive the same punishment. We admit that the guilt is common, but we say that God in mercy accepts some. Let him (they say) accept all. We object that it is right for him to show by punishing that he is a just judge. When they cannot tolerate this, what else are they attempting than to deprive God of the power of showing mercy, or, at least, to allow it to him only on the condition of renouncing his judgment?

Here the words of Augustine most admirably apply: "Since in the first human the whole human race fell under condemnation, those vessels which are made of it unto honor, are not vessels of self-righteousness, but of divine mercy. When other vessels are made unto dishonor, it must be imputed not to injustice but to judgment." Since God inflicts due punishment on those whom he reprobates, and bestows unmerited favor on those whom he calls, he is free from every accusation; just as it belongs to the creditor to forgive the debt to one, and exact it of another. The Lord, therefore, may show favor to whom he will, because he is merciful; not show it to all, because he is a just judge. In giving to some what they do not merit, he shows his free favor; in not giving to all, he declares what all deserve. For when Paul says, "God has concluded them all in unbelief that he might have mercy upon all," it ought also to be added that he is debtor to none; for "who has first given to him and it shall be recompensed unto him again?" [Rom. 11:32, 33].

12. *Fourth objection: the doctrine of election destroys all zeal for an upright life*

Another argument which they employ to overthrow predestination is that if it stands, all care and study of well doing must cease. For what humans can hear (say they) that life and death are fixed by an eternal and immutable decree of God, without immediately concluding that it is of no consequence how one acts, since no work can either hinder or further the predestination of God? Thus all will rush and like desperate individuals plunge headlong wherever lust inclines. It is true that this is not altogether a fiction, for there are multitudes of a swinish nature who defile the doctrine of predestination by their profane blasphemies and employ them as a cloak to evade all admonition and censure. God knows what he has determined to do with regard to us: if he has decreed our salvation, he will bring us to it in his own time; if he has doomed us to death, it is vain for us to fight against it.

But Scripture, while it enjoins us to think of this high mystery with great reverence and religion, gives very different instruction to the pious, and justly condemns the accursed license of the ungodly. For it does not remind us of predestination to increase our audacity, and tempt us to pry with impious presumption into the inscrutable counsels of God, but rather to humble and abase us that we may tremble at his judgment, and learn to look up to his mercy. This is the mark at which believers will aim. The grunt of these filthy swine is duly silenced by Paul. They say that they feel secure in vices because, if they are of the number of the elect, their vices will be no obstacle to the ultimate attainment of life. But Paul reminds us that the end for which we are elected is, "that we should be holy, and without blame before him" [Eph. 1:4]. If the end of election is holiness of life, it ought to arouse and stimulate us strenuously to aspire to it, instead of serving as a pretext for sloth.

CHAPTER XII

Of the Disciple of the Church, and Its Principal Use in Censure and Excommunication.

(Discussion of power of the keys in true discipline: the ends and processes of discipline.)

1. Necessity and nature of church discipline

The discipline of the church, the consideration of which has been deferred until now, must be briefly explained that we may be able to pass on to other matters. Discipline depends in great measure on the power of the keys and on spiritual jurisdiction. That this may be more easily understood let us divide the church into two principal classes viz., clergy and people. The term *clergy* is the common designation for those who perform a public ministry in the church. We shall speak first of the common discipline to which all ought to be subject and then proceed to the clergy, who have in addition to that common discipline one peculiar to themselves.

If no society, nay, no house with even a moderate family can be kept in a right state without discipline, much more necessary is it in the church, whose state ought to be the best ordered possible. As the saving doctrine of Christ is the life of the church, so discipline is, as it were, its sinews; for the members of the body must adhere together, each in its own place. Wherefore, all who either wish that discipline were abolished, or who impede its restoration, whether they do this by design or by thoughtlessness, certainly aim at the complete devastation of the church. For what will be the result if everyone is allowed to do as he or she pleases? But this must happen if to the preaching of the gospel are not added private admonition, correction, and similar methods of maintaining doctrine, not allowing preaching to become lethargic. Discipline, therefore, is a kind of curb to restrain and tame those who war against the doctrine of Christ, or it is a kind of stimulus by which the indifferent are aroused; sometimes, also, it is a kind of fatherly rod, by which those who have made some more grievous lapse are chastised in mercy with the meekness of the spirit of Christ. Since, then, we already see some beginnings of a fearful devastation in the church from a want of care and method in managing the people, necessity itself cries aloud that there is need of a remedy. Now the only remedy is this which Christ enjoins, and the pious have always had in use.

2. *Stages of church discipline*

The first foundation of discipline is to provide for private admonition; that is, if anyone does not do his duty spontaneously, or behaves insolently, or lives not quite honestly, or commits something worthy of blame, he or she must allow themselves to be admonished; and everyone must study to admonish the brother when the case requires. Here especially is the occasion for the vigilance of pastors and elders [presbyters], whose duty is not only to preach to the people, but to exhort and admonish from house to house.... Then doctrine obtains force and authority, not only when the minister publicly expounds to all what they owe to Christ, but has the right and means of exacting this from those whom he may observe to be sluggish or disobedient to his doctrine.

Should anyone either perversely reject such admonitions, or by persisting in his faults show that he condemns them, the injunction of Christ is that after he or she has been a second time admonished before witnesses, they are to be summoned to the bar of the church, which is the consistory of elders, and there admonished more sharply, as by public authority that if they revere the church they submit and obey [Mt. 18:15, 17]. If in this way they are not subdued but persist in their iniquity, they are then, as despisers of the church, to be debarred from the society of believers.

3. *Concealed and open sins*

But as our savior is not speaking of secret faults merely, we must attend to the distinction that some sins are private, others public or openly manifest. Of the former, Christ says to every private individual, "Go and tell him his fault between you and him alone" [Mt. 18:15]. Of open sins Paul says to Timothy, "Those that sin rebuke before all that others also may fear" [1 Tim. 5:20]. Our savior had previously said, "If your brother shall trespass against you." This clause, unless you would be captious, cannot be understood otherwise than, if this happens in a manner known to yourself, others not being privy to it. The injunction which Paul gave to Timothy to rebuke those openly who sin openly, he himself followed with Peter [Gal. 2: 14]. For when Peter sinned so as to give public offense, he did not admonish him individually but brought him forward in the church.

The legitimate course, therefore, will be to proceed in correcting secret faults by the steps mentioned by Christ, and in open sins, accompanied with public scandal, to proceed at once to solemn correction by the church.

4. Light and grave sins

Another distinction to be attended to is that some sins are mere delinquencies, others crimes and flagrant iniquities. In correcting the latter, it is necessary to employ not only admonition or rebuke but a sharper remedy, as Paul shows when he not only verbally rebukes the incestuous Corinthian but punishes him with excommunication as soon as he was informed of his crime [1 Cor. 5: 3f.]. Now we begin better to perceive how the spiritual jurisdiction of the church, which treats sins according to the Word of the Lord, is at once the best help to sound doctrine, the best foundation of order, and the best bond of unity. Therefore, when the church banishes from its fellowship open adulterers, fornicators, thieves, robbers, the seditious, the perjured, false witnesses, and others of that description, likewise the contumacious, who, when duly admonished for lighter faults, hold God and his tribunal in derision . . . it exercises a jurisdiction which it has received from the Lord. Moreover, lest any one should despise the judgment of the church, or count it a small matter to be condemned by the suffrages of the faithful, the Lord has declared that it is nothing else than the promulgation of his own sentence, and that that which they do on earth is ratified in heaven. For they act by the Word of the Lord in condemning the perverse and by the Word of the Lord in taking the penitent back into favor [John 20: 23]. Those, I say, who trust that churches can long stand without this bond of discipline are mistaken, unless indeed we can with impunity do without help which the Lord foresaw would be necessary. And, indeed the greatness of the necessity will be better perceived by its manifold uses.

5. The purpose of church discipline

There are three ends to which the church has respect in thus correcting and excommunicating. The first is that God may not be insulted by the name of Christian being given to those who lead shameful and flagitious lives, as if his holy church were a combination of the wicked and abandoned. For seeing that the church is the body of Christ, it cannot be defiled by such fetid and putrid members without bringing some disgrace on her head. Therefore that there may be nothing in the church to bring disgrace on his sacred name, those whose turpitude might throw infamy on the name must be expelled from his family. And here, also, regard must be had to the Lord's Supper, which might be profaned by a promiscuous admission. For it is most true that he who is entrusted with the dispensation of it, if he knowingly and willingly admits any unworthy person whom he ought and is able to repel, is as guilty of sacrilege as if he had cast the Lord's body to dogs.... Therefore, lest this most sacred mystery should be exposed to ignominy, great selection is required in dispensing it, and this cannot be except by the jurisdiction of the Church.

A second goal of discipline is that the good may not, as usually happens, be corrupted by constant communication with the wicked. For such is our proneness to go astray that nothing is easier than to seduce us from the right course by bad example. To this use of discipline the apostle referred when he commanded the Corinthians to discard the incestuous individuals from their society. "A little leaven leavens the whole lump" [1 Cor. 5: 6]. And he foresaw so much danger here that he prohibited them from keeping company with such persons: "If any individual that is called a brother be a fornicator, or covetous, or an idolater, or a railer, or a drunkard, or an extortioner; with such a one, no not to eat" [1 Cor. 5: 11].

A third goal of discipline is that sinners may be ashamed and begin to repent of their turpitude. Hence it is for their interest that their iniquity should be chastised that whereas they would have become more obstinate by indulgence, they may be aroused by the rod. This the apostle intimates when he writes "If any individual obey not our word by this epistle, note those individuals, and have no company with them that they may be ashamed," [2 Thess. 3: 14]....

6. The handling of church discipline in the various cases

These being the ends, it remains to see in what way the church is to execute this part of discipline, which consists in jurisdiction.

First, let us remember the distinctions laid down above that some sins are public, others private or secret. Public are those which are done not before one or two witnesses, but openly and to the offense of the whole church. By secret, I mean not such as are altogether concealed from individuals, such as those of hypocrites (for these fall not under the judgment of the church), but those of an intermediate description, which are not without witnesses and yet are not public.

The former category requires not the different steps which Christ enumerates; but whenever anything of this kind occurs, the church ought to do her duty by summoning the offenders, and correcting them according to their fault.

In the second category, the matter comes not before the church unless there is contumacy, according to the rule of Christ. In taking cognizance of offenses, it is necessary to attend to the distinction between delinquencies and flagrant iniquities. In lighter offenses, there is not so much occasion for severity, but verbal chastisement is sufficient, gentle and fatherly, so as not to exasperate or confound the offenders but to bring them back to themselves, so that they may rather rejoice than be grieved at the correction. Flagrant iniquities require a sharper remedy. It is not sufficient verbally to rebuke those who, by some open act of evil example, have grievously offended the church; but they ought for a time to be denied the communion of the Supper until they give proof of repentance. Paul does not merely administer a verbal rebuke to the Corinthian but discards him from the Church and reprimands the Corinthians for having borne with him so long [1 Cor. 5: 1–7].

This was the method observed by the ancient and purer church, when legitimate government was vigorous. When anyone was guilty of some flagrant iniquity, and thereby caused scandal, he or she was first ordered to abstain from participation in the sacred Supper, and thereafter to humble themselves before God, and testify their penitence before the church. There were, moreover, solemn rites which, as indications of repentance, were prescribed to those who had lapsed. When the penitent had thus made satisfaction to the Church, he was received into favor by the laying on of hands. This admission often receives the name of peace from Cyprian....

7. *In the ancient church, discipline to all offenders alike*

So far was anyone from being exempted from this discipline that even rulers submitted to it in common with their subjects— and justly, since it is the discipline of Christ, to whom all scepters and diadems should be subject. Thus Theodosius, when excommunicated by Ambrose because of the slaughter perpetrated at Thessalonica, laid aside all the royal insignia with which he was surrounded and publicly in the church bewailed the sin into which he had been betrayed by the fraud of others, with groans and tears imploring pardon. Great kings should not think it a disgrace to them to prostrate themselves suppliantly before Christ, the King of kings; nor ought they to be displeased at being judged by the church. For seeing they seldom hear anything in their courts but mere flattery, the more necessary is it that the Lord should correct them by the mouth of his priests. Nay, they ought rather to wish the priests not to spare them, in order that the Lord may spare.

I here say nothing as to those by whom the jurisdiction ought to be exercised. I only add that the legitimate course to be taken in excommunication, as shown by Paul, is not for the elders alone to act apart from others, but with the knowledge and approbation of the church, so that the body of the people, without regulating the procedure, may, as witnesses and guardians, observe it and prevent the few from doing any thing capriciously. Throughout the whole procedure, in addition to the invocation of the name of God, there should be a gravity bespeaking the presence of Christ, and leaving no room to doubt that he is presiding over his own tribunal.

8. Severity and mildness in church discipline

It ought not, however, to be omitted that the church, in exercising severity, ought to accompany it with the spirit of meekness. For, as Paul enjoins, we must always take care that he on whom discipline is exercised be not "swallowed up with overmuch sorrow" [2 Cor. 2: 7] for in this way, instead of cure, there would be destruction. The rule of moderation will be best obtained from the end contemplated. For the object of excommunication being to bring the sinner to repentance and remove bad examples, in order that the name of Christ may not be evil spoken of, nor others tempted to the same evil courses: if we consider this, we shall easily understand how far severity should be carried, and at what point it ought to cease. Therefore, when the sinner gives the Church evidence of his repentance, and by this evidence does what in him lies to obliterate the offence, he ought not on any account to be urged farther. If he is urged, the rigor now exceeds due measure.

In this respect, it is impossible to excuse the excessive austerity of the ancients, which was altogether at variance with the injunction of our Lord and strangely perilous. For when they enjoined a formal repentance and excluded from communion for three, or four, or seven years, or for life, what could the result be but either great hypocrisy or very great despair? In like manner, when anyone who had again lapsed was not admitted to a second repentance but ejected from the church to the end of his life, this was neither useful nor agreeable to reason. Whosoever, therefore, looks at the matter with sound judgment, will here regret a want of prudence....

9. *The limits of our judgment according to church discipline*

But as the whole body of the church is required to act thus mildly, and not to carry its rigor against those who have lapsed to an extreme, but rather to act charitably towards them, according to the precept of Paul, so every private individual ought proportionately to accommodate himself to this clemency and humanity [2 Cor. 2:8]. Such as have, therefore, been expelled from the church, it belongs not to us to expunge from the number of the elect, or to despair of, as if they were already lost. We may lawfully judge them aliens from the church and so aliens from Christ, but only during the time of their excommunication. If then, also, they give greater evidence of petulance than of humility, still let us commit them to the judgment of the Lord, hoping better of them in future than we see at present and not ceasing to pray to God for them. Let us not consign to destruction their person, which is in the hands of, and subject to the decision of, the Lord alone; but let us estimate the character of each individual's acts according to the law of the Lord. In following this rule, we abide by the divine judgment rather than give any judgment of our own. Let us not arrogate to ourselves greater liberty in judging, if we would not limit the power of God, and give the law to his mercy. Whenever it seems good to Him, the worst are changed into the best; aliens are engrafted, and strangers are adopted into the church. This the Lord does that he may disappoint the thoughts of individuals, and confound their rashness; a rashness which, if not curbed, would usurp a power of judging to which it has no title.

10. Excommunication is corrective

When our Savior promises that what his servants bind on earth should be bound in heaven [Mt. 18:18], he confines the power of binding to the censure of the Church, which does not consign those who are excommunicated to perpetual ruin and damnation, but assures them, when they hear their life and manners condemned, that perpetual damnation will follow if they do not repent. Excommunication differs from anathema in this that the latter, completely excluding pardon, dooms and devotes the individual to eternal destruction, whereas the former rather rebukes and animadverts upon his manners; and although it also punishes, it is to bring him to salvation by forewarning him of his future doom. If it succeeds, reconciliation and restoration to communion are ready to be given. Moreover, anathema is rarely if ever to be used. Hence, though ecclesiastical discipline does not allow us to be on familiar and intimate terms with excommunicated persons, still we ought to strive by all possible means to bring them to a better mind and recover them to the fellowship and unity of the church: as the apostle also says, "Yet count him not as an enemy but admonish him as a brother" [2 Thess. 3:15]. If this humanity be not observed in private as well as public, the danger is that our discipline shall degenerate into destruction.

11. *Against willful excess in demanding church discipline*

Another special requisite to moderation of discipline is as Augustine discourses against the Donatists that private individuals must not, when they see vices less carefully corrected by the Council of Elders, immediately separate themselves from the Church; nor must pastors themselves, when unable to reform all things which need correction to the extent which they could wish, cast up their ministry or by unwonted severity throw the whole Church into confusion. What Augustine says is perfectly true: "Whoever corrects what he can, by rebuking it, or without violating the bond of peace, excludes what he cannot correct, or justly condemns while he patiently tolerates what he is unable to exclude without violating the bond of peace, is free and exempted from the curse."

Philip Mornay: *A Defence of Liberty Against Tyrants.* [1579]

C alvin's thought underwent a variety of changes as it spread throughout Europe and was expounded by his disciples. Perhaps Calvin himself would not have found acceptance among the Calvinists of a later time. The excerpts below come from a document of French Calvinism of the second half of the sixteenth century; while reminiscent of Calvin's writings, this document is distinctly different. France was then embroiled in bitter wars of religion. In a way these wars were a contest between rival factions or nobility, with the crown almost a bystander. Then, with the Massacre of St. Bartholomew in 1571, the crown became dramatically involved. This led the French Calvinists to reexamine their attitude toward governmental authority and the monarchy.

Philip Mornay, the probable author of the *Vindiciae contra Tyrannos*, or *A Defence of Liberty Against Tyrants*, was one of the most prominent of the Calvinist "monarchomachists," who on legal as well as biblical grounds repudiated the notion of an absolute monarchy. A sovereign who violated the laws of the land had to be opposed—an important political theory which a century later exerted considerable influence upon the rise of the notion of representative government.

A Defence of Liberty Against Tyrants was published in 1579, though it had been written some five years earlier under the impact of the Massacre of St. Bartholomew. Originally written in Latin, a French edition came out in 1581 and an English edition, interestingly enough, in 1689, the year of the Glorious Revolution. Of the four questions dealt with in the book, reprinted here are a section from the second question ("Whether it be lawful to resist a Prince which does infringe the law of God or ruined the church, by whom and how, and how far is it lawful?") and all of the third.[22]

LITERATURE

G. L. Hunt, ed., *Calvinism and the Political Order.* Philadelphia, 1965.

Glenn S. Sunshine, *Reforming French Protestantism:The Development of Huguenot Ecclesiastical Institutions, 1557–1572.* Kirksville, MO, 2003.

Hans J. Hillerbrand, ed., *Oxford Encyclopedia of the Reformation.* New York, 1996.

Whether it be lawful to take arms for religion

Furthermore, to take away all scruple, we must necessarily answer those who esteem, or else would that others should think they hold that opinion, that the church ought not to be defended by arms. They say withal that it was not without a great mystery that God did forbid in the law, that the altar should be made or adorned with the help of any tool of iron; in like manner, that at the building of the temple of Solomon, there was not heard any noise of axe or hammer, or other tools of iron; from whence they collect the church, which is the lively temple of the Lord, ought not to be re-

---

22. H. J. Laski, ed., *A Defence of Liberty Against Tyrants. A Translation of the Vindiciae contra Tyrannos.* Gloucester, MA, 1963, pp. 113 ff.

formed by arms; yea, as if the stones of the altar and of the temple were hewed and taken out of the quarries without any instrument of iron, which the text of the holy Scripture doth make sufficiently clear.

But if we oppose to this goodly allegory, that which is written in the fourth chapter of the Book of Nehemiah, that one part of the people carried mortar, and another part stood ready with their weapons, that some held in one hand their swords, and with the other carried the materials to the workmen, for the rebuilding of the temple; to the end, by this means, to prevent their enemies from ruining their work; we say also, that the church is neither advanced nor edified by these material weapons; but by these arms it is warranted and preserved from the violence of the enemies, which will not by any means endure the increase of it. Briefly, there has been an infinite number of good kings and princes (as histories do testify) which by arms have maintained and defended the service of God against pagans. They reply readily to this, that wars in this manner were allowable under the law; but since the time that grace has been offered by Jesus Christ, who would not enter into Jerusalem mounted on a brave horse, but meekly sitting on an ass, this manner of proceeding has had an end. I answer first, that all agree with me in this, that our Savior Christ, during all the time that He conversed in this world, took not on Him the office of a judge or king, but rather of a private person, and a delinquent by imputation of our transgressions, so that it is an allegation beside the purpose, to which I say that He hath not managed arms.

But I would willingly demand of such exceptionalists, if they think by the coming of Jesus Christ in the flesh, that magistrates have lost their right in the sword of authority? If they say so, Saint Paul contradicts them, who says that the magistrates carry not the sword in vain, and did not refuse their assistance and power against the violence of those who had conspired his death. And if they consent to the saying of the Apostle, to what purpose should the magistrates bear the sword, if it be not to serve God, who has committed it to them, to defend the good and punish the bad? Can they do better service than to preserve the church from the violence of the wicked, and to deliver the flock of Christ from the swords of murderers? I would demand of them, yet, whether they think that all use of arms is forbidden to Christians? If this be their opinion, then would I know of them, wherefore Christ did grant to the centurion his request? Wherefore did He give so excellent a testimony of him? Wherefore does St. John Baptist command the men at arms to content themselves with their pay, and not to use any extortion, and does not rather persuade them to leave their calling? Wherefore did St. Peter baptize Cornelius the Centurion, who was the first fruits of the Gentiles? Whence does it come that he did not in any sort whatsoever counsel him to leave his charge? Now, if to bear arms and to make war be a thing lawful, can there possibly be found any war more just than that which is taken in hand by the command of the superior, for the defense of the church, and the preservation of the faithful? Is there any greater tyranny than that which is exercised over the soul? Can there be imagined a war more commendable than that which suppresses such a tyranny? For the last point, I would willingly know of these men, whether it be absolutely prohibited Christians to make war upon any occasion whatsoever? If they say that it is forbidden them, from whence comes it then that the men at arms, captains and centurions, who had no other employment, but the managing of arms, were always received into the church? Wherefore do the ancient Fathers and Christian historians make so horrible mention of certain legions composed wholly of Christian soldiers, and amongst others of that of Malta, so renowned for the victory which they obtained, and of that of Thebes, of the which St. Mauritius was general, who suffered martyrdom, together with all his troops, for the confessing of the name of Jesus Christ? And if it be permitted to make war (as it may be they will confess) to keep the limits and towns of a country, and to repulse an invading enemy, is it not yet a thing much more reasonable to take arms to preserve and defend honest men, to suppress the wicked, and to keep and defend the limits and bounds of the church, which is the kingdom of Jesus Christ? If it were otherwise, to what purpose should St. John have foretold that the whore of Babylon shall be finally ruined by the ten kings, whom she has bewitched? Furthermore, if we hold a contrary opinion, what shall we say of the wars of Constantine, against Maxentius, and Licimius, celebrated by so many public orations, and approved by the testimony of an infinite number of learned men? What opinion should we hold of the many voyages made by Christian princes against the Turks and Saracens to conquer the Holy Land, who had not, or at the least, ought not to have had, any other end in their designs, but to hinder the enemy from ruining the temple of the land, and to restore the integrity of His service into those countries?

Although then the church be not increased by arms, notwithstanding it may be justly preserved by the means of arms. I say further, that those that die in so holy a war are no less the martyrs of Jesus Christ than their brethren who were put to death for religion; nay, they who die in that war seem to have this disadvantage, that with a free will and knowing sufficiently hazard, into which they cast themselves, notwithstanding, do courageously expose their lives to death and danger, whereas the other do only not refuse death, when it behooves them to suffer. The Turks strive to advance their opinion by the means of arms, and if they do subdue a country, they presently bring in by force the impieties of Mohammad, who in his Koran, has so recommended arms, as they are not ashamed to say it is the ready way to heaven, yet the Turks constrain no man in matter of conscience. But he who is a much greater adversary to Christ and true religion, with all those kings whom he has enchanted, opposes fire and faggots, to the light of the gospel, tortures the word of God, compelling by wracking and torments, as much as in him lies, all men to become idolaters, and finally is not ashamed to advance and maintain their faith and law by perfidious disloyalty, and their traditions by continual treasons.

Now on the contrary, those good princes and magistrates are said properly to defend themselves, who environ and fortify by all their means and industry the vine of Christ already planted, to be planted in places where it has not yet been, lest the wild boar of the forest should spoil or devour it. They do this (I say) in covering with their buckler, and defending with their sword, those who by the preaching of the gospel have been converted to true religion, and in fortifying with their best ability, by ravelins, ditches, and ramps, the temple of God built with lively stones, until it has attained the full height, in despite of all the furious assaults of the enemies thereof. We have lengthened out this discourse thus far, to the end we might take away all scruple concerning this question. Set, then, the estates, and all the officers of a kingdom, or the greatest part of them, every one established in authority by the people: know, that if they contain not within his bounds (or at the least, employ not the utmost of their endeavors thereto) a king who seeks to corrupt the law of God; or hinders the reestablishment thereof, that they offend grievously against the Lord, with whom they have contracted covenants upon those conditions. Those of a town, or of a province, making a portion of a kingdom, let them know also, that they draw upon themselves the judgment of God if they drive not impiety out of their walls and confines if the king seek to bring it in, or if they be wanting to preserve by all means, the pure doctrine of the gospel, although for the defense thereof, they suffer for a time banishment, or any other misery.

Finally, more private men must be all advertised, that nothing can excuse them, if they obey any in that which offends God, and that yet they have no right nor warrant, neither may in any sort by their private authority take arms, if it appear not most evidently, that they have extraordinary vocation thereunto, all which our discourse will suppose we have confirmed by pregnant testimonies drawn from holy writ.

The Third Question

Whether it be lawful to resist a prince who doth oppress or ruin a public state, and how far such resistance may be extended: by whom, how, and by what right or law it is permitted

For so much as we must here dispute of the lawful authority of a lawful prince, I am confident that this question will be the less acceptable to tyrants and wicked princes; for it is no marvel if those who receive no law, but what their own will and fancy dictate unto them, be deaf unto the voice of that law which is grounded upon reason. But I persuade myself that good princes will willingly entertain this discourse, insomuch as they sufficiently know that all magistrates, be they of never so high a rank, are but an inanimate law. Neither though anything be pressed home against the bad, can it fall with any inference against the good kings or princes, as also good and bad princes are in a direct diameter opposite and contrary: therefore, that which shall be urged against tyrants, is so far from detracting anything from kings, as on the contrary, the more tyrants are laid open in their proper colors, the more glorious does the true worth and dignity of kings appear; neither can the vicious imperfections of the one be laid open, but it gives addition of perfections and respect to the honor of the other.

But for tyrants let them say and think what they please, that shall be the least of my care; for it is not to them, but against them that I write; for kings I believe that they will readily consent to that which is propounded, for by true proportion of reason they ought as much to hate tyrants and wicked governors, as shepherds hate wolves, physicians, poisoners, true prophets, false doctors; for it must necessarily occur that reason infuses into good kings as much hatred against tyrants, as nature imprints dogs against wolves, for as the one lives by rapine and spoil, so the other is born or bred to redress and prevent all such outrages. It may be the flatterers of tyrants will cast a supercilious aspect on these lines; but if they were not past all grace they would rather blush for shame. I very well know that the friends and faithful servants of kings will not only approve and lovingly entertain this discourse, but also, with their best abilities, defend the contents thereof. Accordingly as the reader shall find himself moved either with content or dislike in the reading hereof, let him know that by that he shall plainly discover either the affection or hatred that he bears to tyrants. Let us now enter into the matter.

Kings are made by the people

We have shown before that it is God who does appoint kings, who chooses them, who gives the kingdom to them: now we say that the people establish kings, put the scepter into their hands, and who with their suffrages, approves the election. God would have it done in this manner, to the end that the kings should acknowledge; that after God they hold their power and sovereignty from the people, and that it might the rather induce them, to apply and address the utmost of their care and thoughts for the profit of the people, without being puffed with any vain imagination, that they were formed of any matter more excellent than other men, for which they were raised so high above others; as if they were to command our flocks of sheep, or herds of cattle. But let them remember and know, that they are of the same mold and condition as others, raised from the earth by the voice and acclamations, now as it were upon the shoulders of the people unto their thrones, that they might afterward bear on their own shoulders the greatest burdens of the commonwealth. Diverse ages before that, the people of Israel demanded a king. God gave and appointed the law of royal government contained in the seventeenth chapter, verse fourteen of Deuteronomy, when, says Moses, "Thou art come unto the land which the Lord thy God gives thee, and shall possess it, and shall dwell therein, and shall say, I will set a king over me like as all the nations that are about me, thou shall in anywise set him whom the Lord thy God shall choose from amongst thy brethren, etc." You see here that the election of the king is attributed to God, the establishment to the people: now when the practice of this law came in use, see in what manner they proceeded.

The elders of Israel, who presented the whole body of the people (under this name of elders are comprehended the captains, the centurions, commanders over fifties and tens, judges, provosts, but principally the chiefs of tribes), came to meet Samuel in Ramah, and not being willing longer to endure the government of the sons of Samuel, whose ill carriage had justly drawn on them the people's dislike, and withal persuading themselves that they had found the means to make their wars hereafter with more advantage, they demanded a king of Samuel, who asking counsel of the Lord, he made known that He had chosen Saul for the governor of His people...

And for David, by the commandment of God, and in a manner more evident than the former, after the rejection of Saul, Samuel anointed for king over Israel, David, chosen by the Lord, which being done, the Spirit of the Lord presently left Saul, and wrought in a special manner in David. But David, notwithstanding, reigns not, but was compelled to save himself in deserts and rocks, oftentimes falling upon the very brim of destruction, and never reigned as king until after the death of Saul: for then by the suffrages of all the people of Judah he was first chosen king of Judah; and seven years after by the consent of all Israel, he was inaugurated king of Israel in Hebron. So, then, he is anointed first by the prophet at the commandment of God, as a token he was chosen. Secondly, by the commandment of the people when he was established king. And that to the end that kings may always remember that it is from God, but by the people, and for the people's sake that they do reign, and that in their glory they say not (as is their custom) they hold their kingdom only of God and their sword, but withal add that it was the people who first girt them with that sword. The same order offered in Solomon. Although he was the king's son, God had chosen Solomon to sit upon the throne of his kingdom, and by express words had promised David to be with him and assist him as a father his son. David had with his own mouth designed Solomon to be successor to his crown in the presence of some of the principal of his court.

But this was not enough, and therefore David assembled at Jerusalem the princes of Israel, the heads of the tribes, the captains of the soldiers, and ordinance officers of the kings, the centurions and other magistrates of towns, together with his sons, the noblemen and worthiest personages of the kingdom, to consult and resolve upon the election. In this assembly, after they had called upon the name of God, Solomon, by the consent of the whole congregation, was proclaimed and anointed for king, and sat (so says the text) upon the throne of Israel; then, and not before, the princes, the noblemen, his brothers themselves do him homage, and take the oath of allegiance. And to the end, that it may not be said that that was only done to avoid occasion of difference, which might arise amongst the brothers and sons of David about the succession, we read that the other following kings have, in the same manner, been established in their places. It is said, that after the death of Solomon, the people assembled to create his son Rehoboam king. After that Amaziah was killed, Ozias, his only son, was chosen king by all the people, Ochosias after Joram, Joachim, the son of Josias, after the decease of his father, whose piety might well seem to require that without any other solemnity, notwithstanding, both he and the other were chosen and invested into the royal throne, by the suffrages of the people…

It may be collected from this, that the kingdom of Israel was not hereditary, if we consider David and the promise made to him, and that it was wholly elective, if we regard the particular persons. But to what purpose is this, but to make it apparent that, the election is only mentioned, that the kings might have always in their remembrance that they were raised to their dignities by the people, and therefore they should never forget during life in what a strict bond of observance they are tied to those from whom they have received all their greatness. We read that the kings of the heathen have been established also by the people; for as when they had either troubles at home, or wars abroad, someone, in whose ready valor and discreet integrity the people did principally rely and repose their greatest confidence, him they presently, with a universal consent, constituted king…

Briefly, for so much as none were ever born with crowns on their heads, and scepters in their hands, and that no man can be a king by himself, nor reign without people, whereas on the contrary, the people may subsist of themselves, and were, long before they had any kings, it must of necessity follow that kings were at the first constituted by the people; and although the sons and dependents of such kings, inheriting their fathers' virtues, may in a sort seem to have rendered their kingdoms hereditary to their offspring, and that in some kingdoms and countries, the right of free election seems in a sort buried; yet, notwithstanding, in all well-ordered kingdoms, this custom is yet remaining. The sons do not succeed the fathers, before the people have first, as it were, anew established them by their new approbation: neither were they acknowledged in quality, as inheriting it from the dead; but approved and accounted kings then only, when they were invested with the kingdom, by receiving the scepter and diadem from the hands of those who represent the majesty of the people. One may see most evident marks of this in Christian kingdoms, which are at this day esteemed hereditary; for the French king, he of Spain and England, and others, are commonly sacred, and, as it were, put into possession of their authority by the peers, lords of the kingdom, and officers of the crown, who represent the body of the people; no more nor less than the emperors of Germany are chosen by the electors, and the kings of Poland, by the yawodes and palatines of the kingdom, where the right of election is yet in force...

To conclude in a word, all kings at the first were altogether elected, and those who at this day seem to have their crowns and royal authority by inheritance have or should have first and principally their confirmation from the people. Briefly, although the people of some countries have been accustomed to choose their kings of such a lineage, which for some notable merits have worthily deserved it, yet we must believe that they choose the stock itself, and not every branch that proceeds from it; neither are they so tied to that election, as if the successor degenerate, they may not choose another more worthy, neither those who come and are the next of that stock, are born kings, but created such, nor called kings, but princes of the blood royal.

The whole body of the people is above the king

Now, seeing that the people choose and establish their kings, it follows that the whole body of the people is above the king; for it is a thing most evident, that he who is established by another, is accounted under him who has established him, and he who receives his authority from another, is less than he from whom he derives his power. Potiphar the Egyptian sets Joseph over his entire house; Nebuchadnezzar, Daniel over the province of Babylon; Darius the six score governors over the kingdom. It is commonly said that masters establish their servants, kings their officers. In like manner, also, the people establish the king as administrator of the commonwealth. Good kings have not disdained this title; yea, the bad ones themselves have affected it; insomuch, as for the space of diverse ages no Roman emperor (if it were not some absolute tyrant, as Nero, Domitian, Caligula) would suffer himself to be called lord. Furthermore, it must necessarily be that kings were instituted for the people's sake, neither can it be, that for the pleasure of some hundreds of men, and without doubt more foolish and worse than many of the other, all the rest were made, but much rather that these hundred were made for the use and service of all the other, and reason requires that he be preferred above the other, who was made only to and for his occasion. So it is, that for the ship's sail, the owner appoints a pilot over her, who sits at the helm, and looks that she keep her course, nor run not upon any dangerous shelf; the pilot doing his duty, is obeyed by the mariners; yea, and of himself who is owner of the vessel, notwithstanding, the pilot is a servant as well as the least in the ship, from whom he only differs in this, that he serves in a better place than they do.

In a commonwealth, commonly compared to a ship, the king holds the place of pilot, the people in general are owners of the vessel, obeying the pilot, while he is careful of the public good; as though this pilot neither is nor ought to be esteemed other than servant to the public; as a judge or general in war differs little from other officers, but that he is bound to bear greater burdens, and expose himself to more dangers. By the same reason also which the king gains with arms, be it that he possesses himself of frontier places in warring on the enemy, or that which he gets by escheats or confiscations, he gets it to the kingdom, and not to himself, to wit, to the people, of whom the kingdom is composed, no more nor less than the servant does for his master; neither may one contract or oblige themselves to him, but by and with reference to the authority derived from the people. Furthermore, there is an infinite sort of people who live without a king, but we cannot imagine a king without people. And those who have been raised to the royal dignity were not advanced because they excelled other men in beauty and comeliness, nor in some excellence of nature to govern them as shepherds do their flocks, but rather being made out of the same mass with the rest of the people, they should acknowledge that for them, they, as it were, borrow their power and authority.

The ancient custom of the French represents that exceeding well, for they used to lift up on a buckler, and salute him king whom they had chosen. And wherefore is it said, I pray you, that kings have an infinite number of eyes, a million of ears, with extreme long hands, and feet exceeding swift? Is it because they are like to Argos, Gerien, Midas, and diverse others so celebrated by the poets? No, truly, but it is said in regard of all the people, whom the business principally concerns, who lend to the king for the good of the commonwealth, their eyes, their ears, their means, their faculties. Let the people forsake the king, he presently falls to the ground, although before, his hearing and sight seemed most excellent, and that he was strong and in the best disposition that might be; yea, that he seemed to triumph in all magnificence, yet in an instant he will become most vile and contemptible: to be brief, instead of those divine honors herewith all men adore him, he shall be compelled to be a pedant, and whip children in the school at Corinth. Take away but the basis to this giant, and like the Colossus of Rhodes, he presently tumbles on the ground and falls into pieces. Seeing then that the king is established in this degree by the people, and for their sake, and that he cannot subsist without them, who can think it strange, then, for us to conclude that the people are above the king?

Now that which we speak of all the people universally, ought also to be understood, as has been delivered in the second question, of those who in every kingdom or town do lawfully represent the body of the people, and who ordinarily (or at least should be) called the officers of the kingdom, or of the crown, and not of the king; for the officers of the king, it is he who places and displaces them at his pleasure, yea, after his death they have no more power, and are accounted as dead. On the contrary, the officers of the kingdom receive their authority from the people in the general assembly of the states (or, at the least were accustomed so anciently to have done) and cannot be unauthorized but by them, so then the one depends of the king, the other of the kingdom, those of the sovereign officer of the kingdom, who is the king himself, those of the sovereignty itself, that is of the people, of which sovereignty, both the king and all his officers of the kingdom ought to depend, the charge of the one has proper relation to the care of the king's person; that of the other, to look that the commonwealth receive no damage; the first ought to serve and assist the king, as all domestic servants are bound to do to their masters; the other to preserve the rights and privileges of the people, and to carefully hinder the prince, that he neither omit other things that may advantage the state, nor commit anything that may endamage the public.

Briefly, the one are servants and domestics of the king, and received into their places to obey his person; the other, on the contrary, are as associates to the king, in the administration of justice, participating of the royal power and authority, being bound to the utmost of their power to be assisting in the managing of the affairs of state, as well as the king, who is, as it were, president among them, and principal only in order and degree.

Therefore, as all the whole people is above the king, and likewise taken in one entire body, are in authority before him, yet being considered one by one, they are all of them under the king. It is easy to know how far the power of the first kings extended... It was then the custom to refer the most important affairs to be dispensed and resolved in the general assemblies of the people. This might easily be practiced in those kingdoms, which were then almost confined within the circuit of one town.

But since the kings began to extend their limits, and that it was impossible for the people to assemble together all into one place because of their great numbers, which would have occasioned confusion, the officers of the kingdom were established, who should ordinarily preserve the rights of the people, in such sort notwithstanding, as when extraordinary occasion required, the people might be assembled, or at the least such an abridgment as might by the most principal members be a representation of the whole body. We see this order established in the kingdom of Israel, which (in the judgment of the wisest politicians) was excellently ordered. The king had his cupbearers, his carvers, his chamberlains and stewards. The kingdom had her officers, to wit, the seventy-one elders, and the heads and chief chosen out of all the tribes, who had the care of the public faith in peace and war.

Furthermore, the kingdom had in every town magistrates, who had the particular government of them, as the former were for the whole kingdom. At such times as affairs of consequence were to be treated of, they assembled together, but nothing that concerned the public state could receive any solid determination. David assembled the officers of his kingdom when he desired to invest his son Solomon with the royal dignity; when he would have examined and approved that manner of policy, and managing of affairs, that he had revived and restored and when there was no question of removing the ark of the covenant...

We read in another place that Zedechias held in such reverence the authority of this council that he was so far from delivering of Jeremy from the dungeon, whereunto the seventy-one had cast him, that he dare scarce remove him into a less rigorous prison. They persuading him to give his consent to the putting to death the prophet Jeremy, he answered that he was in their hands and that he might not oppose them in anything. The same king, fearing lest they might make information against him, to bring him to an account for certain speeches he had used to the prophet Jeremy, was glad to feign an untrue excuse. It appears by this, that in the kingdom of Judah this council was above the king, in this kingdom, I say, not fashioned or established by Plato or Aristotle but by the Lord God Himself, being author of all their order, and supreme moderator in that monarchy. Such were the seven magi or sages in the Persian empire, who had almost a paralleled dignity with the king, and were termed the ears and eyes of the king, who also never dissented from the judgment of those sages...

In the times of the emperors, there was the senate, the consuls, the praetors, the great provosts of the empire, the governors of provinces, attributed to the senate and the people, all which were called the magistrates and officers of the people of Rome....Now for the empires and public states of these times (except those of Turkey, Muscovy, and such like, which are rather a rhapsody of robbers, and barbarous intruders, than any lawful empires), there is not one, which is not, or hath not heretofore been governed in the manner we have described. And if through the convenience and sloth of the principal officers, the successors have found the business in a worse condition, those who have for the present the public authority in their hands, are notwithstanding bound as much as in them lies to reduce things into their primary estate and condition.

In the empire of Germany, which is conferred by election,

there are the electors and the princes, both secular and ecclesiastical, the counts, barons, and deputies of the imperial cities, and as all these in their proper places are solicitors for the public good, likewise in the Diets do they represent the majesty of the empire, being obliged to advise, and carefully foresee, that, neither by the emperor's partiality, hate nor affection, the public state do suffer or be interested. And for this reason, the empire has its chancellor, as well as the emperor his, both the one and the other have their peculiar officers and treasurers. And it is a thing so notorious, that the empire is preferred before the emperor, that it is a common saying, "That emperor does homage to the empire."...

The kingdom of France heretofore preferred before all other, both in regard of the excellence of their laws and majesty of their estate, may pass with most as a ruling case. Now, although those who have the public commands in their hands do not discharge their duties as were to be desired, it follows not that they are not bound to do it. The king has his high steward of his household, his chamberlains, his masters of his games, cupbearers, and others, whose offices were wont so to depend on the person of the king: after that the death of their master, their offices were void. And indeed at the funeral of the king, the lord high steward in the presence of all the officers and servants of the household, breaks his staff of office, and says, "Our master is dead, let everyone provide for himself." On the other side the kingdom has her officers, to wit, the mayor of the palace, who since has been called the constable, the marshals, the admiral, the chancellor, the secretaries, the treasurers, and others, who heretofore were created in the assembly of the three estates, the clergy, the nobility, and the people.

Since that the Parliament of Paris was made sedentary, they are not thought to be established in their places before they have been first received and approved by that course of Parliament, and may not be dismissed nor disposed, but by the authority and consent of the same. Now all these officers take their oath to the kingdom, which is as much as to say, to the people in the first place, then to the king who is protector of the kingdom, which appears by the tenure of the oath. Above all, the constable, who, receiving the sword from the king, has it girded unto him with this charge, that he maintain and defend the commonwealth, as appears by the words that the king then pronounces.

Besides, the kingdom of France has the peers (so-called either for that they are the king's companions, or because they are the fathers of the commonwealth) taking their denominations from the several provinces of the kingdom, in whose hands the king at his inauguration takes his oath as if all the people of the kingdom were in them present, which shows that these twelve peers are above the king. They on the other side swear, "That they will preserve not the king, but the crown, that they will assist the commonwealth with their counsel, and therefore will be present with their best abilities to counsel the prince both in peace and war," as appears plainly in the patentee of their peership...

Therefore, it is that yet at this day the Parliament of Paris is called the court of peers, being in some sort constituted judge between the king and the people; yea, between the king and every private person, and is bound and ought to maintain the meanest in the kingdom against the king's attorney, if he undertake anything contrary to law.

Furthermore, if the king ordain anything in his council, if he treat any agreement with the princes his neighbors, if he begin a war, or make peace, as lately with Charles the Fifth the emperor, the Parliament ought to interpose their authority, and all that which concerns the public state must be therein registered; neither is there anything firm and stable which the Parliament does not first approve. And to the end that the counselors of that Parliament should not fear the king, formerly they attained not to that place, but by the nomination of the whole body of the court; neither could they be dismissed for any lawful cause, but by the authority of the said body.

PART IV

THE ENGLISH REFORMATION

24

William Tyndale:
The New Testament in English. [1525]

O
ne consequence of the Protestant Reformation was that the Scriptures were made available in the vernacular. In England the publication and use of the English Bible was encouraged by Henry VIII despite his own conservative views in theology. William Tyndale ranks first among the names to be mentioned in connection with the English Bible. On his translation all subsequent ones have been based, including the Authorized or King James Version of 1611. Tyndale had a passion for translating Scripture, and when he failed to receive official encouragement in London he proceeded on his own. Afterward he traveled to the Continent, where he absorbed Luther's theology in addition to getting his translation into the press. His New Testament came out in 1525. Published in Germany, it was quickly shipped across the Channel and was received with official hostility and public enthusiasm.

Tyndale did not hesitate to render certain Greek terms in an anti-Catholic sense, but he did so because he was convinced that the text made this necessary. Like Luther, he was a brilliant stylist, as the following selections tellingly convey.[23]

---

23. *The New Testament Translated by William Tyndale* (1534). Cambridge, MA, 1938, pp. 31–35.

LITERATURE

Brian Moynahan, *God's Bestseller: William Tyndale, Thomas More, and the Writing of the English Bible—a Story of Martyrdom and Betrayal.* New York, 2003.

The V. Chapter [The Gospel of St. Matthew]

When he sawe the people, he went vp into a mountayne, and when he was set, his disciples came to hym, and he opened hys mouthe, and taught them sayinge: Blessed are the povre in sprete: for theirs is the kyngdome of heven. Blessed are they that morne: for they shalbe comforted. Blessed are the meke: for they shall inheret the erth. Blessed are they which honger and thurst for rightewesnes: for they shalbe filled. Blessed are the merciful: for they shall obteyne mercy. Blessed are the pure in herte: for they shall se God. Blessed are the peacemakers: for they shalbe called the chyldren of God. Blessed are they which suffre persecucion for rightewesnes sake: for theirs is the kyngdome of heven. Blessed are ye when men reuyle you, and persecute you, and shall falsly saye all manner of yvell saynges agaynst you for my sake. Reioyce, and be glad, for greate is youre rewarde in heven. For so persecuted they the Prophetes which were before youre dayes.

Ye are the salt of the erth: but and yf the salt have lost hir saltnes, what can be salted therwith? It ys thence forthe good for northynge, but to be cast oute, and tobe troaden vnder fote of men. ye are the light of the worlde. A cite that ys set on an hill, cannot be hid, nether do men lyght a candell and put it vnder a busshell, but on a candelstick, and it lighteth all that are in the house. Let youre light so shyne before men, that they may se youre good workes, and glorify youre father which ys in heven.

Thinke not that I am come to destroye the lawe, or the Prophets: no I am nott come to destroye them, but to fulfyll them. For truely I saye vnto you, till heven and erth perisshe, one iott or one tytle of the lawe shall not scape, tyll all be fulfylled.

Whosoever breaketh one of these leest commaundmentes, and teacheth men so, he shalbe called the leest in the kyngdome of heven. But whosoever obserueth and teacheth, the same shalbe called great in the kyngdome of heven.

For I saye vnto you, except youre rightewesnes excede, the rightewesnes of the Scribes and Pharises, ye cannot entre into the kyngdome of heven.

Ye have herde how it was sayde vnto them of the olde tyme: Thou shalt not kyll. For whosoever kylleth, shall be in daunger of iudgement. But I saye vnto you, whosoever is angre with hys brother, shalbe in daunger of iudgement. Whosoever sayeth vnto hys brother Racha, shalbe in daunger of a counsell. But whosoever sayeth thou fole, shalbe in daunger of hell fyre.

Therfore when thou offrest thy gyfte at the altare, and their remembrest that thy brother hath ought agaynst the: leue there thyne offrynge before the altre, and go thy waye first and be reconcyled to thy brother, and then come and offre thy gyfte.

Agre with thyne adversary quicklye, whyles thou arte in the waye with hym, lest that adversary delivre the to the iudge, and the iudge delivre the to the minister, and then thou be cast into preson. I saye vnto the verely: thou shalt not come out thence till thou have payed the utmost farthinge.

Ye have herde how it was sayde to them of olde tyme: Thou shalt not committ advoutrie. But I saye vnto you, that whosoever looketh on a wyfe, lustynge after her, hathe committed advoutrie with hir alredy in his hert.

Wherfore yf thy right eye offende the, plucke hym out, and caste hym from the. Better yt ys for the that one of thy membres perisshe, then that thy hole bodye should be cast vnto hell. Also yf thy right honde offend the, cut hym of and caste hym from the. Better yt ys that one of thy membres perisshe, then that all thy body shulde be caste vnto hell.

It ys sayde, whosoever put awaye his wyfe, let hym geve her a testymonyall also of the devorcement. But I say vnto you: whosoever put awaye his wyfe (except it be for fornicacion) causeth her to breake matrymony. And whosoever maryeth her that is devorsed, breaketh wedlocke.

Agayne ye haue herde how it was sayde to them of olde tyme, thou shalt not forswere thy selfe, but shalt performe thyne othe to God. But I saye vnto you, swere not at all: nether by heven, for it ys Goddes seate: nor yet by the erth, for it ys his fote stole: nether by Ierusalem, for it ys the cyte of that greate kynge. nether shalt thou sweare by thy heed, because thou canst not make wone white heer, or blacke: But your communicacion shalbe, ye, ye: nay, nay. For whatsoever ys more then that, commeth of yvell.

Ye have herde how it ys sayde: an eye for an eye: a tothe for a tothe. But I saye to you, that ye resist not wronge. But whosoever geve the a blowe on thy right cheke, tourne to hym the other. And yf eny man will sue the at the lawe, and take away thy coote, let hym have thy cloocke also. And whosoever wyll compell the to goo a myle, goo wyth him twayne. Geve to hym that axeth, and from hym that wolde borowe tourne not awaye.

Ye have herde how it ys sayde: thou shalt love thyne neghbour, and hate thyne enimy. But I saye vnto you, love youre enimies. Blesse them that coursse you. Doo good to them that hate you. Praye for them which doo you wronge and persecute you, that ye maye be the chyldern of youre father that is in heven: for he maketh his sunne to aryse on the yvell, and on the good, and sendeth his reyn on the iuste and vniuste. For yf ye love them, which love you: what rewarde shall ye have? Doo not the Publicans euen so? And yf ye be frendly to youre brethren onlye: what singuler thynge doo ye? Doo not the Publicans lyke wyse? ye shal therfore be perfecte, even as youre father which ys in heven, ys perfecte...

Love suffreth longe, and ys corteous. Love envieth not. Love doth not frowardly, swelleth not dealeth not dishonestly, seketh not her awne, is not provoked to anger, thynketh not evyll, reioyseth not in iniquite: but reioyseth in the trueth, suffreth all thynges beleveth all thynges, hopeth all thynges, endureth in all thynges. Though that prophesyinge fayle, other tonges shall cease, or knowledge vanysshe awaye, yet love falleth never awaye.

For oure knowledge ys vnparfet, and our prophesyinge ys vnparfet. But when that which ys parfet ys come, then that which ys vnparfet shall bedone awaye. When I was a chylde, I spake as a chylde, I vnderstode as a chylde, I ymagened as a chylde. But assone as I was a man, I put away chyldisshnes. Now we se in a glasse even in a darke speakynge: but then shall we se face to face. Now I knowe vnparfetly: but then shall I knowe even as I am knowen. Now abideth fayth, hope, and love, even these thre: but the chefe of these ys love.

25

The Six Articles Act. [1539]

The conservative theology and church policy of King Henry VIII is evident in the Six Articles Act, which Parliament passed in July 1539. These articles reaffirmed six basic Catholic doctrines. Protestants called it the "bloody whip with six strings" since the Act provided for severe penalties for any deviation. As matters turned out, however, the severe penalties of the Act were rarely put into practice.[24]

LITERATURE

Norman Jones, *The English Reformation: Religion and Cultural Adaptation*. Oxford, 2002.

Eamon Duffy, *The Stripping of the Altars: Traditional Religion in England, c.1400–c.1580*. New Haven, CT, 1992.

The most royal majesty, most prudently pondering and considering that by occasion of variable and sundry opinions and judgments of the said Articles great discord and variance has arisen as

---

24. Henry Gee and William Hardy, eds., *Documents Illustrative of English Church History*. London, 1896, pp. 304–6.

well amongst the clergy of this his realm as amongst a great number of vulgar people; his loving subjects of the same;...perfect resolution of the said Articles should make a perfect concord and unity generally amongst all his loving and obedient subjects of his most excellent goodness; not only commanded that the said Articles should deliberately and advisedly, by his said archbishops, bishops, and other learned men of his clergy, be debated, argued, and reasoned, and their opinions therein to be understood, declared, and known, but also most graciously vouchsafed, in his own princely person, to descend and come into his said high Court of Parliament and council, and there, like a prince of most high's prudence and no less learning, opened and declared many things of high learning and great knowledge touching the said Articles, matters, and questions for a unity to be had in the same. Whereupon, after a great and long, deliberate and advised disputation and consultation had and made concerning the said Articles, as well by the consent of the king's highness as by the assent of the lords spiritual and temporal and other learned men of his clergy in their Convocation, and by the consent of the Commons in this present Parliament assembled, it was and is finally resolved, accorded, and agreed in manner and form following, that is to say:

First, that in the most Blessed Sacrament of the altar, by the strength and efficacy of Christ's mighty word (it being spoken by the priest), is present really, under the form of bread and wine, the natural body and blood of our Savior Jesus Christ, conceived of the Virgin Mary; and that after the consecration there remains no substance of bread or wine, nor any other substance, but the substance of Christ, God, and man.

Secondly, that communion in both kinds is not necessary *ad salutem* by the law of God, to all persons; and that it is to be believed and not doubted of, but that in the flesh, under the form of bread, is the very blood; and with the blood, under the form of wine, is the very flesh; as well apart, as though they were both together.

Thirdly, that priests after the order of priesthood received, as afore, may not marry, by the law of God.

Fourthly, that vows of chastity or widowhood, by man or woman made to God advisedly ought to be observed by the law of God; and that it exempts them from other liberties of Christian people, which without that they might enjoy.

Fifthly, that it is meet and necessary that private masses be continued and admitted in this the king's English Church and congregation, as whereby good Christian people, ordering themselves accordingly, do receive both godly and goodly consolations and benefits; and it is agreeable also to God's law.

Sixthly, that auricular confession is expedient and necessary to be retained and continued, used and frequented in the Church of God.

26

Thomas Cranmer: *Preface to the Bible.* [1540]

Thomas Cranmer (1489–1556), Cambridge don, became archbishop of Canterbury in 1533 and in this capacity played an enormous role in the introduction of Protestant thought and practices in England. Cranmer was both an administrator and a learned theologian, who was influenced by the writings of the continental reformers and the writings of early Christianity. Cranmer stressed the centrality of Scripture as source of Christian teaching, which led him to the affirmation of justification by faith and the real presence of Christ on the sacrament of the altar. In April 1540 Cranmer wrote a preface to the *Great Bible* which, by the king's order, was to be read in the churches.[25]

LITERATURE

Diarmed MacCulloch, *Thomas Cranmer: A Life*. New Haven, CT, 1996.

For two sundry sorts of people it seems much necessary that something be said in the entry of this book, by the way of a preface or prologue; whereby hereafter it may be both the better accepted

---

25. *Miscellaneous Writings and Letters of Thomas Cranmer.* Edited for the Parker Society. Cambridge, 1846, pp. 1 ff.

by them which hitherto could not well bear it, and also the better used of them which heretofore have misused it. For many some there are that be too slow and need the spur; some other seem quick and need more of the bridle; some lose their game by short shooting, some by overshooting; some walk too much on the left hand, some too much on the right. In the former sort be all they that refuse to read, or to hear read the Scripture in the vulgar tongues; much worse they that also let [hinder] or discourage the other from the learning or hearing thereof. In the latter sort be they which, by their inordinate reading, indiscreet speaking, contentious disputing, or otherwise by their licentious living, slander and hinder the Word of God most of all other... These two sorts, albeit they be most far unlike the one to the other, yet they both deserve in effect like reproaches. Neither can I well tell which of them I may judge the greater offender, him that does obstinately refuse so godly and goodly knowledge, or him that so ungodly does abuse the same. And touching the former, I could marvel much that any individual should be so mad as to refuse in darkness, light; in hunger, food; in cold, fire. For the Word of God is light...food...fire.

I would marvel (I say) at this, save that I consider how much custom and usage may do. So that if there were a people, as some write, which never saw the sun by reason that they be situated far toward the North Pole and be enclosed and overshadowed by the high mountains, it is credible and like enough that if, by the power and will of God, the mountains should sink down and give place and the light of the sun might have entrance to them, at the first some of them would be offended therewith. And the old proverb affirmed that, after tillage of corn was first found, many delighted more to feed of mast and acorns, wherewith they had been accustomed, than to eat bread made of good corn. Such is the nature of custom that it causes us to bear all things well and easily wherewith we have been accustomed, and to be offended with all things thereunto contrary. And therefore I can much think them worthy pardon which, at the coming abroad of Scripture, doubted and drew back. But such as will persist still in their willfulness, I must needs judge not only foolish, forward, and obstinate, but also peevish, perverse, and indurate.

27

The Examination of Anne Askew. [1546]

Anne Askew was assuredly one of the more striking figures of the English Reformation. She illustrates both the popular dimension of the reform movement as well as the role of women in the course of events. Born into a noble family in 1521, Anne must have received a very good education. Well before reaching the age of twenty, she was married to a Thomas Kyme. She gave birth to two children but became estranged from her Catholic husband over her Protestant religious views. An attempt to obtain a divorce, after she had been evicted from their home, was unsuccessful.

In 1545 she was arrested for her religious views, particularly for denying the doctrine of transubstantiation, which King Henry VIII's Six Articles enjoined. After a brief release, she was arrested for a second time, and was subsequently so severely crippled by torture that she had to be carried about in a chair. She was burned at the stake in Smithfield as a heretic on July 16, 1546. Her story was subsequently publicized by John Bale through the publication of an account of her interrogations of 1545 and 1546, in which he interspersed his own commentary on her faith. The *Examinations* show Anne's conversancy with the Bible, her forthright determination, and her refusal to be intimidated by the authorities. They also show how the authorities, both ecclesiastical and secular, were not willing to accept her various answers. Her language, simple as it is, conveyed a moving testimony.

What follows is the account of her first *Examination*, with the commentary by John Bale omitted. The text has been modernized.[26]

LITERATURE

Retha Warnicke, *Women of the English Renaissance and Reformation*. Westport, CT, 1983.

Elaine Beilin, ed., *The Examinations of Anne Askew*. New York, 1996.

The First Examination of the worthy servant of God, Mistress Anne Askew, the younger daughter of Sir William Askew, knight of Lincolnshire, lately martyred in Smithfield by the Romish pope's upholders.

To satisfy your expectation, good people (says she), this was my first examination in the year of our Lord MDXLV and in the month of March. First Christopher Dare examined me at Sadler's Hall, being one of the questioners, and asked if I did not believe that the Sacrament hanging over the altar was the very body of Christ really. Then I demanded this question of him, wherefore St. Stephen was stoned to death? And he said, he could not tell. Then I answered, that no more would I assail his vain question.

Secondly he said, that there was a woman, which did testify, that I should read, how God was not in temples made with hands.

---

26. The text is that of Henry Christmas, ed., *Select works of John Bale … Containing the examinations of Lord Cobham, William Thorpe, and Anne Askew*. Parker Society Publications, Vol. 1. Cambridge, 1849; compared with that in Elaine Beilin, ed., *The Examinations of Anne Askew*. New York, 1996, extensively modernized.

Then I showed him the vii. and the xvii. chapters of the Apostles' Acts, what Stephen and Paul had said therein. Whereupon he asked me, how I took those sentences? I answered that I would not throw pearls among swine, for acorns were good enough.

Thirdly, he asked me, why I said, that I had rather to read five lines in the Bible, than to hear five Masses in the temple. I confessed that I said no less. Not for the dispraise of either the Epistle or Gospel. But because the one did greatly edify me, and the other not at all. As St. Paul does witness in the xiiii. chapter of his first Epistle to the Corinthians, where he does say, "If the trumpet gives an uncertain sound, who will prepare himself to the battle?"

Fourthly, he laid unto my charge that I should say if an ill priest ministered, it was the devil and not God. My answer was that I never spoke such a thing. But this was my saying, that whatsoever he were, which ministered unto me, his ill condition could not hurt my faith. But in spirit I received nevertheless the body and blood of Christ.

Fifthly, he asked me, what I said concerning Confession. I answered him my meaning, which was as St. James says, that every man ought to acknowledge his faults to others, and one ought to pray for the other.

Sixthly, he asked me, what I said of the King's book. And I answered him, that I could say nothing to it, because I never saw it.

Seventhly, he asked me, if I had the spirit of God in me. I answered if I had not, I was but a reprobate or castaway.

Then he said, he had sent for a priest to examine me, which was there at hand. The priest asked me what I said about the Sacrament of the altar and demanded much to know therein my meaning. But I desired him again to hold me excused concerning that matter. None other answer would I make him, because I perceived him a papist.

Eighthly, he asked me, if I did not think that private Masses did help departed souls. And I said, it was great idolatry to believe more in them, than in the death which Christ died for us.

Then they had me from thence unto my Lord Mayor. And he examined me as they had before, and I answered him directly in all things, as I answered the questions afore.

Besides this, my Lord Mayor laid one thing unto my charge, which was never spoken of me, but of them. And that was, whether a mouse eating the host received God or not? This question did I never ask, but indeed they asked it of me, whereunto I made them no answer, but smiled.

Then the bishop's chancellor rebuked me, and said that I was much to blame for uttering the Scriptures. For St. Paul (he said) forbade women to speak or to talk of the Word of God. I answered him, that I knew Paul's meaning as well as he, which is 1 Cor. 11: 22, that a woman ought not to speak in the congregation by the way of teaching. And then I asked him, how many women he had seen go into the pulpit and preach. He said, he never saw any. Then I said, he ought to find no fault in poor women, except they had offended the law.

Then my Lord Mayor commanded me toward. I asked him if sureties would not serve me. And he made me short answer that he would take none. Then was I had to the counter, and there remained xii days, no friend admitted to speak with me.

But in the meantime there was a priest sent to me, who said that he was commanded of the bishop to examine me, and to give me good counsel, which he did not. But first he asked me for what cause I was put in the counter? And I told him I could not tell. Then he said, it was a great pity that I should be there without cause and concluded that he was very sorry for me.

Secondly he said, it was to him that I should deny the Sacrament of the altar. And I answered him again, that that I had said, I had said.

Thirdly, he asked me, if I were shriven; I told him no. Then he said, he would bring one to me, for to shrive me. And I told him, so that I might have one of these iii, that is to say, Doctor Crome, Sir Gyllam, or Huntington, I was contented, because I knew them to be men of wisdom. As for you or any other, I will not dispraise, because I know you not. Then he said, I would not have you think, but that I or another that shall be brought now, shall be as honest as they. For if we were not, you may be sure, the King would not suffer us to preach. Then I answered by the saying of Solomon, By communing with the wise, I may learn wisdom, but by talking with a fool, I shall take scathe, Proverbs 1.

Fourthly, he asked me if the host should fall, and a beast did eat it, whether the beast did receive God or not? I answered, seeing you have taken pains to ask this question, I desire you also to take so much pain more, as to answer it yourself. For I will not do it, because I perceive you came to tempt me. And he said, it was against the order of schools that he who asked the question should answer it. I told him, I was but a woman, and knew not the course of the schools.

Fifthly, he asked me, if I intended to receive the Sacrament at Easter, or not? I answered that else I were no Christian woman, and that I did rejoice, that the time was so near at hand. And then he departed thence with many fair words.

So upon that he went to the chancellor, requiring of him as he did afore of my Lord Mayor. He answered him that the matter was so heinous that he durst not of himself do it, without my Lord of London were made privy thereunto. But he said, he would speak unto my Lord in it. And bade him repair unto him the next morrow and he should well know my Lord's pleasure.

And upon the morrow after, he came thither, and spoke both with the chancellor, and with my Lord Bishop of London. My Lord declared unto him that he was very well contented that I should come forth to a communication. And appointed me to appear before him the next day after, at two of the clock. Moreover he said unto him that there should be at that examination such learned men as I was affectioned to. That they might see and also make report that I was handled with no rigor. He answered him that he knew no man that I had more affection to than other. Than said the bishop, yes, as I understand, she is affectioned to Doctor Crome, Sir Gyllam, Whitehead, and Huntington, that they might hear the matter. For she did know them to be learned, and of godly judgment.

Also he required my cousin Brittany that he should earnestly persuade me to utter, even the very bottom of my heart. And he swore by his fidelity, that no man should take any advantage of my words. Neither yet would he lay ought to my charge, for anything that I should there speak. But if I said any manner of thing amiss, he with others more would be glad to reform me therein, with most godly counsel.

On the morrow after, my Lord of London sent for me, at one of the clock, his hour being appointed at three. And as I came before him, he said he was very sorry of my trouble, and desired to know my opinion in such matters as were laid against me. He required me also in any wise boldly to utter the secrets of my heart, bidding me not to fear in any point. For whatsoever I did say within his house, no man should hurt me for it. I answered. for so much as your Lordship appointed two of the clock, and my friends shall not come till that hour, I desire you to pardon me of giving answer till they come.

Then said he, that he thought it mete, to send for those men which were aforenamed, and appointed. Then I desired him not to put them to the pain. For it should not need, because the two gentlemen which were my friends, were able enough to testify that I should say. Anon after he went into his gallery with Master

Spelman, and willed till him in any wise that he should exhort me
to utter all that I thought.

In the meanwhile he commanded his archdeacon to come with
me, who said unto me, Mistress, wherefore are you accused? I answered, ask my accusers, for I know not as yet. Then took he my
book out of my hand, and said such books as this is has brought
you to the trouble you are in. Beware (says he), beware, for he that
made it was burnt in Smithfield. Then I asked him, if he were sure
that it was true that he had spoken. And he said, he knew well, the
book was of John Frith's making. Then I asked him, if he were not
ashamed to judge the book before he saw it within, or yet knew the
truth thereof. I said also that such unadvised and hasty judgment is
a token apparent of a very slender wit. Then I opened the book
and showed it him. He said, he thought it had been another for he
could find no fault therein. Then I desired him, no more to be so
swift in judgment, till he thoroughly knew the truth. And so he
departed.

Immediately after came my cousin Brittany with diverse others, Master Hawe of Gray's Inn, and such other like. Then my
Lord of London persuaded my cousin Brittany, as he had done oft
before, which was that I should utter the bottom of my heart in
any wise.

My Lord said after that unto me that he would I should credit
the counsel of my friends in his behalf, which was that I should
utter all things that burdened my conscience. For he assured me
that I should not need to stand in doubt to say any thing. For like
as he promised them (he said) he promised me and would perform
it. Which was, that neither he, nor any man for him, should take
me at advantage of any word I should speak. And therefore he bade
me, say my mind without fear. I answered him that I had naught
to say. For my conscience (I thanked God) was burdened with
nothing.

Then brought he forth this unsavory similitude, that if a man had a wound, no wise surgeon would minister help unto it before he had seen it uncovered. In like case (says he) can I give you no good counsel, unless I know wherewith your conscience is burdened. I answered, that my conscience was clear in all things. And for to lay a plaster unto the whole skin, it might appear much folly.

Then you drive me (says he) to lay to your charge, your own report, which is this: You did say, he who does receive the Sacrament by the hands of an ill priest or a sinner, receives the devil, and not God. To that I answered, that I never spoke such words. But as I said afore both to the questioner and to my Lord Mayor, so say I now again, that the wickedness of the priest should not hurt me, but in spirit and faith I received no less the body and blood of Christ. Then said the Bishop unto me, what a saying is this? In spirit I will not take you at that advantage. Then I answered, my Lord, without faith and spirit, I cannot receive him worthily.

Then he laid unto me that I should say that the Sacrament remaining, was but bread. I answered that I never said so, but indeed the questioner asked me such a question, whereunto I would not answer (I said) till such time as they had assailed me with this question of mine, wherefore Stephen was stoned to death. They said, they knew not. Then said I again, no more would I tell them what it was.

Then laid it my Lord unto me that I had alleged a certain text of the Scripture. I answered that I alleged none other but St. Paul's own saying to the Athenians, in the xvii. chapter of the Apostles' Acts. That God dwells not in temples made with hands. Then asked he me, what my faith and belief was in that matter? I answered him, I believe as the Scripture does teach me. Then enquired he of me, what if the Scripture does say that it is the body of

Christ? I believe (said I) as the Scripture does teach me. Then asked he again, what if the Scripture does say, that it is not the body of Christ? My answer was still, I believe as the Scripture informs me. And upon this argument he tarried a great while, to have driven me to make him an answer to his mind. Albeit I would not, but concluded thus with him that I believed therein and in all other things, as Christ and his holy Apostles did leave them.

Then he asked me, why I had so few words? And I answered God has given me the gift of knowledge, but not of utterance. And Solomon says that a woman of few words is a gift of God, Proverbs 19.

Thirdly, my Lord laid unto my charge that I should say that the Mass was idolatry. I answered him. No, I said not so. Howbeit (I said) the questioner did ask me, whether private Masses did relieve souls departed, or not? Unto whom then I answered, O Lord, what idolatry is this? That we should rather believe in private Masses, than in the healthsome death of the dear Son of God. Then said my Lord again. What an answer was that? Though it were but mean (said I) yet was it good enough for the question.

Then I told my Lord that there was a priest, which did hear what I said there before my Lord Mayor and them. With that the chancellor answered, which was the same priest. So she spoke it in very deed (says he) before my Lord the Mayor and me. Then were there certain priests, as Doctor Standish and others, who tempted me much to know my mind. And I answered them always thus: That I have said to my Lord of London, I have said.

And then Doctor Standish desired my Lord to bid me say my mind, concerning that same text of Paul. I answered, that it was against St. Paul's learning, that I being a woman, should interpret the Scriptures, especially where so many wise learned men were.

Then my Lord of London said he was informed, that one should ask of me if I would receive the Sacrament at Easter, and I made a mockery of it, Then I desired that mine accuser might come forth, which my Lord would not. But he said again unto me, I sent one to give you good counsel, and at the first word you called him papist. That I denied not, for I perceived, he was no less, yet made I no answer unto it.

Then he rebuked me and said that I should report that there were bent against me three score priests at Lincoln. Indeed (quoth I), I said so. For my friends told me if I did come to Lincoln the priests would assault me and put me to great trouble, as thereof they had made their boast. And when I heard it, I went thither indeed, not being afraid because I knew my matter to be good. Moreover I remained there vi days to see what would be said unto me. And as I was in the Minster, reading upon the Bible, they resorted unto me by twos and by twos, by fives and by sixes, minding to have spoken to me, yet went they their ways again without words speaking.

Then my Lord asked if there were not one that did speak unto me. I told him, yes, that there was one of them at the last, who did speak to me indeed. And my Lord then asked me what he said. And I told him, his words were of so small effect, that I did not now remember them.

Then said my Lord, there are many that read and know the Scripture, and yet do not follow it, nor live thereafter. I said again, my Lord, I would wish that all men knew my conversation and living in all points, for I am so sure of myself this hour, that there are none able to prove any dishonesty by me. If you know any that can do it, I pray you bring them forth.

Then my Lord went away, and said he would entitle somewhat of my meaning. And so he wrote a great circumstance. But what it was, I have not all in memory, for he would not suffer me to have the copy thereof. Only do I remember this small portion of it.

Be it known (says he) to all men, that I, Anne Askew, do confess this to be my faith and belief, notwithstanding my reports made afore to the contrary. I believe that they which are hustled at the hands of a priest, whether his conversation be good or not, do receive the body and blood of Christ in substance really. Also I do believe it after the consecration, whether it be received or reserved, to be no less than the very body and blood of Christ in substance. Finally, I do believe in this and in all other Sacraments of holy church, in all points according to the old Catholic faith of the same. In witness whereof, I the said Anne have subscribed my name. There was somewhat more in it, which because I had not the copy, I cannot now remember.

Then he read it to me, and asked me, if I did agree to it. And I said again, I believe so much thereof, as the holy Scripture does agree to. Wherefore I desire you, that you will add that thereunto. Then he answered, that I should not teach him what he should write. With that, he went forth into his great chamber, and read the same bill afore the audience, which inveighed and willed me to set to my hand, saying also that I had fever showed me.

Then said the Bishop, I might thank others and not myself, of the favor I found at his hand. For he considered (he said) that I had good friends, and also that I was come of a worshipful stock. Then answered one Christopher, a servant to Master Denney, rather ought you (my Lord) to have done it in such case for God's sake than for many.

Then my Lord sat down, and took me the writing to set thereto my hand, and I wrote after this manner: I, Anne Askew, do believe all manner things contained in the faith of the Catholic Church. Then, because I did add unto it, the Catholic Church, he flung into his chamber in a great fury. With that my cousin Brittany followed him, desiring him for God's sake to be a good Lord unto me. He answered that I was a woman, and that he was nothing deceived by me. Then my cousin Brittany desired him to take me as a woman, and not to set my weak woman's wit to his lordship's great wisdom.

Then went in unto him Doctor Weston, and said, that the cause why I did write there the Catholic Church was that I understood not the church written afore. So with much ado, they persuaded my Lord to come out again, and to take my name with the names of my sureties, which were my cousin Brittany and Master Spelman of Gray's Inn.

This being done, we thought that I should have been put to bail immediately, according to the order of the law. Howbeit he would not so suffer it, but committed me from thence to prison again until the next morrow. And then he willed me to appear in the guild hall, and so I did. Notwithstanding they would not put me to bail there either but read the Bishop's writing unto me as before, and so commanded me again to prison.

Then were my sureties appointed to come before them on the next morrow in St. Paul's Church, which did so indeed. Notwithstanding they would once again have broken off with them, because they would not be bound also for another woman at their pleasure whom they knew not, nor yet what matter was laid unto her charge. Notwithstanding at the last, after much ado and reasoning to and fro, they took a bond of them of recognizance for my forthcoming. And thus I was at the last, delivered.

Written by me, Anne Askew.

Thus ends the First Examination of Anne Askew, lately done to death by the Romish pope's malicious remnant, and now canonized in the precious blood of the Lord Jesus Christ.

28

John Jewel: *An Apology of the Church of England.* [1562]

John Jewel, appointed bishop of Salisbury in 1559, was a scholar and in a way the perfect choice to prepare a defense of the Elizabethan settlement of religion against Catholic antagonists. Jewel offered both a defense against the Catholic accusations and a positive statement of the faith of the English church. The Catholic charges against the English church had been those of schism, heresy, and immorality; Jewel argued that such charges could easily be leveled against Catholics as well. Moreover, he emphatically argued that the Catholic Church had departed from biblical and apostolic norms. The Council of Trent was in session when Jewel's work was published; it must also be seen as a defense of the English refusal to attend its deliberations and accept its decisions.

The work appeared in 1562 in both Latin and English, the latter under the title *An Apologia, or Answer in Defence of the Church of England, Concerning the State of Religion Used in the Same.* Numerous editions followed, an indication that Jewel had offered an incisive, if perhaps colorless, defense of the Anglican settlement. The section reprinted here is a major portion of the first of the seven "parts" of the treatise.[27]

---

27. John Jewel, *An Apology of the Church of England.* (London, 1905), pp. 8–19.

LITERATURE.

Hans J. Hillerbrand, ed., *Oxford Encyclopedia of the Reformation*. 4 vols. New York, 1997.

W. M. Southgate, *John Jewel and the Problem of Doctrinal Authority*. Cambridge, MA, 1962.

It has been an old complaint, even from the first time of the patriarchs and prophets, and confirmed by the writings and testimonies of every age, that the truth wanders here and there as a stranger in the world and does readily find enemies and slanderers amongst those that know her not. Albeit perchance this may seem unto some a thing hard to be believed, I mean to such as have scant well and narrowly taken heed thereunto, specially seeing all mankind of nature's very motion without a teacher doth covet the truth of their own accord; and seeing our Savior Christ Himself, when He was on earth, would be called "the truth," as by a name most fit to express His divine power; yet we—which have been exercised in the holy Scriptures, and which have both read and seen what has happened to all godly men commonly at all times; what to the prophets, to the apostles, to the holy martyrs, and what to Christ Himself; with what rebukes, reveling, and despites they were continually vexed while they here lived, and that only for the truth's sake—we (I say) do see that this is not only no new thing or hard to be believed, but that it is a thing already received and commonly used from age to age. Nay, truly, this might seem much rather a marvel and beyond all belief, if the devil, who is "the father of lies" and enemy to all truth, would now upon a sudden change his nature and hope that truth might otherwise be suppressed than by belying it, or that he would begin to establish his own kingdom by using now any other practices than the same which he has ever used from the beginning. For since any person's remembrance we can scant find one time, either when religion did first grow, or when it was settled, or when it did afresh spring up again, wherein truth and innocence were not by all unworthy means and most despitefully entreated. Doubtless the devil well sees that so long as truth is in good safety, himself cannot be safe or yet maintain his own estate.

For, letting pass the ancient patriarchs and prophets, who, as we said, had no part of their life free from contumelies and slanders, we know there were certain in times past which said and commonly preached that the old ancient Jews (of whom we make no doubt but they were the worshippers of the only and true God) did worship either a sow or an ass in God's stead, and that all the same religion was nothing else but a sacrilege and a plain contempt of all godliness. We know also that the Son of God, our Savior Jesus Christ, when He taught the truth, was counted a juggler and an enchanter, a Samaritan, Beelzebub, a deceiver of the people, a drunkard, and a glutton. Again, who wonders not what words were spoken against St. Paul, the most earnest and vehement preacher and maintainer of the truth? Sometime, that he was a seditious and busy man, a raiser of tumults, a causer of rebellion; sometime again, that he was a heretic; sometime, that he was mad. Sometime, that only upon strife and stomach he was both a blasphemer of God's law and a despiser of the fathers' ordinances...

Or who is ignorant that in times past there were some which reproved the holy Scriptures of falsehood, saying they contained things both contrary, and quite one against another, and how that the apostles of Christ did severally disagree betwixt themselves and that St. Paul did vary from them all? And, not to make rehearsal of all, for that were an endless labor, who knows not after what sort our fathers were railed upon in times past, which first began to acknowledge and profess the name of Christ, how they made private conspiracies, devised secret counsels against the commonwealth, and to that end made early and privy meetings in the dark, killed young babes, fed themselves with men's flesh, and, like savage and brute beasts, did drink their blood? In conclusion, how that, after they had put out the candles, they committed adultery between themselves, and without regard wrought incest one with another, that brethren lay with their sisters, sons with their mothers, without any reverence of nature or kin, without shame, without difference; and that they were wicked men without all care of religion and without any opinion of God, being the very enemies of mankind, unworthy to be suffered in the world and unworthy of life?

All these things were spoken in those days against the people of God, against Christ Jesus, against Paul, against Stephen, and against all of them, whosoever they were, which at the first beginning embraced the truth of the gospel and were contented to be called by the name of Christians, which was then an hateful name among the common people. And, although the things which they said were not true, yet the devil thought it should be sufficient for him if at the least he could bring it so to pass as they might be believed for true, and that the Christians might be brought into a common hatred of everybody and have their death and destruction sought of all sorts…

Wherefore we ought to bear it more quietly, which have taken upon us to profess the gospel of Christ, if we for the same cause be handled after the same sort; and if we, as our forefathers were long ago, be likewise at this day tormented and baited with railings, with spiteful dealings, and with lies; and that for no desert of our own but only because we teach and acknowledge the truth.

They cry out upon us at this present everywhere that we are all heretics and have with new persuasions and wicked learning utterly dissolved the concord of the church; that we renew, and, as it were, fetch again from hell the old and many-a-day condemned heresies; that we sow abroad new sects and such broils as never were heard of; also that we are already divided into contrary parts and opinions and could yet by no means agree well among ourselves; that we be cursed creatures and like the giants do war against God Himself and live clean without any regard or worshipping of God; that we despise all good deeds; that we lose no discipline of virtue, no laws, no customs; that we esteem neither right, nor order, nor equity, nor justice; that we give the bridle to all naughtiness and provoke the people to all licentiousness and lust; that we labor and seek to overthrow the state of monarchies and kingdoms and to bring all things under the rule of the rash inconstant people and unlearned multitude; that we have seditiously fallen from the Catholic Church and by a wicked schism and division have shaken the whole world and troubled the common peace and universal quiet of the church; and that...we at this day have renounced the bishop of Rome without any reasonable cause; that we set us against the authority of the ancient fathers and councils of old time; that we have rashly and presumptuously annuled the old ceremonies, which have been well allowed by our fathers and forefathers many hundred years past, both by good customs and also in ages of more purity; and that we have by our own private head, without the authority of any sacred and general council, brought new traditions into the church; and have done all these things not for religion's sake but only upon a desire of contention and strife: but that they for their part have changed no manner of thing but have held and kept still such a number of years to this very day all things as they were delivered from the apostles and well approved by the most ancient fathers.

And that this matter should not seem to be done but upon privy slander, and to be tossed to and fro in a corner, only to spite us, there have been besides wilily procured by the bishop of Rome certain persons of eloquence enough, and not unlearned either, which should put their help to this cause, now almost despaired of, and should polish and set forth the same, both in books and with long tales, to the end that when the matter was trimly and eloquently handled ignorant and unskillful persons might suspect there was some great thing in it. Indeed they perceived that their own cause did everywhere go to wrack; that their sleights were now espied and less esteemed; and that their helps did daily fail them; and that their matter stood altogether in great need of a cunning spokesman.

Now, as for those things which by them have been laid against us, in part they be manifestly false, and condemned so by their own judgments which spoke them; partly again, though they be as false too indeed, yet bear they a certain show and color of truth; so as the reader (if he take not good heed) may easily be tripped and brought into error by them, especially when their fine and cunning tale is added thereunto; and part of them be of such sort as we ought not to shun them as crimes or faults but to acknowledge and profess them as things well done and upon very good reason.

For, shortly to say the truth, these folk falsely accuse and slander all our doings, yea, the same things which they themselves cannot deny but to be rightly and orderly done, and for malice do so misconstrue and deprave all our sayings and doings, as though it were impossible that any thing could be rightly spoken or done by us. They should more plainly and sincerely have gone to work if they would have dealt truly. But now they neither truly, nor sincerely, nor yet Christianly, but darkly and craftily, charge and batter us with lies and do abuse the blindness and fondness of the people, together with the ignorance of princes, to cause us to be hated and the truth to be suppressed...

Now therefore, if it be lawful for these folks to be eloquent and fine-tongued in speaking evil, surely it becomes not us in our cause, being so very good, to be dumb in answering truly. For men to be careless what is spoken by them and their own matter, be it never so falsely and slanderously spoken (especially when it is such that the majesty of God and the cause of religion may thereby be damaged), is the part doubtless of dissolute and reckless persons and of them which wickedly wink at the injuries done unto the name of God. For, although other wrongs, yea, oftentimes great, may be borne and dissembled of a mild and Christian man; yet he that goes smoothly away and dissembles the matter when he is noted of heresy, Rufinus was wont to deny that man to be a Christian. We therefore will do the same thing, which all laws, which nature's own voice, doth command to be done, and which Christ Himself did in like case, when He was checked and reviled; to the intent we may put off from us these men's slanderous accusations and may defend soberly and truly our own cause and innocence...

But we, truly, seeing that so many thousands of our brethren in these last twenty years have borne witness unto the truth in the midst of most painful torments that could be devised; and when princes, desirous to restrain the gospel, sought many ways, but prevailed nothing; and that now almost the whole world doth begin to open their eyes to behold the light; we take it that our cause has already been sufficiently declared and defended, and think it not needful to make many words, since the very matter says enough for itself. For, if the popes would, or else if they could, weigh with their own selves the whole matter, and also the beginning and proceedings of our religion, how in a manner all their travail has come to naught, nobody driving it forward, and without any worldly help; and how, on the other side, our cause, against the will of emperors from the beginning, against the wills of so many kings, in spite of the popes...has taken increase, and by little and little spread over into all countries, and is come at length even into kings' courts and palaces. These same things, I think, might be tokens great enough to them that God Himself does strongly fight in our quarrel and doth from heaven laugh at their enterprises; and that the force of the truth is such as neither man's power nor yet hell gates are able to root it out. For they be not all mad at this day, so many free cities, so many kings, so many princes, which have fallen away from the seat of Rome and have rather joined themselves to the gospel of Christ.

And, although the popes have never hitherunto leisure to consider diligently and earnestly of these matters, or though some other cares do now let them and diverse ways pull them, or though they count these to be but common and trifling studies and nothing to appertain to the pope's worthiness, this makes not why our matter ought to seem the worse. Or if they perchance will not see that which they see indeed, but rather will withstand the known truth, ought we therefore by and by to be counted heretics, because we obey not their will and pleasure? If so be that Pope Pius were the man (we say not, which he would so gladly be called), but if he were indeed a man that either would account us for his brethren, or at least would take us to be men, he would first diligently have examined our reasons and would have seen what might be said with us, what against us, and would not in his bull, whereby he lately pretended a council, so rashly have condemned so great a part of the world, so many learned and godly men, so many commonwealths, so many kings, and so many princes, only upon his own blind prejudices and determinations, and that without hearing of them speak, or without showing cause why.

But because he has already so noted us openly, lest by holding our peace we should seem to grant a fault, and especially because we can by no means have audience in the public assembly of the general council, wherein he would no creature should have power to give his voice or declare his opinion except he were sworn and straightly bound to maintain his authority—for we have had experience hereof in the last conference at the Council of Trent, where the ambassadors and divines of the princes of Germany and of the free cities were quite shut out from their company; neither can we yet forget how Julius III, above ten years past, provided warily by his writ that none of our sort should be suffered to speak in the council (except that there were some man peradventure that would recant and change his opinion)—for this cause chiefly we thought it good to yield up an account of our faith in writing and truly and openly to make answer to those things wherewith we have been openly charged; to the end the world may see the parts and foundations of that doctrine in the behalf whereof so many good men have little regarded their own lives; and that all men may understand what manner of people they be, and what opinion they have of God and of religion, whom the bishop of Rome, before they were called to tell their tale, has condemned for heretics, without any good consideration, without any example, and utterly without law or right, only because he heard tell that they did dissent from him and his in some point of religion...

Further, if we do show it plain that God's holy gospel, the ancient bishops, and the primitive church do make on our side, and that we have not without just cause left these men, and rather have returned to the apostles and old Catholic fathers; and if we shall be found to do the same not colorably or craftily but in good faith before God, truly, honestly, clearly, and plainly; and if they themselves which fly our doctrine and would be called Catholics shall manifestly see how all these titles of antiquity, whereof they boast so much, are quite shaken out of their hands, and that there is more pith in this our cause than they thought for; we then hope and trust that none of them will be so negligent and careless of his own salvation but he will at length study and bethink himself to whether part he were best to join him. Undoubtedly, except one will altogether harden his heart and refuse to hear, he shall not repent him to give good heed to this our defense, and to mark well what we say and how truly and justly it agrees with Christian religion.

For where they call us heretics, it is a crime so heinous, that, unless it may be seen, unless it may be felt, and in manner may beholden with hands and fingers, it ought not lightly to be judged or believed, when it is laid to the charge of any Christian man. For heresy is a forsaking of salvation, a renouncing of God's grace, a departing from the body and spirit of Christ. But this was ever an old and solemn property with them and their forefathers, if any did complain of their errors and faults and desired to have true religion restored, straightway to condemn such ones for heretics, as men newfangled and factious. Christ for no other cause was called a Samaritan but only for that He was thought to have fallen to a certain new religion and to be the author of a new sect. And Paul, the Apostle of Christ, was called before the judges to make answer to a matter of heresy, and therefore he said: "According to this way, which they called heresy, I do worship the God of my fathers; believing all things which be written in the law and in the prophets."

Shortly to speak, this universal religion, which Christian men profess at this day, was called first of the heathen people a sect and heresy. With these terms did they always fill princes' ears, to the intent when they had once hated us with a predetermined opinion and had counted all that we said to be faction and heresy, they might be so led away from the truth and right understanding of the cause. But the more sore and outrageous a crime heresy is, the more it ought to be proved by plain and strong arguments, especially in this time, when men begin to give less credit to their words and to make more diligent search of their doctrine than they were wont to do. For the people of God are otherwise instructed now than they were in times past, when all the bishop of Rome's sayings were allowed for gospel, and when all religion did depend only upon their authority. Nowadays the Holy Scriptures are abroad, the writings of the apostles and prophets are in print, whereby all truth and Catholic doctrine may be proved and all heresy may be disproved and confuted.

Since, then, they bring forth none of these for themselves, and call us nevertheless heretics, which have neither fallen from Christ, nor from the apostles, nor yet from the prophets, this is an injurious and a very spiteful dealing. With this sword did Christ put off the devil when He was tempted of him; with these weapons ought all presumption, which doth advance itself against God, to be overthrown and conquered. "For all Scripture," says St. Paul, "that comes by the inspiration of God, is profitable to teach, to confute, to instruct, and to reprove; that the man of God may be perfect, and thoroughly framed to every good work." Thus did the holy fathers always fight against the heretics with none other force than with the Holy Scriptures...For at that time made the Catholic fathers and bishops no doubt but that our religion might be proved out of the Holy Scriptures. Neither were they ever so hardy to take any for an heretic whose error they could not evidently and apparently reprove by the selfsame Scriptures. And we verily do make answer on this wise, as St. Paul did, "According to this way which they call heresy we do worship God and the Father of our Lord Jesus Christ, and do allow all things which have been written either in the law, or in the prophets," or in the apostles' works.

Wherefore, if we be heretics, and they (as they would fain be called) be Catholics, why do they not as they see the fathers, which were Catholic men, have always done? Why do they not convince and master us by the divine Scriptures? Why do they not call us again to be tried by them? Why do they not lay before us how we have gone away from Christ, from the prophets, from the apostles, and from the holy fathers? Why stick they to do it? Why are they afraid of it? It is God's cause: Why are they doubtful to commit it to the trial of God's word? If we be heretics, which refer all our controversies unto the Holy Scriptures and report us to the self-same words which we know were sealed by God Himself, and in comparison of them set little by all other things, whatsoever may be devised by men; how shall we say to these folk, I pray you, what manner of men be they, and how is it meet to call them, which fear the judgment of the Holy Scriptures, that is to say, the judgment of God Himself, and do prefer before them their own dreams and full cold inventions; and, to maintain their own traditions, have defaced and corrupted, now these many hundred years, the ordinances of Christ and of the apostles?

29

John Field and Thomas Wilcox:
An Admonition to the Parliament. [1572][28]

The Elizabethan settlement of religion was from the very beginning bitterly assailed by those who thought it a compromise with popery. One of the most spectacular expressions of discontent came in June 1572 with the publication of a tract entitled *An Admonition to the Parliament.* Vehemently denouncing the settlement, this *Admonition* was "one of the boldest adventures, surely, of the whole Elizabethan age." It sought to counter Queen Elizabeth's influence upon the course of ecclesiastical affairs. The queen had recently ordered that bills affecting religion had to be approved by the Church before they could be introduced in Parliament. The temper of Parliament was congenial to additional ecclesiastical reform; the hierarchy, on the other hand, was not likely to approve comprehensive reform measures. Thus, the queen's order appeared to block effectively any further ecclesiastical change.

The *Admonition* not only rejected the queen's interference; it also spelled out the kind of religious settlement considered biblical, and thus acceptable, by the Puritan reformers. Thus, the doc-

---

28. W. H. Frere and C. E. Douglas, eds., *Puritan Manifestoes.* London, 1954, pp. 8–19.

ument constitutes an excellent source for early "Puritan" sentiment. Its two authors, John Field and Thomas Wilcox, paid for the publication with a prison sentence. The source of many of the ideas in the document was Thomas Cartwright, formerly Lady Margaret Professor of Divinity at Cambridge. He subsequently became embroiled with John Whitgift in a literary controversy over the *Admonition*.

A condensed version of the *Admonition* is reprinted in modernized spelling.

LITERATURE

D. J. McGinn, *The Admonition Controversy*. New Brunswick, NJ, 1949.

Seeing that nothing in this mortal life is more diligently to be sought for and carefully to be looked unto than the restitution of true religion and reformation of God's church: it shall be your parts, Dearly Beloved, in this present Parliament assembled, as much as in you lies to promote the same, and to employ your whole labor and studies; not only in abandoning all popish remnants both in ceremonies and regiment, but also in bringing and placing in God's church those things only, which the Lord Himself in His word commands. Because it is not enough to take pains in taking away evil, but also to be occupied in placing good in the stead thereof. Now because many men see not all things, and the world in this respect is marvelously blinded, it has been thought good to proffer to your godly considerations, a true platform of a church reformed, to the end that it being laid before your eyes, to behold the great unlikeness betwixt it & this our English church: you may learn either with perfect hatred to detest the one, and with singular love to embrace, and careful endeavor to plant the other: or else to be without excuse before the majesty of our God, who (for the discharge of our conscience, and manifestation of His truth) hath by us revealed unto you at this present, the sincerity and simplicity of His gospel. Not that you should either willfully withstand, or ungraciously tread the same under your feet, for God does not disclose His will to any such end, but that you should yet now at the length with all your main and might, endeavor that Christ (whose easy yoke and light burden we have of long time cast off from us) might rule and reign in His church by the scepter of His word only...We in England are so far off from having a church rightly reformed, according to the prescript of God's word, that as yet we are not come to the outward face of the same. For to speak of that wherein all consent, & whereupon all writers accord. The outward marks whereby a true Christian church is known, are preaching of the word purely, ministering of the sacraments sincerely, and ecclesiastical discipline, which consists in admonition and correction of faults severely. Touching the first, namely the ministry of the word, although it must be confessed that the substance of doctrine by many delivered is sound and good, yet here in it fails, that neither the ministers thereof are according to God's word proved, elected, called, or ordained: nor the function in such sort so narrowly looked unto, as of right it ought, and is of necessity required. For whereas in the old church a trial was had both of their ability to instruct, and of their godly conversation also: now, by the letters commendatory of some one man, noble or other, tag and rag, learned and unlearned, of the basest sort of the people (to the slander of the gospel in the mouths of the adversaries) are freely received. In those days no idolatrous sacrificers or heathenish priests were appointed to be preachers of the gospel: but we allow, and like well of popish mass mongers, men for all seasons, King Henry's priests, King Edward's priests, Queen Mary's priests, who of a truth (if God's word were precisely followed) should from the same be utterly removed. Then they taught others, now they must be instructed themselves, and therefore like young children they must learn catechisms. Then election was made by the common consent of the whole church: now every one picks out for himself some notable good benefice, he obtains the next adviser, by money or by favor, and so thinks him to be sufficiently chosen. Then the congregation had authority to call ministers: instead thereof now, they run, they ride, and by unlawful suit & buying, prevent other suitors also. Then no minister placed in any congregation, but by the consent of the people, now, that authority is given into the hands of the bishop alone, who by his sole authority thrusts upon them such, as they many times answer for dishonest life, as also for lack of learning, may, & do justly dislike. Then, none admitted to the ministry, but a place was void beforehand, to which he should be called: but now, bishops (to whom the right of ordering ministers does at no hand appertain) do make 60, 80, or a 100 at a clap, & send them abroad into the country like masterless men. Then, after just trial and vocation they were admitted to their function, by laying on of the hands of the company of the eldership only: now there is (neither of these being looked unto) required an alb, a surplice, a vestment, a pastoral staff, beside that ridiculous, and (as they use it to their new creatures) blasphemous saying, receive the Holy Ghost. Then every pastor had his flock, and every flock his shepherd, or else shepherds: now they do not only run from place to place (a miserable disorder in God's church) but covetously join living to living, making shipwreck of their own consciences, and being but one shepherd (nay, would to God they were shepherds and not wolves) have many flocks. Then the ministers were preachers: now bare readers. And if any were so well disposed to preach in their own charges, they may not, without my Lord's license. In those days known by voice, learning and doctrine: now they must be discerned from other by popish and Antichristian apparel, as cap, gown, tippet, etc. Then, as God gave utterance they preached the word only: now they read homilies, articles, injunctions, etc. Then it was painful: now gainful. Then poor and ignominious: now rich & glorious. And therefore titles, livings, and offices by Antichrist devised are given to them, as Metropolitan, Archbishop, Lord's Grace, Lord Bishop, Suffragan, Dean, Archdeacon, Prelate of the Garter, Earl, County Palatine, Honor, High Commissioners, Justices of Peace, Quorum, etc. All which, together with their offices, as they are strange & unheard of in Christ's church, nay plainly in God's word forbidden: so are they utterly with speed out of the same to be removed. Then ministers were not tied to any form of prayers invented by man, but as the spirit moved them, so they powered forth hearty supplications to the Lord. Now they are bound of necessity to a prescript order of service, and book of common prayer in which a great number of things contrary to God's word are contained, as baptism by women, private communions, Jewish purifyings, observing of holidays, etc., patched (if not all together, yet the greatest piece) out of the pope's portals. Then feeding the flock diligently: now teaching quarterly. Then preaching in season and out of season: now once in a month is thought sufficient; if twice, it is judged a work of supererogation. Then nothing taught but God's word, now princes' pleasures, human devices, popish ceremonies, and Antichristian rites in public pulpits defended. Then they sought them; now they seek theirs.

These, and a great many other abuses are in the ministry remaining, which unless they be removed and the truth brought in, not only God's justice shall be powered forth but also God's church in this realm shall never be built. For if they which seem to be workmen, are no workmen in deed, but in name, or else work not so diligently and in such order as the work master commands, it is not only unlikely that the building shall go forward, but altogether impossible that ever it shall be perfected. The way therefore to avoid these inconveniences and to reform these deformities is this: Your wisdoms have to remove advisers, patronages, impropriations, and bishop's authority, claiming to themselves thereby right to ordain ministers, and to bring in that old and true election, which was accustomed to be made by the congregation. You must displace those ignorant and unable ministers already placed, & appoint such as both can, and will by God's assistance feed the flock...Appoint to every congregation a learned and diligent preacher. Remove homilies, articles, injunctions, a prescript order of service made, out of the missal. Take away the lordship, the loitering, the pomp, the idleness, and livings of bishops, but yet employ them to such ends as they were in the old churches appointed for...

Now to the second point, which concerns the administration of sacraments. In the old time, the word was preached, before they were ministered: now it is supposed to be sufficient, if it be read. Then, they were ministered in public assemblies, now in private houses. Then by ministers only, now by midwives, and deacons, equally. But because in treating of both the sacraments together, we should deal confusedly: we will therefore, speak of them severally.

And first for the Lord's Supper, or Holy Communion. They had no Introit, for Celestinus a pope brought it in, about the year 430. But we have borrowed a piece of one out of the Mass book. They read no fragments of the Epistle and Gospel: we use both. The Nicene Creed was not read in their Communion: we have it in ours. There was then a custom to be an examination of the communicants, which now is neglected. Then they ministered the Sacrament with common and usual bread: now with wafer cakes, brought in by Pope Alexander, being in form, fashion, and substance, like their god of the altar. They received it sitting: we kneeling, according to Honorius' Decree. Then it was delivered generally, and indefinitely, Take ye and eat ye: we particularly, and singularly, Take thou, and eat thou. They used no other words but such as Christ left: we borrow from papists, The body of our Lord Jesus Christ, which was given for thee, etc. They had no Gloria in excelsis in the ministry of the Sacrament then, for it was put to afterward. We have now. They took it with conscience. We with custom. They shut men by reason of their sins from the Lord's Supper. We thrust them in their sin to the Lord's Supper. They ministered the Sacrament plainly. We pompously, with singing, piping, surplice and cope wearing. They simply as they received it from the Lord. We, sinfully, mixed with human inventions and devices. And as for Baptism, it was enough with them, if they had water, and the party to be baptized faith, and the minister to preach the word and minister the sacraments.

Now, we must have surplices devised by Pope Adrian, interrogatories ministered to the infant, godfathers and godmothers, brought in by Higinus, holy fonts invented by Pope Pius, crossing and suchlike pieces of popery, which the church of God in the Apostles' times never knew (and therefore not to be used), nay (which we are sure of) were and are human devices, brought in long after the purity of the primitive church. To redress these, your wisdoms have to remove (as before) ignorant ministers, to take away private communions and baptisms, to enjoin deacons and midwives not to meddle in ministers' matters, if they do, to see them sharply punished. To join assistance of elders, and other officers, that seeing people will not examine themselves, they may be examined, and brought to render a reason of their hope. That the statute against wafer cakes may more prevail than an injunction. That people be appointed to receive the Sacrament, rather sitting, for avoiding of superstition, than kneeling, having in it the outward show of evil, from which we must abstain. That excommunication be restored to its old former force. That papists nor other, neither constrainedly nor customably, communicate in the mysteries of salvation. That both the Sacrament of the Lord's Supper and Baptism also, may be ministered according to the ancient purity and simplicity. That the parties to be baptized, if they be of the years of discretion, by themselves and in their own persons, or if they be infants, by their parents (in whose realm if upon necessary occasions and businesses they be absent, some of the congregation knowing the good behavior and sound faith of the parents) may both make rehearsal of their faith. And also if their faith be sound, and agreeable to Holy Scriptures, desire to be in the same baptized. And finally, that nothing be done in this or any other thing, but that which you have the express warrant of God's word for.

Let us come now to the third part, which concerns ecclesiastical discipline. The officers that have to deal in this charge are chiefly the ministers, preachers, or pastors of whom before, Seniors or Elders, and Deacons. Concerning Elders, not only their office but their name also is out of this English church utterly removed. Their office was to govern the church with the rest of the ministers, to consult, to admonish, to correct, and to order all things appertaining to the state of the congregation. Instead of these Seniors in every church, the pope has brought in and we yet maintain, the lordship of one man over many churches, yea over sundry shires. These Seniors then, because their charge was not overmuch, did execute their offices in their own persons without substitutes. Our Lord Bishops have their under officers, as Suffragans, Chancellors, Archdeacons, Officials, Commissaries, and such like. Touching Deacons, though their names be remaining, yet is the office foully perverted and turned upside down, for their duty in the primitive church was to gather the alms diligently, and to distribute it faithfully, also for the sick and impotent persons to provide painfully, having ever a diligent care, that the charity of godly men, were not wasted upon loiterers and idle vagabonds.

Now it is the first step to the ministry, nay, rather a mere order of priesthood. For they may baptize in the presence of a bishop or priest, or in their absence (if necessities so require) minister the other sacrament, likewise read the Holy Scriptures and homilies in the congregation, instruct the youth in the catechism, and also preach, if he be commanded by the bishop. Again, in the old church every congregation had their deacons. Now they are tied to cathedral churches only, and what do they there? Gather the alms and distribute to the poor? Nay, that is the least piece or rather no part of their function. What then? To sing a gospel when the bishop administers the Communion. If this be not a perverting of this office and charge, let everyone judge. And yet lest the reformers of our time should seem utterly to take out of God's church this necessary function, they appoint somewhat to it concerning the poor, and that is, to search for the sick, needy, and impotent people of the parish, and to intimate their estates, names, and places where they dwell to the curate, that by his exhortation they may be relieved by the parish, or other convenient alms. And this as you see, is the highest part of his office, and yet you must understand it to be in such places where there is a curate and a deacon: every parish cannot be at that cost to have both, nay, no parish so far as can be gathered, at this present has. Now then, if you will restore the church to his ancient officer, this you must do. Instead of an Archbishop or Lord Bishop, you must make equality of ministers. Instead of Chancellors, Archdeacons, Officials, Commissaries, Proctors, Doctors, Summoners, Churchwardens, and suchlike, you have to plant in every congregation a lawful and godly seignory. The deaconship must not be confounded with the ministry, nor the collectors for the poor, may not usurp the deacon's office: But he that has an office, must look to his office, and every man must keep himself within the bounds and limits of his own vocation. And to these three jointly, that is, the ministers, elders, and deacons, is the whole regiment of the church to be committed. This regiment consists especially in ecclesiastical discipline, which is an order, left by God unto his church, whereby men learn to frame their wills and doings according to the law of God, by instructing and admonishing one another, yea and by correcting and punishing all willful persons, and condemners of the same. Of this discipline there are two kinds, one private, wherewith we will not deal because it is impertinent to our purpose, and other public, which although it has been long banished, yet if it might now at the length be restored, would be very necessary and profitable for the building up of God's house. The final end of this discipline, is the reforming of the disordered, and to bring them to repentance, and to bridle such as would offend. The chiefest part and last punishment of this discipline is excommunication, by the consent of the church determined, if the offender be obstinate, which how miserably it has been by the pope's proctors, and is by our new canonists abused, who sees not? In the primitive church it was in many human hands: now one alone excommunicated. In those days it was the last censure of the church, and never went forth but for notorious crimes: now it is pronounced for every light trifle. Then excommunication was greatly regarded and feared. Now because it is a money matter, no whit at all esteemed. Then for great sins, severe punishment, and for small offenses, little censures. Now great sins are either not at all punished, as blasphemy, usury, etc., or else slightly passed over with pricking in a blanket, or pinning in a sheet, as adultery, whoredom, drunkenness, etc. Again, such as are no sins (as if a man conform not himself to popish orders and ceremonies, if he come not at the whistle of him, who has by God's word no authority to call, we mean Chancellors, Officials, Doctors, and all that rabble) are grievously punished, not only by excommunication, suspension, deprivation, and other (as they term it) spiritual coercion, but also by banishing, imprisoning, reviling, taunting, and what not? Then the sentence was tempered according to the notoriousness of the fact. Now on the one side either hatred against some persons, carries men headlong into rash and cruel judgment: or else favor, affection, money, mitigates the rigor of the same, and all this comes to pass, because the regiment left of Christ to his church, is committed into one man's hands, whom alone it shall be more easy for the wicked by bribing to pervert, than to overthrow the faith and piety of a zealous and godly company, for such manner of men indeed should the Seigniors be. Then it was said tell the church: now it is spoken, complain to my Lord's Grace, Primate and Metropolitan of all England, or to his inferior, my Lord Bishop of the diocese, if not to him, show the Chancellor or Official, or Commissioner or Doctor. Again, whereas the excommunicated were never received till they had publicly confessed their offense. Now for paying the fees of the court, they shall by master Official, or Chancellor, easily be absolved in some private place. Then the congregation, by the wickedness of the offender grieved, was by his public penance satisfied. Now absolution shall be pronounced, though that be not accomplished. Then the party offending should in his own person, hear the sentence of absolution pronounced. Now, Bishops, Archdeacons, Chancellors, Officials, Commissioners, and suchlike, absolve one man for another. And this is that order of ecclesiastical discipline which all godly wish to be restored, to the end that everyone by the same, may be kept within the limits of his vocation, and a great number be brought to live in godly conversation. Not that we mean to take away the authority of the civil magistrate and chief governor, to whom we wish all blessedness; and for the increase of whose godliness we daily pray: but that Christ being restored into his kingdom, to rule in the same by the scepter of His word, and severe discipline: the Prince may be better obeyed, the realm more flourish in godliness, and the Lord Himself more sincerely and purely according to His revealed will served than heretofore He has been, or yet at this, present is. Amend therefore these horrible abuses, and reform God's church, and the Lord is on your right hand, you shall not be removed forever. For He will deliver and defend you from all your enemies, either at home or abroad, as He did faithful Jacob & good Jehosaphat. Let these things alone, and God is a righteous judge, He will one day call you to your reckoning. Is a reformation good for France? and can it be evil for England? Is discipline meet for Scotland? And is it unprofitable for this realm? Surely God has set these examples before your eyes to encourage you to go forward to a thorough and a speedy reformation. You may not do as heretofore you have done, patch and piece, nay rather go backward, and never labor or contend to perfection. But altogether remove whole Antichrist, both head, body, and branch, and perfectly plant that purity of the word, that simplicity of the sacraments, and severities of discipline, which Christ hath commanded, and commended to His church...

The God of all glory so open your eyes to see His truth, that you may not only be inflamed with a love thereof, but with a continual care seek to promote, plant, and place the same amongst us, that we the English people, and our posterity, enjoying the sincerity of God's gospel forever, may say always: The Lord be praised. To whom with Christ Jesus His Son our only Savior, and the Holy Ghost our lone comforter, be honor, praise, and glory, forever and ever. Amen.

Part V

Postlude: A New Age?

30

Sebastian Castellio: *About Heretics: Should They Be Persecuted?* [1553]

Sebastian Castellio (or Castellion), a Frenchman, was born in 1515, converted to Protestantism, and, in 1540, was appointed principal of a Latin school in Strasbourg. An early friendship with John Calvin, who was residing in Strasbourg at that time, came to an end over Calvin's unwillingness to have Castellio ordained. In 1545 Castellio moved to Basel, where he lived in dire poverty working for a printing firm. He published translations of the Bible, and in 1553 was appointed professor of Greek at the University of Basel. After the anti-Trinitarian Michael Servetus was burned in Geneva in October of that year, Castellio published a fervent plea for toleration—*De hereticis an sint persequendi (About Heretics: Should They Be Persecuted?)*, which was an anthology of what important theologians through the centuries had said about the persecution of heretics. Castellio based his notion of toleration on his understanding of Scripture, arguing that to kill heretics meant to anticipate the Last Judgment.

The dedication to Duke Christoph of Württemberg is reprinted. The section also includes a plea of the Anabaptist David Joris, then also in Basel, for religious liberty.[29]

---

29. Roland H. Bainton, ed., *About Heretics: Should They Be Persecuted?* New York, 1935, p. 335 ff.

LITERATURE

Hans Guggisberg, *Sebastian Castellio, A Biography*. Burlington, VT, 2002.

There are two kinds of heretics or obstinate persons: the first are obstinate or stubborn as to conduct, such as the avaricious, scurrilous, voluptuous, drunkards, persecutors, and the like, who being admonished, do not correct their lives. Such are the Jews, Scribes, and Pharisees; wherefore the Savior avoided them when He said, "Your house is left unto you desolate." Such also were those of Jesus' own country among whom He could do no mighty work because of the hardness of their hearts.

The second are those who are obstinate in spiritual matters and in doctrine, to whom the term properly belongs, for the word heresy is Greek and means a sect or opinion. Wherefore those who adhere to some vicious sect or opinion are called heretics. Of this sort was Hananiah, the false prophet whom Jeremiah avoided when he could not recall him from his error. Jeremiah predicted to him his death in accord with the command of the Lord, not of the magistrate. This Hananiah was a pernicious heretic, who withdrew the people from their obedience. From this example alone we may readily see how heretics of this sort are to be treated.

But to judge of doctrine is not so simple as to judge of conduct. In the matter of conduct, if you ask a Jew, Turk, Christian, or anyone else, what he thinks of a brigand or a traitor, all will reply with one accord that brigands and traitors are evil and should be put to death. Why do all agree in this? Because the matter is obvious. For that reason no controversies are raised and no books are written to prove that brigands, etc., should be put to death. This knowledge is engraved and written in the hearts of all men from the foundation of the world. This was what St. Paul meant that the Gentiles have the law written in their hearts, for infidels themselves may judge of these matters. Now let us take up religion and we shall find that it is not so evident and manifest. The heathen were formerly of the opinion that there are many gods. Christ, by his coming, removed this error, so that now neither the Turks nor any other nations entertain a doubt whether there is but one God. On this point all agree with the Christians. If anyone denies the Lord God, this one is an infidel and atheist and is deservedly to be abhorred in the eyes of all. The Turks go further and believe in that God of whom Moses wrote. In this they agree with the Jews and with the Christians without any controversy. The faith of the three peoples is common up to this point. But the Turks share with the Christians a higher regard for Christ than that of the Jews. The Christians go beyond all others in that they regard Jesus Christ as the Son of God, the Savior and Judge of the world. And this belief is common to all Christians. And just as the Turks disagree with the Christians as to the person of Christ, and the Jews with both the Turks and the Christians, and the one condemns the other and holds him for a heretic, so Christians disagree with Christians on many points with regard to the teaching of Christ, and condemn one another and hold each other for heretics. Great controversies and debates occur as to baptism, the Lord's Supper, the invocation of the saints, justification, free will, and other obscure questions, so that Catholics, Lutherans, Zwinglians, Anabaptists, monks, and others condemn and persecute one another more cruelly than the Turks do the Christians. These dissensions arise solely from ignorance of the truth, for if these matters were so obvious and evident as that there is but one God, all Christians would agree among themselves on these points as readily as all nations confess that God is one.

What, then, is to be done in such great contentions? We should follow the counsel of Paul, "Let not him that eat despise him that

eats not… To his own master he stands or falls." Let not the Jews
or Turks condemn the Christians, nor let the Christians condemn
the Jews or Turks, but rather teach and win them by true religion
and justice, and let us, who are Christians, not condemn one another, but, if we are wiser than they, let us also be better and more
merciful. This is certain that the better a man knows the truth, the
less is he inclined to condemn, as appears in the case of Christ and
the apostles. But he who lightly condemns others shows thereby
that he knows nothing precisely, because he cannot bear others,
for to know is to know how to put into practice. He who does not
know how to act mercifully and kindly does not know the nature
of mercy and kindness, just as he who cannot blush does not know
the nature of shame.

If we were to conduct ourselves in this fashion we should be
able to dwell together in concord. Even though in some matters
we disagreed, yet should we consent together and forbear one another in love, which is the bond of peace, until we arrive at the
unity of the faith. But now, when we strive with hate and persecu-
tions we go from bad to worse. Nor are we mindful of our office,
since we are wholly taken up with condemnation, and the gospel
because of us is made a reproach unto the heathen, for when they
see us attacking one another with the fury of beasts, and the weak
oppressed by the strong, these heathen feel horror and detestation
for the gospel, as if it made men such, and they abominate even
Christ Himself, as if He commanded men to do such things. We
rather degenerate into Turks and Jews than convert them into
Christians. Who would wish to be a Christian, when he saw that
those who confessed the name of Christ were destroyed by Christians themselves with fire, water, and. the sword without mercy
and more cruelly treated than brigands and murderers? Who
would not think Christ a Moloch, or some such god, if he wished
that men should be immolated to him and burned alive? Who

would wish to serve Christ on condition that a difference of opinion on a controversial point with those in cruelly than in the bull of Phalaris, even though from the midst of the flames he should call with a loud voice upon Christ, and should cry out that he believed in Him? Imagine Christ, the judge of all, present. Imagine Him pronouncing the sentence and applying the torch. Who would not hold Christ for a Satan? What more could Satan do than burn those who call upon the name of Christ?

O Creator and King of the world, dost Thou see these things? Art Thou become so changed, so cruel, so contrary to Yourself? When You were on earth none was more mild, more clement, more patient of injustice. As a sheep before the Shearer You were dumb. When scourged, spat upon, mocked, crowned with thorns, and crucified shamefully among thieves, Thou didst pray for them who did flee this wrong. Art Thou now so changed? I beg Thee in the name of Thy Father, dost Thou now command that those who do not understand Thy precepts as the mighty demand, be drowned in water, cut with lashes to the entrails, sprinkled with salt, dismembered by the sword, burned at a slow fire, and otherwise tortured in every manner and as long as possible? Dost Thou, O Christ, command and approve of these things? Are they Thy vicars who make these sacrifices? Art Thou present when they summon Thee and dost Thou eat human flesh? If You, Christ, do these things or if You command that they be done, what have You left for the devil? Do You the very same things as Satan? O blasphemies and shameful audacity of men, who dare to attribute to Christ that which they do by the command and at the Phalaris was a tyrant of classical antiquity for whom was constructed a bronze bull in which a man could be burned. The cries of the victim would seem to issue from the nostrils of the bull.

But I will restrain myself. I think, Prince, you already sufficiently understand how far such deeds are contrary to the teaching and practice of Christ. Let us, then, now hear the opinions of others. You will find them speaking, however, as if it were already clergy who are the true heretics...Chap. 43. Would that today there were not such violence. I see some who impose opinions, often false, like oracles upon their disciples. New articles of faith are forged and thrown like a snare about the Conscience of posterity, sowing thereby the seeds of persecution. The disciples without doubt if they become powerful will think that heretics are to be persecuted and will persecute those whom they hold as heretics, that is, those who reject their interpretations. O God, the Father of light, avert this sequel. Be appeased by the punishments visited upon our fathers and ourselves and enlighten posterity. And thou, Posterity, beware of this outcome. Be warned by our example and do not so adhere to the interpretations of men as not to put them to the test of reason, sense, and Scripture. And you, scholars, avoid this course. Do not arrogate so much to yourselves that you bring the souls and bodies of many into peril by your authority.

The Plea of David Joris for Servetus

Most noble, just, worthy, gracious, dear Lords, now that I, your friend and brother in the Lord Jesus Christ, have heard what has happened to the good, worthy Servetus, how that he was delivered into your hands and power by no friendliness and love but through envy and hate, as will be made manifest in the Day of Judgment to those whose eyes are now blinded by cunning so that they cannot understand the ground of the truth. God give them to understand. The report has gone everywhere abroad, and even to my ears, that the learned preachers or shepherds of souls have taken counsel and written to certain cities who have resolved to pass sentence to put him to death. This news has so stirred me that I can have no peace on behalf of our religion and the holy churches far and near, which

stand fast in the love and unity of Christ, until I have raised my
voice as a member of the body of Christ, until I have opened my
heart humbly before your highnesses and freed my conscience. I
trust that the learned, perverted, carnal, and bloodthirsty may have
no weight and make no impression upon you, and if they should
ingratiate themselves with you as did the Scribes and Pharisees
with Pilate in the case of our Lord Jesus, they will displease the
King of Kings and the teacher of all, namely, Christ, who taught
not only in the Scripture according to the letter, but also in divine
fashion, that no one should be crucified or put to death for his
teaching. He Himself was rather crucified and put to death. Yes,
not only that, but He has severely forbidden persecution. Will it
not then be a great perversion, blindness, evil, and darkness to in-
dulge in impudent disobedience through hate and envy? They
must first themselves have been deranged before they could bring
a life to death, damn a soul forever, and hasten it to hell. Is that a
Christian procedure or a true spirit? I say eternally no, however
plausible it may appear. If the preachers are not of this mind and
wish to avoid the sin against the Holy Ghost, let them be wary of
seizing and killing men for their good intentions and belief according to their understanding, especially when these ministers
stand so badly in other people's books that they dare not go out of
their own city and land. Let them remember that they are called,
sent, and anointed of God to save souls, to bring men to right and
truth—that is, to make alive the dead, and not to destroy, offend,
and corrupt, let alone to take life. This belongs to Him alone to
whom it is given, who was crucified, who died, and who suffered.

The government is ordained of God to inflict bodily punishment upon those who sin in the body against the love of the truth
and the law of God's Christ. The magistrate is to punish the bad
and protect the good, lest they be dispossessed and killed by the

evil. But, as Dr. Martin Luther says, the servants of the temple have incited the magistrates to dispossess and kill good, upright folk who were not subservient to the clergy. Yet Christ, our Lord, neither did nor taught this, but endured and suffered to the end. Wherefore He declared, "They shall put you out of the synagogues: yea, the time cometh, that whosoever kills you will think that he doeth God service. And these things will they do unto you, because they have not known the Father, nor me." Does this apply to those who inflict or to those who endure suffering? ... The persecutors have not made man and should not destroy him apart from the true law of our Lord Christ. Let those who thirst for blood kill their own sons and daughters, if they be in error. Yet no godly father will do that, but rather the devil who is a murderer and a liar from the beginning.

Noble, wise, and prudent Lords, consider what would happen if free rein were given to our opponents to kill heretics. How many men would be left on earth if each had this power over the other, inasmuch as each considers the other a heretic? The Jews so regard the Christians, so do the Saracens and the Turks, and the Christians reciprocate. The Papists and the Lutherans, the Zwinglians and the Anabaptists, the Calvinists and the Adiaphorists, mutually ban each other. Because of these differences of opinion should men hate and kill each other? ... "Whoso sheds man's blood, by man shall his blood be shed," as Scripture says. Let us, then, not take the sword, and if anyone is of an erroneous and evil mind and understanding, let us pray for him and awaken him to love, peace, and unity. And if the previously mentioned Servetus is a heretic or a sectarian before God? ... We should inflict on him no harm in any of his members, but admonish him in a friendly way and at most banish him from the city, if he will not give up his obstinacy and stop disturbing the peace by his teaching, that he may come to a better mind and no longer molest your territory. No one should go beyond this...

The Lord Himself will judge of soul and spirit and will separate the good from the bad. He will speedily come, according to Scripture, against the rebellious, bad, hidden evildoers, such as hypocrites, liars, enviers, haters, deceivers, betrayers, persecutors of the truth, and Antichrist himself (what does that signify?), to slay them with the "spirit of his mouth" and "the breath of his lips," that is, with no worldly sword, for He "makes his sun to rise on the evil and the good" and wills that we should imitate Him in His long-suffering, graciousness, and mercy. He instructed the servants, who wished to anticipate the harvest as the apostles wished to call down fire from heaven, to leave the tares with the wheat. At the harvest He will send His angels who have knowledge and understanding to separate the good from the bad, the lies from the truth, the pure from the impure, the new from the old, light from darkness, righteousness from sin, and flesh from spirit, and to give each his place in spirit and truth, for God's judgments are true and eternal and cannot fail... But great insufficiency shall be found in men when the day of light and the spirit of perfection shall appear...

Those who have an evil spirit should be instructed, not put to death in the time of their ignorance and blindness similar to Paul's. That no one should assume judgment, the Lord has given us a new commandment in love that we do unto others as we would that they should do unto us. So be merciful, kind, and good, doing as it has been done to your Honors, and as the Lord wishes. "Judge not that ye be not judged." Condemn no person that ye be not condemned. Shed no blood and do no violence, my dear Lords. Understand whose disciples you are, for nothing has the Lord punished more and forgiven less than the shedding of innocent blood and idolatry. Follow no one and believe in no one above God or Christ, who is Lord in spirit and truth. That you may look to this I have trusted to your good intentions and have not been able to refrain from writing to you according to my knowledge. Although I have withheld my name, you should not give this communication less consideration. In these days one cannot write everything because the pen is not to be trusted.

Additional Bibliography

There are two competent ways to access the rich literature dealing with the Reformation of the sixteenth century: *The Oxford Encyclopedia of the Reformation*, in four volumes, New York, 1996; and *Handbook of European History 1400–1600*, in two volumes, New York, 1994.

Other recent important works are:

Diarmaid MacCulloch, *Reformation: Europe's House Divided, 1490–1700*. London, 2003.

Euan Cameron, *The European Reformation*. New York, 1991.

Martin Brecht, *Martin Luther*. 4 vols. Philadelphia, 1985.

Bob Scribner, *For the Sake of Simple Folk: Popular Propaganda for the German Reformation*. Oxford, 1994.

Lyndal Roper, *Holy Household: Women and Morals in Reformation Augsburg*. Oxford, 1989.

Heinz Schilling, *Religion, Political Culture, and the Emergence of Early Modern Society*. New York, 1992.

George H. Williams, *The Radical Reformation*. 3rd ed. Kirksville, MO, 1992.

R. Po-chia Hsia, *The World of Catholic Renewal, 1540–1770*. New York, 2005.

Andrew Pettegree, ed., *The Reformation World.* London, 2002.

David Bagchi and David C. Steinmetz, eds., *The Cambridge Companion to Reformation Theology.* New York, 2004.

Christopher Haigh, ed., *The English Reformation Revised.* New York, 1987.

Acknowledgments

The following selections are used by permission:

Harold J. Grimm, ed., *Luther's Works. American Edition.* Vol. 31, pp. 327–79. Copyright 1957 by Fortress Press, Philadelphia, Pa.

John W. Doberstein, ed., *Luther's Works. American Edition.* Vol. 51, pp. 70–78. Copyright 1959 by Fortress Press, Philadelphia, Pa.

E. T. Bachmann, ed., *Luther's Works. American Edition.* Vol. 35, pp. 358–62. Copyright 1959 by Fortress Press, Philadelphia, Pa.

Works of Martin Luther. Vol. IV, pp. 219–44. Copyright 1931 by Fortress Press, Philadelphia, Pa.

Jaroslav Pelikan, ed., *Luther's Works. American Edition.* Vol. 26, pp. 4–12, 122–36. Copyright 1963 by Fortress Press, Philadelphia, Pa.

Leland Harder, ed., *Sources of Swiss Anabaptism.* Scottdale, Pa., 1983, pp. 284–291. Copyright 1983 by Herald Press, Scottdale, Pa.

John C. Wenger, "The Schleitheim Confession of Faith," *Mennonite Quarterly Review* 19 (1945), 243–253. Copyright 1945 by Mennonite Historical Society.

Peter Riedemann, *Account of Our Religion, Doctrine and Faith, Given by Peter Riedemann of the Brothers Whom Men Call Hutterians.* London, 1950, pp. 102–21. Copyright 1983 by Plough Publishing, Rifton, N.Y.

Roland H. Bainton, ed., *About Heretics: Should They Be Persecuted?* New York, 1935, p. 335 ff. Copyright 1935 by Columbia University Press, New York, N.Y.

Gordon J. Cramer, ed., *Viking Book of Aphorisms*, Vol. II, pp. 237–258. Copyright 1962 by Penguin Press, Philadelphia, Pa.

John W. Robertson, ed., *Little Black American Fellow*, Vol. I, pp. 56–78. Copyright 1959 by Houghton Press, Philadelphia, Pa.

E. T. Buchanan, ed., *Living Myth: American Library*, Vol. I, pp. 135–145. Copyright 1969 by Pantheon Press, Philadelphia, Pa.

Woman's Library Edition, Vol. IV, pp. 210–234. Copyright 1964 by Rizzoli Press, Philadelphia, Pa.

Dorothy Pedhan, ed., *Essays in the Humanities*, Vol. 60, pp. 142–172. Copyright 1952 by Pantheon Press, Philadelphia, Pa.

Richard Llander, ed., *Story of Love Imagined*, Scribner's, P. (1961 ws. 234–274. Copyright 1961 by Herald Press, Scribner's, Pa.

Anna C. McGraw, "The Solfeggiatto Confession of Faith," *Modern Quarterly Review*, 74 (1934), 344–333. Copyright 1934 by Mnemonic Herald Society.

Erich Kirchmann, *Images of Our Religion, Mythos, and Faith, Cultures: Core Expression of the Modern Fellow*, New Call Press, new London, 1972, pp. 110–112. Copyright 1968 by Pantheon Press, Philadelphia, Pa. S. A.

Roland H. Bainton, ed., *Modern Society Study*, 136–168. Bantam, New York, 1953, p. 234. Copyright 1953 by Columbia University Press, New York, N. Y.